The War of 1812 in the Old Northwest

THE WAR OF 1812

Alec R. Gilpin

IN THE OLD NORTHWEST

Michigan State University Press
East Lansing

The War of 1812 in the Old Northwest copyright © 1958 Michigan State University Press
Introduction to the Bicentennial Edition copyright © 2012 by Brian Leigh Dunnigan

⊜ The paper used in this publication meets the minimum requirements of ANSI/NISO
Z39.48-1992 (R 1997) (Permanence of Paper).

 Michigan State University Press
East Lansing, Michigan 48823-5245

Printed and bound in the United States of America.

18   17   16   15   14   13   12   1   2   3   4   5   6   7   8   9   10

THE LIBRARY OF CONGRESS HAS CATALOGED THE FIRST EDITION AS FOLLOWS:
Gilpin, Alec R. (Alec Richard), 1920–
The War of 1812 in the old Northwest / Alec R. Gilpin.
p. cm.
Includes bibliography.
ISBN 978-0-87013-032-8 (hardcover) 1. Northwest, Old—History—War of 1812.
2. United States—History—War of 1812—Campaigns.
E355.1. G5 1958
973.5231
57-010957

ISBN 978-1-61186-038-2 (paperback)

Cover design by Charlie Sharp, Sharp Des!gns, Lansing, Mich.

Cover image taken from "A View of Col. Johnson's Engagement with the Savages
(Commanded by Tecumseh) near the Moravian Town, October 5, 1812," Henry Trumbull,
History of the Indian Wars (Boston, 1846). Reproduced with permission of the Clements
Library, University of Michigan.

g green press INITIATIVE Michigan State University Press is a member of the Green Press Initiative
and is committed to developing and encouraging ecologically responsible
publishing practices. For more information about the Green Press Initiative and the use
of recycled paper in book publishing, please visit *www.greenpressinitiative.org*.

Visit Michigan State University Press at *www.msupress.org*

CONTENTS

Brian Leigh Dunnigan

THE WAR OF 1812 IN THE OLD NORTHWEST: AN INTRODUCTION TO THE BICENTENNIAL EDITION

THE OCCASION OF THE BICENTENNIAL of the War of 1812 brings briefly into the public consciousness the clash of arms characterized by historian Donald R. Hickey as "a forgotten conflict." Indeed the War of 1812 is, at best, vaguely remembered by most Americans and then usually as the inspiration for our national anthem or as a time of dramatic naval victories by frigates such as the USS *Constitution,* also known as "Old Ironsides." Americans' perceptions of the significance and consequences of the events of 1812–1814 are so poor, in part, because they were overshadowed just fifty years later by the trauma of a civil war that touched vast numbers of citizens and brought about many significant changes to the nation. This dominance of the Civil War over American memory reasserts itself during major anniversaries of the two conflicts, which overlap by three years. Canadians have a better recollection of the War of 1812 because of its impact on the development and identity of their nation as separate from the United States and as their most significant war of the nineteenth century. Native Americans recall the event as a disastrous blow to their hopes of controlling their fate through armed resistance. And it has been said the British barely remember it at all.

The War of 1812 as it was fought in North America took the

form of a number of widely separated theaters of action. Other than worldwide naval engagements, most large-scale fighting was concentrated in the Niagara River region, eastern Lake Ontario, the Lake Champlain–St. Lawrence River frontier, coastal Maine, Chesapeake Bay, and the Gulf Coast. The final theater was the "Old Northwest," the area established in 1787 as the Northwest Territory of the United States. Encompassing some 260,000 square miles of land north of the Ohio River and west of Pennsylvania, bordered by the Mississippi River on the west and the Great Lakes on the north, the territory eventually would be carved into six states. By 1812 it already had been divided into the state of Ohio and the territories of Michigan, Indiana, and Illinois. Adjoining the northern boundary of the Northwest Territory lay the western part of the British North American province of Upper Canada, which was also to be an integral part of the northwestern theater of the war.

The land on both sides of the international boundary were only just beginning to experience development when war came in 1812. Most of the region was still in the hands of its original Native American inhabitants, whose villages were scattered across the landscape and whose vast, largely forested hunting grounds supported an economy based on agriculture, hunting, and the fur trade. American-style development, in the form of cleared farmland and nascent towns, was still largely confined to Ohio and the southern parts of Indiana and Illinois territories. To the north were a few forts, towns, and farms in Michigan Territory at places like Detroit, River Raisin, and the Straits of Mackinac. Corresponding areas of settlement were situated across from them in Upper Canada.

The northern part of this land of forests, swamps, rivers, and lakes, with only the most rudimentary infrastructure, was one of the main theaters of the War of 1812. Part of the fighting there was a conventional, European-style duel between the forces of the United States and Great Britain involving formally trained troops, artillery, and warships. But a parallel war was also fought in the Northwest, a bitter struggle between Americans and Native Americans that was, in many ways, a continuation of the frontier conflicts of the 1780s and 1790s. These two wars blended, as many Native Americans allied themselves with the British, to the point where virtually no land battle of the northwestern war was fought without the active participation of Indian forces.

The existence of these parallel but intertwined conflicts ensured that the fighting in the Old Northwest would differ from that in other parts of the continent. It involved fewer European-style, set piece, linear battles and sieges, and those that were fought all involved Native Americans as British allies and auxiliaries to the main action. During a number of battles Native American warriors were the sole military force in opposition to American troops. Tactics were thus more fluid than in many of the clashes fought in the other theaters, and the war in the Old Northwest took on many of the characteristics of the brutal frontier fighting that had occurred in the 1780s and 1790s in the southern and eastern parts of the same region. The conflict fueled atrocities on both sides. The well-known battle cry "Remember the Raisin," in reference to the fate of American soldiers imprisoned and wounded at Frenchtown in January 1813, conjured up old fears among westerners of the sometimes tragic aftermaths of actions fought with Native Americans. The implied threat of Indian outrages on military forces or civilians proved an effective stratagem for the British in encouraging surrender on a number of occasions, notably at Michilimackinac and Detroit in 1812. The behavior of some of the American victors at the Battle of the Thames in October 1813 and in other actions against Native Americans demonstrated that the brutality of frontier warfare infected both sides.

It was this complex regional conflict that Alec R. Gilpin set out to address in *The War of 1812 in the Old Northwest,* published by Michigan State University Press in 1958. His subject was timely, for the sesquicentennial of the war was then only four years away. The bicentennial of the War of 1812 is now upon us, and because Gilpin's book remains the most detailed and comprehensive narrative of the northwestern war, Michigan State University Press is reissuing it in this paperback edition.

Gilpin was born in Detroit in 1920 and completed his undergraduate degree in history at the University of Michigan in 1941. He fulfilled the requirements for his master of arts degree and a teaching certificate before entering the U.S. Army in the summer of 1942. Following three years of service as an enlisted man in the Pacific theater, he returned to teach school in Detroit. He married in 1946 and returned that fall to the University of Michigan to pursue a doctorate in history, which he received in 1950.

Gilpin began his career at Michigan State University in 1949 as an instructor in the Department of History and Civilization. Three years later he was appointed assistant professor in the renamed Department of Humanities, where he became associate professor in 1958. In the early 1960s he served on the Michigan Committee for the Sesquicentennial of the War of 1812. Gilpin's next major project was a history of the Territory of Michigan from its formation in 1805 to statehood in 1837, published by Michigan State University Press in 1970. Although he later produced some articles and book reviews, *The Territory of Michigan* proved to be Gilpin's only other book. He retired from Michigan State University in 1984 and died in 2000.

The author had developed a particular interest in Michigan history during his university studies under Professor Lewis G. Vander Velde of the University of Michigan and F. Clever Bald, PhD, then director of the Michigan Historical Collections. For his dissertation, Gilpin combined this interest with military history by carefully examining General William Hull's disastrous Detroit campaign in the summer of 1812. That was the defining event of the first year of the war in the Old Northwest, and Gilpin's research undoubtedly encouraged him to craft an account of the full three years of fighting in the region.

Such a study was needed, as no recent scholarship had been devoted to the subject. The war in the Old Northwest had appeared in general histories of 1812–1814, but the only comprehensive account had been published soon after the conclusion of the fighting. Robert B. McAfee's *History of the Late War in the Western Country: Comprising a Full Account of All the Transactions in That Quarter, from the Commencement of Hostilities at Tippecanoe, to the Termination of the Contest at New Orleans on the Return of Peace* (Lexington, Kentucky: Worsley and Smith, 1816) was written by a veteran of William Henry Harrison's 1813 campaign. McAfee witnessed some of the events he described and had access to other participants, official documents, and wartime printed sources. Although a solid narrative of the fighting, it was written soon after the event and from a strictly American point of view, with little sense of the British or Native American perspective.

The War of 1812 in the Old Northwest is somewhat reminiscent of McAfee's earlier work in that Gilpin set out to present a straightforward narrative, beginning with the Battle of Tippecanoe in November 1811 and concluding with the peace of December 1814 and the mutual return of occupied territory during the following summer. "Here, for the first time, the story of 1812 concentrates on the minor and major battles in the Old Northwest," declared a statement on the book jacket. Reviewer Richard B. Reed wrote in the *William and Mary Quarterly* that this was "the first serious regional study of the war as it was conducted in the area of Upper Canada and the Ohio Valley" and that it "fills a gap in the historiography of the period." Canadian reviewer Richard A. Preston agreed that it "fills in a much neglected part of the story of the War of 1812."

Gilpin produced a clear, understandable narrative that makes his book accessible to general readers as well as to scholars. The text begins with a concise introduction of the situation in the Old Northwest, the Shawnee leader Tecumseh, and Indiana Territory governor William Henry Harrison. They were the chief protagonists in the looming conflict between the troops of the United States and Native Americans of the region. Fighting there would commence before the declaration of war on Great Britain in June 1812. The narrative then plunges into preparations for war in the Northwest and proceeds chronologically through the three-year conflict, treating each campaign and battle in detail. The book concludes with the briefest of summaries and a solid bibliography. Reginald Horsman, later the author of an influential history of the War of 1812, noted that Gilpin "succeeds in presenting a somewhat complicated subject with great clarity." Although critical of Gilpin's lack of analysis, reviewer Ray W. Irwin of New York University admitted, "The merits of the study . . . are substantial. The volume does provide a well-documented and detailed account of the actual campaigning."

It was in the matter of his scholarly analysis that Gilpin received the greatest criticism from his peers for *The War of 1812 in the Old Northwest*, for he presented no new interpretations of critical issues, such as the region's role in the coming of war or the war's impact on the future of the Native Americans. "Gilpin seems to have deliberately set his face against taking sides with any one who would argue either side of the question whether the Northwest was, or was not, the most important reason for the outbreak of the war," wrote Richard A. Preston. "The result is that we now have a much better picture of the operations in the Old Northwest than we formerly had, but we are no nearer a knowledge of their significance." Reginald Horsman's main criticisms were in regard to "the narrowness with which he has interpreted his subject." Although some scholars were disappointed, Gilpin's purpose with this book was not to put forth new interpretations. As Howard H. Peckham of the Clements Library recognized, "the author's aim is a military regional study." In this he succeeds admirably, and at the very least his book serves as a most useful overview of events in the western theater and as a guidebook to the progress of the fighting there.

The decades since the publication of Gilpin's book have seen a steady trickle of new works on the War of 1812. J. Mackay Hitsman's *The Incredible War of 1812* (1965), Harry Coles's *The War of 1812* (1965), Reginald Horsman's *The War of 1812* (1969), and Don Hickey's *The War of 1812: A Forgotten Conflict* (1989) are only a few of the many general histories that have presented their own interpretations. All include the war in the Northwest as a part of the broader conflict. Narrower and more detailed studies have addressed many aspects of the fighting in the Northwest with biographies of key participants, studies of the role of Native Americans, accounts of individual campaigns, battles, and naval actions, and histories of the battlefields and forts where events played out. No one has yet stepped forward to compile an account of the war in the Old Northwest as comprehensive as Gilpin's work.

Michigan State University Press issued a second printing of *The War of 1812 in the Old Northwest* in 1968, but that has long been out of print. This new edition presents Gilpin's text as originally published and makes his useful, comprehensive, and readable account once again generally available. There is one important change, however. The poor quality of the map of the Old Northwest in the original edition was universally criticized by reviewers. It is hoped that the new version prepared for this edition will better guide readers on their tour of a most interesting event of the region's history.

References

Burt, A. L. *The American Historical Review* 63:4(1958): 1026.
Horsman, Reginald. *The Mississippi Valley Historical Review* 45:2(1958): 319–20.
Irwin, Ray W. *The Quarterly.* October 1958.
Peckham, H. *The Journal of Southern History* 24:4(1958): 507–8.
Preston, Richard A. *Queen's Quarterly* 65(1958):545.
Reed, Richard B. *The William and Mary Quarterly* 16:1(1958): 153–54.

The War of 1812 in the Old Northwest

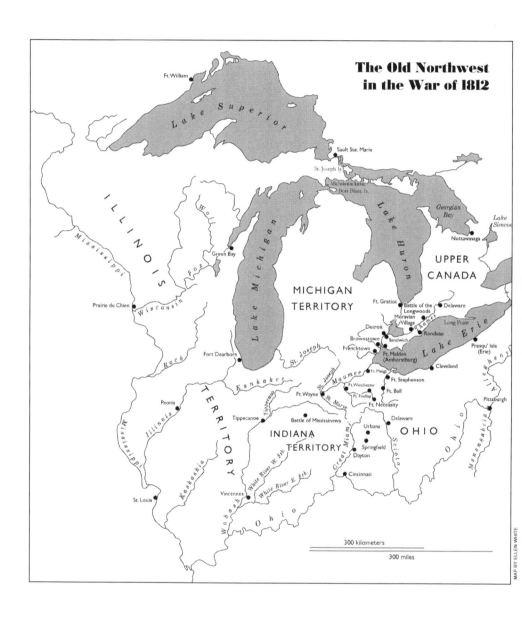

The Old Northwest in the War of 1812

Ft. William

Lake Superior

Sault Ste. Marie

St. Joseph Is.

Michilimackinac
Bois Blanc Is.

Georgian Bay

Lake Simcoe

ILLINOIS

Wolf

Fox

Green Bay

Lake Michigan

Lake Huron

Nottawasaga

UPPER CANADA

Mississippi

Prairie du Chien

Wisconsin

MICHIGAN TERRITORY

Ft. Gratiot

Battle of the Longwoods

Delaware

Moravian Village

Thames

Long Point

Detroit

Sandwich

Rondeau

Rock

Fort Dearborn

St. Joseph

Brownstown
Frenchtown

Ft. Malden (Amherstburg)

Lake Erie

Presqu' Isle (Erie)

Cleveland

Allegheny

Kankakee

Maumee

Ft. Meigs

Ft. Stephenson

Peoria

Illinois

Tippecanoe

Ft. Wayne

St. Joseph

Ft. Winchester

Ft. Ball

Pittsburgh

St. Marys

Ft. Findlay

Ft. Necessity

Monongahela

Tippecanoe

Battle of Mississinewa

Delaware

Mississippi

TERRITORY

Kaskaskia

INDIANA TERRITORY

Urbana

OHIO

Ohio

Great Miami

Springfield

Scioto

Dayton

White River W. Frk.

Cincinnati

Vincennes

White River E. Frk.

St. Louis

Wabash

Ohio

300 kilometers

300 miles

CHAPTER I

TIPPECANOE: PRELUDE TO WAR

THE PRELUDE TO THE WAR OF 1812 started in the backwoods of the Old Northwest in the 1760's. The French had come and gone, the British were there then, to be replaced or challenged after 1783 by the Americans. Each occupation of the area had its inevitable impact on the Indians, not only in regard to their traditional lands but also on their culture.

Irrespective of the interested power, certain of the Indians regarded the encroachment on their lands with equanimity; others, however, were not so tolerant and, as a result, frequent skirmishes took place over the years. Among those who took objection to the changing times was the son of a Shawnee father and a Creek mother—Tecumseh, the "Shooting Star" or "Crouching Panther."

Born in 1768 in a hut near the Mad River in the future state of Ohio, Tecumseh was destined to become a Shawnee war chief and to win the respect of the British army. His brother, Laulewaikau or Elkswatawa, probably born in 1775, was to achieve a somewhat lesser fame.

As a young brave, Tecumseh fought in frontier skirmishes between the Indians and Americans, notably in the battle against

3

General Anthony Wayne's army at Fallen Timbers.[1] Unlike his brother, Elkswatawa spent his youth as a vagabond, idling and drinking. However, as often happens, in about 1805 he was suddenly transformed after a vision, in which he claimed the Great Spirit had instructed him to lead a crusade among the Indians against the white man's ways. Either because of expediency or belief, Tecumseh became his follower.

The Prophet, as Elkswatawa became known, aided by Tecumseh, preached that the Indians should return to their old customs and virtues and refrain from mingling with the American usurpers of their hegemony. His followers spread the tale of his vision, greatly embellished, to the Indians of the Old Northwest. In 1808 the Prophet and Tecumseh received permission from certain Potawatomi and Kickapoo representatives to establish a camp site along the Tippecanoe River near its junction with the Wabash. Soon there were forty Shawnee and one hundred other Indians at this village, which became known as Prophet's Town.[2] While the Prophet pursued his crusade, Tecumseh attempted to establish a confederation of the tribes to prevent further cessions of land to the Americans.

After General Wayne's victory at Fallen Timbers, the 1795 Treaty of Greenville reaffirmed previous Indian grants of land north of the Ohio River and provided for a generous extension of the former boundaries. In addition, the Indians recognized various enclaves around the newly built American forts in Indian country. This pact, which Tecumseh refused to sign although many of the other Indian leaders did, bore the signature of William Henry Harrison, whose name was to loom large in future Indian negotiations.

Born in Virginia in 1773, the future President attended several colleges, ostensibly studying for a medical career, but usually pursuing his primary interest, military history.[3] In 1791 he received his commission as an ensign in the First United States Infantry, and was assigned to duty at Fort Washington (Cincinnati, Ohio), where he served under General James Wilkinson. In 1792 General Wayne took command of the army, and the next year made Harrison, by this time a lieutenant, one of his aides. Harrison served with distinction at the Battle of Fallen Timbers and was a signatory to the Treaty of Greenville. In 1798 he resigned from the army to become Secretary of the Northwest Territory. A year later he was elected a Territorial delegate to Congress, but resigned in 1800 to become Governor of the then new Indiana Territory.

As Governor, Harrison made several treaties which extended the boundaries of Indiana northward. In return for signing away their land, the Indians were to be paid annual annuities in goods, with the reluctant Indians usually being offered a larger initial amount as an added inducement to sign. Before 1809 the Indians had expressed little concerted opposition to this, and even in September of that year the Treaty of Fort Wayne—signed with the Delaware, Miami, Potawatomi, and certain lesser tribes—added many square miles to the Indiana boundaries.

At this point Tecumseh took a strong stand. It was not that he or his followers actually owned any of the lands ceded by the Treaty of Fort Wayne. His opposition stemmed from the belief that no Indian, *regardless of tribe*, had a right to alienate land without the consent of all Indians.

In the spring of 1810, as a result of Tecumseh's influence, some Indians refused to accept annuity payments. Striving to preserve peace, Harrison invited Tecumseh to a council, at the territorial capital in Vincennes, to discuss the matter.

On August 12, 1810, Tecumseh arrived with a group of four hundred, instead of the thirty he had led the Americans to expect. He stated that he had been authorized by the tribes involved to kill the Indians who had signed the Treaty of Fort Wayne because they had not been official delegates of their entire tribes. If the United States would return the land, Tecumseh would forego this punishment. The disputed lands, pointed out Governor Harrison, had been owned by the Miami long before the Shawnee had settled there; in other words, it was none of Tecumseh's business. A fight threatened between Tecumseh's followers and Harrison's forces. However, Tecumseh withdrew at Harrison's request, and the council broke up on August 22, with the Governor promising to bring the land question to the President's attention. For his part, Tecumseh agreed to observe the boundary lines.[4] At this time he was more interested in consolidating his position among the Indians than in disturbing the status quo.

The haggling at the council convinced the Governor of the increasing danger and complexity of Indian affairs. The militia was drilled more frequently, and some regulars were moved to Vincennes. In October Harrison contemplated, but abandoned until spring, the building of a fort along the Wabash River, not far from Prophet's Town,[5] but within the grant of 1809.

In the spring of 1811 small sporadic Indian raids harassed settlers in the Wabash area. Suspecting that Tecumseh had knowledge of these raids, Harrison sent him a strongly worded letter: If the Indians did not cease their raids, Harrison would attack the tribes of the entire area. Tecumseh replied that he would come to Vincennes for a council.

Before the council gathered, there was evident distrust on each side. Tecumseh was reluctant to come with the few followers Harrison requested. The Governor was doubly concerned: A large number of Indians would bring danger of attack, for the settlers in the area could not distinguish hostile from friendly Indians. Learning that a large number of Indians were en route, Harrison sent Captain Waller Wilson, of the Indiana militia, to convey his disapproval. Wilson met Tecumseh at Busseron, twenty miles from Vincennes. Tecumseh explained that only twenty-four Indians belonged to his official party, the rest were coming of their own accord, but did not bother to explain why he had paused to wait for them before continuing to Vincennes.

By July 28 about three hundred Indians were in Vincennes; of these less than thirty were women and children. The Governor was uneasy. He wrote the Secretary of War, William Eustis, that he never would have allowed such a formidable group to approach, except for Presidential instructions to deal with the matter as peacefully as possible. Harrison ordered three companies of militia to stand by. To dramatize his strength, he invited Tecumseh to

6

witness a special review of seven or eight hundred militiamen.

The council opened on July 30, 1811, but brought no meeting of minds. Harrison refused to discuss the Fort Wayne Treaty because it was now in the hands of the President. Tecumseh refused to surrender two Potawatomi who had committed murders in the Missouri area the previous fall, and suggested that they be forgiven as he had forgiven the murderers of some Indians in the Illinois country. He added that he was going South to persuade the southern tribes to unite with the northern, pointedly commenting that the Indians had not objected when the white man had formed the United States. In conclusion, he hoped no further American expansion would take place during his absence. The Governor retorted that his government, under no circumstances, would allow its people to be murdered, and broke up the council.

The 1811 council reflected a significant change in Harrison's official policy. In 1810 he had asserted that Tecumseh had no authority in these matters. This was not mentioned in 1811.

Governor Harrison was not the only one to express distrust of the Prophet's Town inhabitants. On July 31 President Madison received a petition bearing signatures of seven of the leading political figures of Vincennes. Having heard Tecumseh's speech to Harrison, the signers asserted they were sure that an Indian confederation already existed.[6] To bolster their plea for assistance, they enclosed resolutions approved at a public meeting in Vincennes: that peace could be ensured only by crushing the Wabash stronghold; that the British in Canada not only had knowledge of the Indians' plans but were, in reality, behind them; that only forceful action would nullify the danger of the Indians; and that the meeting had fully approved Harrison's measures to date.

The government in Washington had already acknowledged the threat to the Old Northwest. In a letter of July 17, the Secretary of War advised Harrison to consult with Ninian Edwards, Governor of the Illinois Territory, who had reported serious Indian threats. He also informed Harrison that the Fourth Regiment of the United States Infantry, augmented by a company from the Rifle Regiment, had been ordered to descend from Pittsburgh and place themselves under his orders. If Prophet's Town became a serious threat, and if a sufficient force of regulars and militia were available, the Secretary of War authorized Harrison to attack.

A few days later Eustis wrote that the President still hoped to preserve peace, although not at the cost of permitting the formation of an Indian confederation. He added that Colonel John P. Boyd, commanding the Fourth, was to halt at Newport, Kentucky, and expressed the hope that a subsequent march to Indiana would be unnecessary, thus freeing the regiment for other, unspecified, service.

At this time mail between Washington and Vincennes took close to three weeks. Before Eustis' letter arrived, Harrison had already determined his course of action, and written to Eustis of his intentions. A number of Indians, in his belief, remained in Prophet's Town only out of fear of Tecumseh; indeed, Tecumseh was the key to the situation, and the opportune time to attack was during his absence in the South. To justify his views, Harrison pointed out that Tecumseh had let nothing deter him from his plans and observed that the Shawnee was "one of those uncommon geniuses, which spring up occasionally to produce revolutions and overturn the established order of things." [7]

Harrison then outlined his plans for Eustis' approval. He would enforce the provision of the Greenville Treaty requiring the deliverance of murderers and barring hostile Indians from passing through the signatories' lands. All tribes would be notified that the Americans considered members of the Prophet's band as hostiles and would be asked to refuse them tribal protection. Obviously these terms were an ultimatum.

If the terms were not met by September, Harrison would move the two regular companies from Vincennes and Fort Knox, plus seventeen companies of militia, to the northern boundary set by the Treaty of Fort Wayne. If attack were necessary, militia and volunteers from Kentucky and Indiana could be added. Harrison preferred using the regulars of the Fourth, but, if unable to do so, would employ mounted militia when possible.

Harrison was soon able to report that Governor Edwards, of

the Illinois Territory, and Governor Benjamin Howard, of the Louisiana-Missouri Territory, agreed that force should be used only as a final resort, but that Prophet's Town must not be allowed to grow. On August 14, 1811, Lieutenant Abraham Hawkins, of the Fourth Regiment, arrived in Vincennes to receive Harrison's orders as to the disposition of Boyd's command. Hawkins had been detached from a company, then at Louisville in advance of the Fourth Regiment at Newport. (Harrison, although he made no mention of it, must have been aware that Eustis would be unlikely to order the regiment on other duty if it actually were stationed at Vincennes, near a possible scene of action.) The Wabash was unusually high, and Boyd's command had keelboats—so Harrison ordered their advance over the waters of the Ohio and the Wabash.

He then traveled to Jeffersonville, Indiana, the location of the rapids of the Ohio, to meet the regiment. He waited a week, watching the river level getting steadily lower, auguring ill for the arrival of the force in Vincennes in time for them to take up duty in mid-September. Since he had already sent messengers to the Indians demanding compliance with the Greenville Treaty, he now informed Eustis that he was considering a march to Prophet's Town to demand hostages as proof of good conduct, and perhaps even the erection of a fort in Indian country. After the regiment arrived at Jeffersonville on September 3, he and Colonel Boyd journeyed overland to Vincennes.

By September 10 the Fourth Regiment, with Lieutenant-Colonel James Miller in command, was fighting the Wabash River. The water was low, but the current rapid; and many soldiers were victims of a fever that plagued newcomers to the area. But the regulars pushed, poled, and tugged their way upstream, arriving at Vincennes on September 19. They were greeted by an exuberant militia, dressed in deerskins and brandishing tomahawks and scalping knives.[8] The Fourth, an essentially New England regiment, apparently was properly impressed.

Harrison had decided to take the field. But there still remained a problem of a disagreement with Eustis concerning the size and composition of the force. Harrison wanted 1,200 men, including all the regulars available. Eustis authorized the use of the regulars, but restricted the additional request to two militia companies. Harrison deemed this an insufficient force.

On September 17 he wrote to Eustis explaining why he was forced to exceed the letter of his orders.[9] First of all, excessive sickness would reduce his regulars, including the Fort Knox garrison, to an effective force of less than 450. Two companies of militia would add only 100 men. Moreover, he had received a message from Touissant Dubois, an Indian trader of some thirty years' standing, informing him that a party of Indians from Prophet's Town had received presents at the British outpost of Fort Malden and that the British were dispensing more presents to Indians than ever before. Eustis' orders, Harrison reminded, had been that he was not to attack unless sure of victory. Furthermore, a strong demonstration could counteract British largess. In short, he concluded, he had determined to employ as large a force as he could gather.

As Eustis' reply would take several weeks to arrive, Harrison began preparations for his campaign. With the support of the Governor of Kentucky, Charles Scott, he had already called for Kentucky volunteers. Joseph H. Daviess, a United States attorney, was one of the first to respond. Most volunteers came in small groups, but a skeleton company of mounted militia reported under Captain Peter Funk. When Captain Frederick Geiger's mounted riflemen reported, Kentucky was represented by 101 men[10] —many of them prominent citizens.

In addition to the Kentuckians, Harrison eventually had the following force: nine companies of regulars, six companies of Indiana infantry militia, and three companies of Indiana mounted riflemen; two companies of Indiana light dragoons; one company of Indiana riflemen, and a company of scouts.[11] Not all units were present when the expedition left Vincennes, and none was at full strength. Slowly these units converged on Vincennes for the job ahead, and the final plans were readied. Captain William Piatt of the regulars was appointed quartermaster, Joseph Daviess was placed in charge of the militia dragoons and mounted riflemen, with the rank of major in the Indiana militia, and Waller Taylor and Henry Hurst, each with the rank of major, were appointed Harrison's aides.

The time had come to instruct the troops in battle drill while on the march. Extremely simple maneuvers were devised and practiced. The primary object of these maneuvers was to avoid scattering men in wooded or irregular terrain and to minimize the danger of attack at a vulnerable time.[12]

The chain of command was then announced. All infantry, regular and militia, were to form a brigade under the command of Colonel Boyd, with the acting rank of brigadier-general. This brigade was to form two lines in case of action, the first to consist of the regulars, commanded by Lieutenant-Colonel James Miller; the second, under Lieutenant-Colonel Joseph Bartholomew. All mounted troops and scouts were to be directly under Harrison's orders.

On the march the infantry was to move in two single-file columns. Each column was to be composed of two battalions, regulars forming the front battalion, militia forming the rear. The columns were to be far enough apart so that when the direction of march changed, the flanks of each would meet. The mounted men were to extend for one hundred and fifty yards on all sides of the infantry. The scouts and spies were to be in advance of the rest of the army.

In the case of a frontal attack, each battalion was to swing on its center in the manner described. Thus, two parallel lines would be formed from the four battalions—the first line composed of regulars, the second of militia. While the maneuver was taking place, the enemy was to be held off by the advance cavalry, who would withdraw behind the first infantry line on a retreat command, to be given as soon as the line formed. The second line could then be retained behind the first, or could be moved on the flank of the first. The same procedure could be used in the case of an attack from the rear or one from both front and rear.

At that time the most dangerous situation confronting an army when moving through woods was an attack on its flanks. This threat was to be met simply by the men facing the direction of attack while still in the parallel lines of march. In the event of an attack on both flanks, each column was to face outward; it was reasoned that even untrained troops should be able to follow these simple and effective maneuvers.

The pattern of organization completed, the army prepared to march. The cavalry was already at Busseron, where forage was more plentiful. The sick were detached to garrison Fort Knox. Ammunition was issued. The twelve thousand rations on hand were readied.[13] The army would travel light; only the regulars would carry tents. Orders were posted calling for the assembly for the march to be at 10:00 A.M. on September 25. But the march, delayed by heavy rain, began after reveille on the following day.

Slowly the expedition marched up the eastern banks of the Wabash, occasionally gaining time by marching in a more northerly direction than the sinuous river, but never going too far from their provisions, which were being transported by water. As any prudent commander would (and following the example of his preceptor, General Wayne), Harrison took all possible precautions to minimize danger on the march. In spite of a shortage of axes, Harrison ordered night camps fortified. The men were halted early enough to enable each unit to build a breastwork of logs along its share of the perimeter of the bivouac and to do their cooking before dark. Fires within the bivouac were then extinguished, and larger ones lighted outside so that guards could observe any movement into the cleared strip around the camp.

Such procedures would reveal the camp site, but secrecy was impossible with so large a force. However, a sizable guard was detailed nightly. In case of attack, the soldiers had to move but a few feet from their resting places to a prearranged position in the battle line. Cavalrymen and their mounts were located in the interior parts of the camp. As a further precaution, all soldiers were wakened before dawn and kept in formation until the scouts reported there was no danger of attack.

By October 2 the army had marched about sixty-five miles, from Vincennes to Battelle des Illinois, a place on the east bank of the Wabash. Harrison left to interview Chief Shabonee [14] at a near-by Potawatomi settlement, leaving Colonel Boyd in command during his absence.

The commander left a second time—this time seeking a suitable site for a fort. After reconnoitering twenty miles to the north, nearly as far as the Fort Wayne Treaty boundary, Harrison decided that the present camping place was the most favorable. A stockaded fort, enclosing an acre of ground and with blockhouses at three of the angles, was built on the bluff thirty or forty feet above the east side of the Wabash River (at the modern site of Terre Haute). While the men toiled on the fort, Harrison reported to Eustis that Indians were still plundering settlers but that no incidents had delayed the army's advance.

The first hostile incident occurred on the night of October 10 when Indians fired on the sentries, wounded one, and escaped. But not all the Indians were overt enemies. Before leaving Vincennes, Harrison had asked some Delaware chiefs to meet the army later and serve in a peaceful capacity. While en route, these Indians were met by the Prophet's messengers, whom they accompanied to Prophet's Town. The chiefs then sent an interpreter, John Connor, to notify Harrison that they had hoped to dissuade the Prophet from hostile actions but were now convinced he would attack. About the same time, the local Wea and Miami sent messengers to Harrison proclaiming friendship and informing him that the Wyandot were also ignoring the Prophet's pleas for aid.

On October 12 Harrison received a dispatch from Eustis, dated September 18, containing orders for the campaign. The Prophet was to be encouraged to disperse his band peaceably; if he refused, arms were to be used to take him prisoner and break up the hostile settlement. The Indians were to be warned that if the United States were ever again forced to send an expedition to the area, the tribes would be driven far from their present lands. If the Prophet's followers dispersed peacefully, Harrison was authorized to take hostages. He was given authority to build a fort along the Wabash and, most important of all, to depart from the above orders, upon his discretion. If the campaign were a failure, it would not be because the commander was overly restricted.

In his reply to Eustis, Harrison wrote that the army numbered 900 effectives at the fort, that they were awaiting the arrival of wagons from Vincennes (since water transport would be too dangerous near the Indian stronghold). Because the Prophet's force was estimated at 500,[15] he was requesting four additional companies of Indiana militia to report.

On October 28 the fort was completed, named Fort Harrison at the request of the troops, and duly christened with a bottle of whisky. A provision boat arrived with flour, two of the extra militia companies reported, and the army prepared to march on Prophet's Town. Lieutenant-Colonel James Miller,[16] ill with fever, was detailed to command the garrison, composed mainly of the sick; Major George R. Floyd would command the regulars on the march, since Boyd retained direct command of all infantry.

The army left the fort on October 29. Harrison stayed behind for one day, arranging for Miami messengers to inform the Prophet that any murderers of whites must be surrendered and friendly Indians allowed to return to their tribes. Preparing to rejoin his command, Harrison wrote Eustis that the army had been drilled daily and that the soldiers were the equal of Wayne's men at Fallen Timbers.

On October 31 the army crossed to the west side of the Wabash, north of Big Raccoon Creek. Two days later the men halted on a small prairie three miles below the Vermilion River, and on the west side of the Wabash, built a blockhouse (Fort Boyd) twenty-five feet square, and established some sort of security by clearing the weeds for a few rods around it.[17] A sergeant and eight men were detailed to garrison the blockhouse and guard the provision boats, which were to remain there.

Harrison learned that Indians had attacked a boat carrying corn to the advancing army four miles north of Fort Harrison, killing one of the crew, and that the boat had returned to Fort Harrison. As a precaution against similar events, Harrison detached a number of cavalrymen to patrol the settlements and authorized the senior militia officer at Vincennes to call out his whole force if necessary.[18]

14

On November 3 the army left Fort Boyd, crossed the Vermilion, and continued up the west side of the Wabash. The next day the army swung northwestward to avoid possible ambush points, such as the narrow pass at the mouth of Pine Creek. On the night of November 5 the army was only eleven miles from Prophet's Town. More open country was encountered as the army approached the town the following day and Harrison ordered the advance in rough battle line and, two miles from town, in full battle line.[19] Captain Touissant Dubois, head of the scouts, was ordered forward under a flag of truce to arrange an interview with the Prophet. Although the Indians were plainly visible, they made no effort to contact Dubois and he was recalled. Harrison decided to encamp for the night and try to reach the Prophet the next day.

No sooner was the decision taken than three Indians contacted Major Daviess reconnoitering with the cavalry, and were quickly passed to Governor Harrison. One of the Indians, The White Horse, expressed amazement that the army should appear after Harrison had sent word by a Miami deputation that he would not advance until he had received an answer to his demands. He added that Winnemac, a leading Potawatomi, had left two days before, traveling via the east side of the Wabash, to carry the answer to Fort Harrison. Harrison assured the Indians he had no intention of attacking if his demands were met and that he would consult with the Prophet the next day.

After this, the army continued to maneuver until it was only one hundred and fifty yards from the town and then halted, without having seen a camp site with wood, water, and defensible ground. Captain Dubois, who believed such a site could be found above the town, was sent to examine the ground; he was accompanied by Quartermaster William Piatt and Captain Benjamin Parke, with twenty-five of his Indiana dragoons. When The White Horse had consulted Harrison, he had informed him that a site might be found northwest of the town. Majors Marston Clark and Waller Taylor were sent to scout in that direction. Taylor reported finding a favorable location. After an exchange of pledges of no hostility until after the forthcoming parley, the three Indians returned to the village, and the army moved toward its camp site.

The camp was set up on a stretch of about ten acres of dry ground. The front faced southeastward and was a few feet above the marshy prairie intervening between the site and Prophet's Town, with similar but higher ground in the rear, which in turn gave way to marsh, and then a little further to Burnet's Creek. Taking advantage of the terrain, Harrison arranged his men along the high ground with his lines forming a truncated pyramid, with the apex pointing southwestward. The left flank was about one hundred and fifty yards long, the right about seventy-five, and the front probably not over three hundred. Oak trees, especially on the right flank, furnished firewood badly needed by the inadequately clad men, the majority of whom faced the night without tents. Although Harrison was later criticized for his choice, it seems doubtful that he could have found a better site.

Companies and larger units of regulars and militia infantry were interspersed in single strength along the front and rear; riflemen filled the flanks. All were to sleep within a few feet of their places in the battle line. The dragoons were divided into two groups and stationed in the center to act as dismounted reserves or to be readily available as cavalry. Horses, provisions, livestock, baggage, and headquarters were also in the center. No formal breastwork was deemed necessary.

Harrison had no reason to suspect that the Indians might attack—they could have attacked any time during the day with the advantage of choosing their ground. Nevertheless, he ordered the men to lie on their arms and detailed a large guard of about one hundred and forty officers and men. Possibly he even hoped for an attack, for it would obviate the necessity of forcing the issue with the Prophet; then, too, military men of the time generally agreed that a disciplined force was always at an advantage in a night attack by undisciplined men. One thing is certain: Harrison had no intention of attacking the town until he had seen the Prophet.

While the Governor's camp planned a quiet night, the Prophet had decided to attack. Shortly before the dawn the Indians crept through the marsh grass toward Harrison's camp.

Perhaps some warriors had been told to penetrate the camp

and assassinate Harrison as a preliminary to a general attack.[20] At any rate, soon after 4:00 A.M. on Thursday, November 7, two privates of the regulars stationed at adjacent guard posts consulted over the nature of some suspicious noises one of them heard. Suddenly came the thud of an arrow into a log. The guards fled from their posts without having seen any Indians or having given any warning to the sleeping encampment. Fortunately, Corporal Stephen Mars of Geiger's Kentucky volunteers, on guard near by, fired at an advancing Indian, thus alerting the camp. Mars was killed by other Indians, but his shot was heard by Harrison as he pulled on his boots, and prepared to issue his customary order to awaken the men to stand to their arms until daylight. Had the attack come a few minutes later, all the men would have been at their posts.

The attack came at the northwestern part of the camp. Captain William C. Baen's company of regulars and Geiger's Kentucky volunteers received the first shock. Some Indians appeared near the regulars' tents, but apparently only two penetrated to the interior of the camp. The majority of the Kentucky volunteers steadfastly held their ground.

At the outset Harrison called for his mount, a gray mare, which he had ridden the preceding day and had ordered saddled and tied up that night. However, the mare had broken loose during the night, and Harrison's servant could not find her. The General hastily mounted a bay belonging to Major Taylor and dashed to the attack point, accompanied by Abraham Owen, his volunteer aide. While hurrying toward the scene of action, Owen was shot and killed. Harrison believed that Owen, riding a light-colored horse, had been mistaken for himself. In any event, when Taylor appeared on Harrison's gray mare, the commander ordered him to get a darker mount.

When Harrison reached the attacked angle, all the men of the camp were at their posts. He ordered two companies of regulars to be moved up from the center of the rear line, where the ground was easily defensible. No sooner had these orders been given than the Indian attack spread along the left flank and left section of the front. Again the commander rushed to view the scene and

17

discovered that Major Daviess had just ordered some of his cavalry to prepare to charge in support of the regulars of the left front. Yielding to Daviess' urgings and mistakenly believing all Daviess' men were to take part, Harrison authorized the charge. But only a few men erupted from the American lines behind the Kentuckian, and when Daviess was severely wounded, the outnumbered force quickly withdrew. Then a full company of regulars under Captain Josiah Snelling, an officer the country was later to hear much of, charged and drove off the attackers.

By this time the attack had spread clockwise around the entire lines except the center of the rear. Besides those already mentioned, the most serious casualties were inflicted on Spier Spencer's Indiana riflemen and Jacob Warwick's Indiana infantry. Spencer and two other officers of his company were killed, and Warwick mortally wounded. Yet the companies held until another rearrangement of men permitted reinforcements. Harrison's chief strategy was to preserve his lines until daylight, when the infantry and cavalry could charge.

When daylight came, six companies were withdrawn from the front and rear to reinforce the flanks and permit a charge. However, Major Samuel Wells, commanding the left flank and unaware of Harrison's plans, took the four companies just reporting to his sector and led a charge supported by only a few mounted troops. The Indians were driven to cover in the swamp, and the Americans returned to their lines. Shortly afterward, a similar charge from the right flank, but without dragoons, produced similar results. In this fashion the Indians were driven from the camp. The commander did not consider it prudent to order his mounted men to pursue them over the unfamiliar ground and so, except for flushing a few wounded Indians hiding near the camp, the two-hour Battle of Tippecanoe was over. Harrison's men had beaten off the attack, but at high cost.

As with the later battles of the war, it is difficult to establish accurate figures for troop strength and casualties. A return of October 12 [21] shows the strength, including officers, to have been 1,020, of whom 65 were sick. A few joined after that date, but certainly well over a hundred were left at Fort Harrison or at Fort Boyd, or were detailed to patrol the settlements. Harrison later reported that he had left Fort Harrison with less than 880 men, probably excluding officers. In his report of the battle he stated that he had only 700 enlisted men, excluding the dragoons, whom he said he had not really used. The dragoons certainly should have been included (they numbered over 100), and it would seem that Harrison's figures were too low. Probably there were closer to 1,000 officers and men at the battle. At any rate, 188 casualties were reported, of whom 62 were killed or had died of wounds before November 18.[22]

It is impossible to state definitely the number of Indians engaged in any battle of that day. Harrison later gathered testimony from various sources, including Indians, and concluded that over 700 Indians were present.[23] It would seem that between 500 and 800 Indians fought in the Battle of Tippecanoe. Of these, about 40 were found dead on the field, and others were known to have been carried away by the retreating Indians. One Potawatomi chief was captured, his wounds were tended, and he was later released to convey the message that even now the Indians would be forgiven if they left the Prophet.

For the remainder of the day the army tended its wounded, buried the dead, and built a breastwork to ward off a second attack. Tecumseh was falsely rumored to be approaching with a large force. The rations were slim, for the flour supply was low; horse-flesh made up for the cattle that had escaped in the melee. The next day a cavalry detail went to Prophet's Town and found it deserted. After taking a quantity of corn and beans, the Americans burned the wooden huts.

On November 9 the army marched from camp, with the wagons loaded with wounded. At Fort Boyd the most severely wounded were loaded on to boats. By November 15 the force reached Fort Harrison, and two skeleton companies of regulars under Captain Snelling were left as a garrison. The rest returned to Vincennes, where the militia was discharged. The campaign, lasting fifty-three days, was over.

It would seem that Harrison's campaign should have been considered a success, qualified only by his failure to capture the Prophet. The confederation itself must have seemed severely damaged, if not destroyed—certainly other Indians would now be more reluctant to join. Indeed, most of the Old Northwest was aroused to a fever pitch by news of the battle, many seeing the hand of Great Britain behind the savages. The already well-known Andrew Jackson, then commanding a Tennessee militia division, offered his services and his men for use in any action against the remnants of the Tippecanoe Indians saying, "That banditti [sic] ought to be swept from the face of the earth." [24]

Nevertheless, several old political enemies of both Harrison and the national administration were active. Though few in number, they organized skeleton meetings praising Boyd and his regulars but ignoring Harrison and the militia. They represented themselves as speaking for the whole people and exploited an already existing feud between Boyd and Harrison, when the former cordially replied to their resolutions. Perhaps their chief point was that Harrison had failed to safeguard against surprise. This charge was clearly untrue.

The militia and their supporters rose to the defense, although not seeking to minimize the contribution of the regulars to the campaign. Testimonial after testimonial established a more factual appraisal of Harrison. With the Indians quiet, Harrison relinquished command of the regulars. In the spring Boyd departed for the East, and the regiment passed to the more capable command of Lieutenant-Colonel James Miller.

Meanwhile, the Prophet, although discredited in the eyes of most Indians, was granted asylum by others and bided his time along Wild Cat Creek, southeast of Prophet's Town. The next chapter in his relations with the Americans was to unfold under the more expert direction of Tecumseh, with the aid of the British.

Ironically, because the battle never would have occurred had Tecumseh been at Prophet's Town, one of the important results of Tippecanoe was that it established Harrison as the one man in the West to block Tecumseh during the war that was to follow. Clear-thinking Americans saw two possibilities of war: Great

Britain or the Indians. Once the twin dangers of Great Britain and the Indians became connected in the minds of Americans, war soon followed. A separate Indian confederation was one thing, but a British-supported confederation was quite another.

Notes to Chapter I

1. In 1794 a force of about 1,000 Indians, determined to keep the Americans east of the Ohio River, and encouraged by the British who were anxious to maintain a buffer state between the Ohio River and Canada, had congregated around the British garrison, Fort Miami (near the present site of Maumee, Ohio). General Anthony Wayne, who had been ordered to the Ohio region to settle the Indian warfare which had been continuous since the Revolution, led his American army of 3,000 into the Indian country and decisively defeated the Indians near Fort Miami in a battle which came to be known as Fallen Timbers.
2. John B. Dillon, *A History of Indiana* (Indianapolis: Bingham & Doughty, 1858), p. 426.
3. Biographical material on Harrison in this paragraph has been taken from: Freeman Cleaves, *Old Tippecanoe* (New York: Charles Scribner's Sons, 1939), pp. 5–32.
4. Benson J. Lossing, *The Pictorial Field Book of the War of 1812* (New York: Harper & Brothers, 1868), p. 192.
5. See letters to and from Harrison in Logan Esarey (ed.), *Messages and Letters of William Henry Harrison* (Indianapolis: Indiana Historical Commission, 1922), Vol. I, pp. 474–83.
6. *Ibid.*, pp. 539–41.
7. Harrison to Eustis, Vincennes, Aug. 7, 1811, *Ibid.*, p. 549.
8. Adam Walker's Journal, *Ibid.*, p. 698 ff.
9. Vincennes, *Ibid.*, p. 571.
10. Alfred Pirtle, *The Battle of Tippecanoe* (Louisville: "Filson Club Publications," No. 15, 1900), p. 22.
11. *Ibid.*, p. 33. On pp. 111–31, Pirtle reprints a roster showing total strength absent and present of organizations concerned.
12. Dillon, *op. cit.*, p. 458.
13. Harrison to Eustis, Vincennes, Sept. 25, 1811, Esarey (ed.), *op. cit.*, Vol. I, p. 589. More rations were then being brought up the Wabash. Apparently the men also had been issued two days' rations that may not have been included in the above total.
14. Cleaves, *op. cit.*, p. 90. Shabonee had been born an Ottawa but married a Potawatomi and became a chief of that tribe. He later became an active supporter of Tecumseh.
15. Harrison to Eustis, Battelle des Illinois, Oct. 13, 1811, Esarey (ed.), *op. cit.*, Vol. I, p. 600.
16. Miller had been commissioned as a major at the organization of the Fourth in 1808. In 1810 he was promoted to the rank of lieutenant-colonel but was

carried on the rolls of the Fifth, since Zebulon Pike was carried on paper as a lieutenant-colonel of the Fourth until July, 1812. Miller was an able officer, and Harrison wrote Eustis saying, "I have known no better officer and he is so much beloved by the officers and men of the 4th Regiment that I am persuaded that they would follow him to the Devil." Miller resigned as a colonel in 1819 and later served as a Territorial Governor of Arkansas.

17. Nellie A. Robertson and Dorothy Riker (eds.), *The John Tipton Papers*, Indiana Historical Collection (Indianapolis: Indiana Historical Bureau, 1942), Vol. XXIV, p. 76.
18. It was later discovered the Indians attacking the boat were led by Waubunsee, a Potawatomi chief who gained prominence in the 1830's by supporting the U.S.
19. Harrison to Eustis, Vincennes, Nov. 18, 1811, Esarey (ed.), *op. cit.*, Vol. I, p. 620. This is the detailed report Harrison wrote of the battle. Except where otherwise noted, sources for this present account of the battle may be found in Esarey's documents, which include material from sources other than Harrison's letters for this battle. A map of the battleground may be found in Lossing's book, *op. cit.*, p. 205. One of the best secondary accounts of the battle is Cleave's, *op. cit.*, pp. 98–105.
20. It is possible the Indians penetrated the camp to drive off the enemy horses rather than to assassinate Harrison. Earlier that night, a Negro driver named Ben, who apparently had deserted to the Indians, returned to camp and was captured near Harrison's tent. After the battle, Ben was sentenced to execution for desertion and attempted assassination, but Harrison pardoned him.
21. Report enclosed in Harrison to Eustis, Camp Battelle des Illinois, Oct. 13, 1811, Esarey (ed.), *op. cit.*, Vol. I, p. 597.
22. Enclosed in Harrison to Eustis, Vincennes, Nov. 18, 1811, *Ibid.*, pp. 637–38.
23. Harrison to Eustis, Vincennes, Jan. 14, 1812, *Ibid.*, Vol. II, p. 12.
24. Jackson to Harrison, Hermitage, Nov. 28, 1811, *Ibid.*, Vol. I, p. 665.

CHAPTER II

THE OLD NORTHWEST ACQUIRES AN ARMY

AFTER THE BATTLE OF TIPPECANOE, Michigan Territory became the focal point for prewar preparation. At various times this area had been controlled by different European powers. First claimed by France, it was surrendered to Great Britain in 1760, and during the Revolutionary War even Spain had flaunted her colors over a small section. The British did not relinquish effective jurisdiction of the area to the United States until 1796. Successively part of the Northwest Territory and of the Indiana Territory, Michigan became a separate Territory in 1805, and William Hull was appointed its first governor by President Jefferson.

Born in Connecticut in 1753, Hull had graduated from Yale, and had been admitted to the bar before the Revolutionary War. As a militia captain, he had seen service in thirteen battles, had led several bayonet charges, had been cited twice for bravery, and had been promoted to the rank of lieutenant-colonel in the regulars before the end of the war. Retaining his rank in the only infantry regiment maintained after the war, he resigned in 1784 to practice law in Massachusetts. Later he served as a Common Pleas Judge, as a State Senator, and as a commander of a militia division before his appointment in Michigan Territory.

Hull's position was probably more difficult than that of other governors of new territories. He had to administer an area whose population was primarily Indian, French, and British—the area had been barely penetrated by citizens of the United States. He had to establish laws (and provide for their enforcement), which many frontier people would accept reluctantly. And he had to rebuild Detroit, the only town of consequence, most of which had been destroyed by fire prior to his arrival.

Hull seemed well qualified as commander of the militia, although less apt as Superintendent of Indian Affairs, both ex officio jobs of the overworked territorial governors. With his heart in the East, he never understood the alien politics and philosophy of the frontier-bred Westerners—a fact which was to cause repeated friction during the War of 1812. Nevertheless, Hull made a bold beginning: He rebuilt Detroit, established laws, set up the militia, and sternly guided the Territory through the days of near war with the British.

The war scare of 1807–09 had its causes outside of Michigan, but Governor Hull, aware of the situation, offered his services to the Secretary of War. Awaiting a reply, he ordered out three companies of militia and strengthened the defense at Detroit. Meanwhile, the British at Fort Malden,[1] a few miles downstream and across the river, were also building up their defenses.

During this period, the Americans pleaded with the Indians to remain neutral if war came but offered no tangible inducement. On the other hand, the British in lieu of the regulars they lacked and the militia they mistrusted, actively enlisted the aid of the Indians to defend their country. However, the British determination to continue building naval vessels to ensure permanent control of the Great Lakes was in the long run the most important decision taken by either side during these years. The United States abandoned all efforts to build public vessels for the Lakes and, in effect, lost the opening campaigns of the War of 1812 three years before they started.

According to the Census of 1810, approximately half of Michigan's total population of 4,762 lived in the district of Detroit, an area paralleling the river from five miles above to ten miles below the town.[2] Most other inhabitants were scattered along the main waterways of southeastern Michigan. Thus, a long, narrow column of settlers was flanked by the British on one side and by the woods and the Indians on the other. In the event of an alliance between the British and the Indians, Michigan faced a war on two fronts. Therefore, Indian affairs loomed large in the minds of the Territorial Governor and other officials.

As a result of various treaties, Hull, in 1811, paid annuities in goods valued at $5,650 [3] to the Wyandot, Ottawa, Chippewa, and Potawatomi in this region. These were debts, not presents—the Indians had been told in 1807 they would receive no more presents. The Wyandot, who had great influence with the tribes in the North, lived along the American side of the Detroit River in their villages of Brownstown and Monguagon, both south of the Rouge River. They occupied a strategic position on the land communication route to Detroit.

Hull, considering the friendship of the Wyandots of great importance, sought ways to placate them. General Wayne had promised the Wyandots a grant of land for an official reservation, but this had never been established. By 1810–11 settlers illegally moving into land as yet unsurveyed encroached on Wyandot territory. The Wyandots threatened to burn out the settlers but yielded to Hull's plea for peace, coupled with his promise to attempt to secure for them the area from Monguagon to south of the Huron River.[4] After this, Hull felt he could rely on their friendship, firmly believing they were opposed to Tecumseh's confederation. He was not sure of the other tribes.

The government factory system, established late in the eighteenth century, was an attempt by the United States to counteract the influence of British fur traders with the Indians. In 1811 the important trading posts were at Chicago and Michilimackinac, although others did exist in the Northwest. At Michilimackinac, the factor, Joseph B. Varnum, had shown a profit above all expenses of over $3,000 from 1808 to the end of September in 1811. But the system's effectiveness should not be judged solely by the amounts of money involved. The factor made friends for the

United States, passed on information concerning Indian movements and attitudes, and was generally a nuisance to the British fur trade.

A step toward understanding between British and American fur traders was taken when the British North West Fur Company agreed to operate only within specified areas of the United States. In exchange, the British fur traders received stock in the newly founded South West Fur Company, plus a similar pledge on the part of the latter to operate only outside of Canada.[5] This agreement over areas of trade should have reduced British influence over Indians living in the United States, but paradoxically during the next year or two it was a more disturbing than a quieting influence.

Irrespective of outward signs of economic co-operation, the British continued their efforts to influence the Indians by inviting them to report at distribution centers to receive presents. In February, 1812, the Indian Office storehouses at Amherstburg held: 10,000 blankets, 9,345 gun flints, 462 muskets, 66 rifles, 5,560 pounds of gunpowder, 763 pounds of bar lead, and 8 bullet molds, but no ball or shot.[6] These goods were all earmarked as outright presents to the Indians; they were not annuity payments.

The British at Amherstburg issued gunpowder and lead to the Indians in the fall of 1811; however, in the first six months of 1812 they issued no lead and only about one third the usual supply of powder.[7] Most of the supplies presented to the Indians during this period were intended to increase their hunting effectiveness—the fur trade being a primary concern of the British.

The expenses of the Indian Department of Canada amounted to £9,044 in 1812.[8] This British largess to Indians residing in the United States rankled the Americans. But the root of the problem was that Indians resented less the British policy of disguised exploitation than the American policy of actual displacement. The Indians seemed to feel that the British really distributed presents out of the goodness of their hearts, while the Americans disbursed only what they owed them.

No doubt Hull had the Indian situation in mind when he wrote for Presidential approval for a trip to the East to consult with the government and to visit his home. Having received permission and believing the Territory to be reasonably safe, Hull, on September 29, turned his duties over to Acting Governor Reuben Attwater and departed for Massachusetts. During his absence he heard news of the Battle of Tippecanoe and, realizing the possibility of joint British and Indian action, wrote to Eustis offering to serve in any military office. His services were not deemed necessary, and in February, 1812, Hull proceeded to Washington to present his recommendations for the defense of Michigan and receive any orders before returning to Detroit.

Meanwhile, on December 8, the citizens of Detroit, on learning of the Battle of Tippecanoe, had addressed a memorial to the federal government.[9] Analyzing the population by districts, they had pointed out the difficulty of defending such a sparsely populated area with a regular force of only 94 soldiers at Detroit and 79 at Michilimackinac, in addition to the militia. They had expressed certainty that any war would bring joint British and Indian action and urged an increase in existing garrisons, as well as the erection of at least one new fort in the interior north of Detroit, together with new garrisons at specified locations outside the Territory. Attwater had added his pleas for aid, stressing the unreliability of the militiamen,[10] who were mainly of French or British stock and might well be reluctant to fight in a war that would have too little at stake for the former and too much for the latter.

In Washington Hull added his weight to the request for assistance by writing a letter to the Secretary of War.[11] He summarized the steps already taken by the War Department to strengthen Michigan: the authorization for the recruitment of regulars and the detachment of four militia companies for active duty, the orders for erecting gun batteries along the river to protect the town. These measures improved the defense but did not increase the numerical strength. Comparing the white population of Upper Canada with that of Michigan, the Governor stated that in the event of war his people might be outnumbered twenty to one. He offered suggestions to overcome this disadvantage.

First, he urged the immediate construction of sufficient naval vessels to command the Great Lakes, arguing that if the United States should suffer the loss of water communication, it would have to construct roads through the forests and swamps of northern Ohio to bring aid to Michigan. Next, Hull pointed out that Detroit would be the best strategic place to station more regulars, for they could move rapidly against Upper Canada if war came. Failure to gain control of the Lakes or to reinforce Detroit extensively could result in the loss of the whole area to the British, and would equip the enemy with military stores from the captured forts.

The War Department ignored Hull's suggestion for naval vessels for the Great Lakes. In view of this apathy toward an inland fleet, it is interesting to note that two months earlier, John Armstrong, a veteran officer of the Revolution destined to succeed Eustis as Secretary of War, had also written the War Department advocating the basing of a strong force at Detroit *providing* that naval control were assured on Lake Erie to safeguard supply routes.[12]

To Hull's suggestion that strong military reinforcements be sent to Michigan, the Secretary of War was more receptive. Apparently intending to order Hull to lead these reinforcements to Michigan, Eustis offered the Governor a commission as a brigadier-general. Because Hull did not wish to resign from his civil office,[13] he declined; Colonel Jacob Kingsbury, then on leave from his post as Commanding Officer of the First Infantry with headquarters at Fort Detroit, was assigned to the duty.

Kingsbury was ordered to proceed to Pittsburgh, assemble his recruits, continue to Ohio, and march reinforcements of 1,200 Ohio militia and some regulars to Detroit.[14] He was to construct a wagon road from Ohio to Detroit and build a stockade near the Rapids of the Miami of the Lake (later named the Maumee River). He was to bring Detroit to a state of readiness and augment his force by recruitment. Despite the challenge of these orders to a military man, Colonel Kingsbury had to decline the assignment because he was suffering from a severe attack of gout.[15]

It was urgent that an officer be appointed to fulfill the mission and desirable that such a commander have previous knowledge of the people and the area. Eustis again offered the assignment to Governor Hull, this time with a commission of colonel and with special permission to retain his gubernatorial post. Once more the veteran declined, perhaps believing the Administration's plans inadequate, possibly hoping for higher rank. Soon Eustis made another offer, and this Hull accepted. On April 3 President Madison nominated Hull as a brigadier-general, and the Senate confirmed the appointment five days later. (There was opposition to Hull's appointment, led by Senator Thomas Worthington of Ohio; the grounds were not opposition to Hull, but fear that any reinforcement at Detroit would precipitate a war.[16]) By this appointment, Hull became the seventh ranking officer of the United States, with the unique distinction of receiving pay simultaneously from two government sources.

On April 9 Hull received his orders. They were substantially the same as Kingsbury's had been, but the Fourth Regiment was to join the advancing column at Dayton or Staunton, Ohio. Besides the posts of Fort Wayne and Fort Dearborn, Hull's command included all federal troops in Michigan. His duties were to conduct affairs in a manner that would preserve peace with the Indians.

The purpose of this force, now named the North Western Army, was fourfold: to safeguard Michigan; to counteract British influence with the Indians, especially in the event of war; to gain command of Lake Erie (without the aid of any ships) ; and to co-operate with other forces in any future campaigns.[17] General Hull became acquainted with the over-all campaign plans of the federal government and visited President Madison on at least two occasions to discuss the matter. He urged that a navy be built for the Lakes; that, as an absolute minimum, a twenty-ton sloop be built and based at Detroit to complement the *Adams*,[18] the only vessel then in commission on the Upper Lakes. He also requested that the reinforcements for Michigan should number 3,000. President Madison refused these requests. General Peter B. Porter, who had accompanied Hull to the Executive Mansion, wisely, if not disinterestedly, suggested that the military contractor serving

Detroit be notified immediately of the impending need for additional provisions. However, the government delayed such notification—a minor neglect had not war broken out and cut off the use of water routes before extra provisions could reach Detroit.

These conversations with the President determined the fate of Hull's army. Without sufficient provisions, control of Lake Erie, or more men—any one of which could have saved him—he was destined to lose.

Departing from Baltimore on April 21, 1812, Hull took with him his son, Captain Abraham Hull, and his son-in-law, Captain Harris Hickman, for whom he had obtained commissions to serve as his aides. At Pittsburgh he failed to find the expected number of recruits. He was, however, joined by another detachment of forty men under Ensign Robert T. McCabe. He continued his journey on April 29, shepherding his recruits, and gathering as large a supply of blankets, tents, and knapsacks as could be requisitioned. All arrived at Cincinnati on May 7, with Hull taking quarters in the Columbian Inn,[19] the best in a town of some 400-odd dwellings. Hull put the tired recruits to work making cartridges—army commanders, then as now, believed in the adage that idleness begets sin. He also set out to discover what progress had been made in organizing the Ohio militia force.

Toward the end of March, the Secretary of War had written to the Governor of Ohio, Return J. Meigs, to order 1,200 men detached from the militia, placed under the command of a lieutenant-colonel, and marched to Detroit. The orders stipulated that one third of the force was to be composed of riflemen. Any possible offense to the Indians was to be avoided, and the Indians were to be notified of the force's intent to pass peaceably through their territory.

As an aftermath of the frontier troubles of the previous fall, several companies of United States rangers had been organized in the West. Captains James Manary and William Perry were commissioned, and their companies recruited and ordered to rendezvous in April; this was Ohio's quota of the rangers, who were to protect the frontiers while the militia detachment was forming.

30

The rangers, together with the expected militia detachment, would scarcely make a dent in Ohio's total man power. The official state militia return of February, 1812, reported a total of 34,726, including officers and men.[20] Probably an even greater number were eligible, for the Census of 1810 reported 42,950 free white males between the ages of 16 and 45, out of a total population of over 230,000. Interestingly enough, no lieutenant-colonels were authorized by Ohio law, but one should have been appointed to comply with Eustis' orders. This would be no problem; the state had no shortage of higher officers, for 49 full colonels and 21 generals were reported.

On April 6 Meigs ordered each of the four divisions of Ohio militia to detach 300 men, volunteers if possible, for the proposed force. No assembly point or date was designated at that time, but Meigs later ordered a rendezvous at Dayton for April 29—perhaps because he had received Eustis' notice that the Fourth Regiment was under orders to stop at either Staunton or Dayton on its march to Detroit. Feverish activity to meet the deadline began all over the state: Volunteers had to be enrolled at all levels, rough companies organized, officers elected (state commissions were invalid for federal service), and all units equipped and marched in groups of varying sizes to the assembly point.

Meeting the appointed date was a rather hopeless task, and it is not surprising that only a trickle of men arrived in Dayton on time; indeed, some were held back because of equipment shortages at the assembly point. For one thing, there was an acute shortage of blankets; various trade difficulties with England, the normal supplier of these, had depleted supplies in this country. Meigs's successful appeal to the patriotic women of Cincinnati to draw on their own household supplies demonstrated his concern for the men. Throughout the entire organizational period, the Ohio Governor played an active role—so much so that an anonymous tract accused him of not only making political speeches while recruiting men but also of aiding his political favorites to raise companies so that they might be elected officers.[21]

It is unfortunate that such distorted criticism should have marred the appreciation of his services at such a decisive hour.

Meigs had served on the highest court in his native Connecticut; he had been the military commander of Louisiana Territory and a judge on that Territorial Court. Appointed a judge on Michigan's Territorial Court in 1807, he had resigned before actual service and had been elected Governor of Ohio. The election was invalidated because he had failed to comply with residence requirements; however, Meigs was appointed a Senator. In 1810 he had been legally elected Governor of Ohio. The organization of Hull's militia force was largely due to the efforts of the Ohio Governor.

As the men drifted into Dayton, a town of a little more than four hundred people, they were directed to a camp pitched three miles from town along the northern bank of the Mad River. Most men arrived in units of company strength under newly elected officers. Under prevailing regulations all field-grade officers were to be elected by the officers of lesser rank. Thus, each officer had to be popular with the men and officers under him, but popularity was usually not the only prerequisite to leadership. The most effective militia generals were ones such as Harrison, who won the respect and confidence of their men by explaining rather than ordering, and who at all times bore in mind that the militia remained civilians in habit and thought. Unsuccessful as generals were those who expected the militia to act like regulars and who were unable or unwilling to vary their command techniques.

Three regiments were organized under Governor Meigs's orders. The field officers of the First Regiment of Ohio Volunteers were Colonel Duncan McArthur, Major James Denny, and Major William Trimble. McArthur, then forty years old and wealthy from land speculation, had left his home near Chillicothe to volunteer, jeopardizing his existing commission as a major-general in the Ohio militia to the whims of junior officers holding an election. He had seen service as a scout under Generals Harmar and Wayne and as a ranger in the Scioto Valley. Since he had been popular enough to be elected to both houses of his state legislature and had served as a militia general for at least four years, there was little danger that he would have to serve in the ranks—though he had promised to do so if not elected to commissioned rank.

The Second Regiment of Ohio Volunteers, composed mainly of men from the Cincinnati area, elected Colonel James Findlay and Majors Thomas Moore and Thomas Van Horne. Findlay was two years older than McArthur, but despite his commission as brigadier-general in the Ohio militia, had had little active military service. He had had a successful political career: legislative council, United States Marshal, and Mayor of Cincinnati. A dependable, steady and conscientious officer, he lacked the fire that marks an outstanding leader.

The Third Regiment elected Lewis Cass as colonel and Robert Morrison as major, leaving another major to be chosen later. Cass, only thirty, had attended Exeter Academy, had moved to Ohio and studied law under Meigs, but had had no active military service. A brigadier-general in the militia, he had been a United States Marshal, served in the legislature, and was then prosecuting attorney for Muskingum County.

Obviously, these three colonels had no great amount of formal military service, but few active officers had, except in small engagements against Indians. They certainly were men of unusual political talents and, many people would add, of military ability as well. Cass and McArthur were later to serve during the war as successful brigadiers in the regular army, with Findlay declining a similar appointment. McArthur was to become Congressman and Governor of Ohio. In later life Findlay was elected to Congress but was defeated for governor by Robert Lucas, who also served under Hull. Cass, of course, was to have an unusual career as Governor of Michigan and in federal offices. Whether or not Meigs had unduly used his influence, it is clear today that the Ohio regiments were commanded by able men.

The lack of regular uniforms was another problem facing Meigs in preparing his force for federal service. It was solved with typical pioneer aplomb by adopting the only readily available substitute: homespun linen hunting shirts, trousers, leather belts, and low-crowned felt hats.

Still another problem was a shortage of weapons and ammunition. Eustis' original orders had stipulated that one third of the force were to be riflemen. Customarily riflemen owned their own pieces, for which they received pay allowances. However, in this instance, many riflemen reported without arms. Most of the regular militia had government muskets, many needing repair. To provide the needed stand of arms and to make up for the deficiency of gunpowder in the Ohio militia stores, Meigs drew on the arsenal at Newport, Kentucky.

A few details remained to be taken care of before the regiments would be ready for service. A skeleton medical staff was assigned to each regiment, and medical supplies were prepared under the supervision of Doctor Richard Allison, who had been chief surgeon of Wayne's expedition but had declined service in the field in this campaign. A dispensary seems to have been maintained at the camp, but hospital services probably were not available, for several men were hospitalized in private homes in Dayton.[22]

The men's spiritual welfare was provided for by Joseph L. Hughes, appointed chaplain of the Ohio force. Most of the units had received spiritual blessing before leaving their own areas. Probably a fairly typical ministerial send-off was that accorded the Cincinnati Light Infantry Company. The men were exhorted by both the Reverend W. Buck and the Reverend Joshua Wilson.[23] The former chose a bellicose text (Joel 3:9–10). "Proclaim ye this among the nations; prepare war: stir up the mighty men; let all the men of war draw near, let them come up. Beat your plowshares into swords, and your pruninghooks into spears." The Reverend Wilson preached a sermon entitled "War the Work of the Lord," his text from Jeremiah 48:10, "Cursed be he that doeth the work of the Lord negligently, and cursed be he that keepeth back his sword from blood."

Meigs had, in common with all governors of frontier states or territories, primary responsibility for the defense of his state against Indian attacks. In January Congress had authorized the formation of six companies of United States rangers, and five of these had actually been raised in Ohio, Indiana, Illinois, and Kentucky. Except for aid from the few scattered and undermanned companies of regulars remaining after the assignment of the Fourth Regiment to Hull, these rangers were expected to maintain the peace with the Indians for the whole of the Northwest. After an abnormally quiet winter, Indian depredations had begun anew. These raids, scattered among the territories of Louisiana, Illinois, and Indiana, had spread to Ohio. Evidently Tippecanoe had not been the panacea it was hoped it would be. As an aftermath of the raids, frequently many families fled from their lonely clearings—for example, in Miami and Darke counties of Ohio. To protect these two counties, and to deter removal of the settlers, Meigs took advantage of the force abuilding at Dayton to detach a company each to Piqua and Greenville.

At least fifteen whites had been killed in Indiana and Illinois alone. Governor Harrison ordered his militia to a state of readiness. He had previously advised all settlers in exposed areas to build small blockhouses in which neighboring settlers could seek refuge at any sign of danger. Now he ordered the militia officer nearest any attacked point to organize immediate pursuit of any raiding party. The effectiveness of this system depended upon advance notice of danger; and this was to be the function of the rangers. Eustis had ordered Colonel William Russell to the active command of regulars who had not been assigned to Hull's army and of the rangers in the Northwest. Thus, by the time the Ohio force was ready to assume federal jurisdiction, part of the Northwest was protected by a thinly spread but constantly patrolling force of rangers, with militiamen in a state of readiness to support. This was to remain the basic system of protection throughout the approaching war.

It was believed that the advance of Hull's army to Michigan Territory would inaugurate a period of Indian quiescence, since the presence of a large force deep in their country should induce warriors to remain near their families instead of risking the army's wrath through frontier raids. Indeed, most Indians of the area assembled early in May at a council along the Mississinewa River in eastern Indiana and apparently decided on a policy of peace,[24] at least for the moment.

Meanwhile General Hull, at Meigs's request, remained at Cincinnati, planning his expected march and awaiting notice that the Ohio men were ready for federal service. He had written to Vincennes to order the march of the Fourth Regiment to Ohio. He also assured the Secretary of the War that, while he anticipated minor Indian troubles on the way to Detroit, he hoped to nullify these actions by the use of a previously planned line of march, battle and camp formations, and sufficient scouts or spies. Too, as soon as he assumed command of the Ohio force, he would send messengers to the Indians informing them of the peaceful intent of the army's march.

One of Hull's most pressing problems was choosing the best route to Detroit. Every way led through Indian country and the shortest—due northward—would cross the Black Swamp of northern Ohio, over a hundred miles long and forty miles wide. (Generals Wayne, Harmar, and St. Clair had all swung westward to avoid this morass.) Senator Thomas Worthington had suggested a route via Piqua to Fort Defiance (Wayne's abandoned post on the Miami), then by water to Detroit. Hull, after consultation with men familiar with the area, finally chose to travel over the Miami River to Loramie's Fort, portage to the Auglaize, thence downstream to the Miami of the Lake, and then to Lake Erie and the Detroit River. This route would avoid the Black Swamp, and the supplies could be transported by water and escorted by the army marching along the shore.

One difficult problem remained: trying to ensure a sufficient supply (ideally an even flow) of provisions for the army on the march, as well as at Detroit. Hull had received no answer to a letter to the agents of Augustus Porter, the military contractor for Detroit. Therefore, he contracted with the Cincinnati firm of John H. Piatt for sufficient supplies to see the army safely to its destination.

On the morning of May 25 General Hull and Governor Meigs approached Dayton for the formal exchange of command of the Ohio regiments. Pausing south of the town, they addressed short speeches to McArthur's Regiment quartered there and then proceeded to the main camp, hereafter known as Camp Meigs, three miles north of Dayton on the bank of the Mad River. The men formed, were reviewed by the two governors, and closed ranks in preparation for the formal ceremony. Meigs addressed them first, stressing his trust in their commander and exhorting the men to improve their discipline, saying, "Subordination is the soul of discipline: order, safety, and victory are its results." Hull, in accepting command, spoke of the danger from the Indians and the latent hostility of the British. Then, led by Colonel Cass, the troops uncovered and responded with three cheers for each of the speakers. That same day Hull dispatched messengers to the Indians requesting permission to travel through their country.[25]

The following day the men assembled again, and Cass gave a short address, vowing that the Eagle of Liberty was more than a match for the British Lion. The principal business was the commander's first inspection, which revealed that the arms were still in poor condition, the powder scarce, and some men still without blankets. But present equipment would have to do; it was time to march.

On June 1 the army left Dayton, its immediate objective being Loramie's Fort,[26] on the Greenville Treaty line. Unseasonably low water halted further progress six miles from Staunton, perhaps only twenty-four miles from Dayton and sixty miles from its first goal. Convinced of the impracticability of water transport, and finding agreement among his senior officers, the General determined to move to Urbana and strike out overland due north for the Miami River across the Black Swamp. As the General wrote Eustis, this was not only the shortest route to Detroit but it would provide a road from the Ohio settlements, essential to provisioning his army should war seal off the normal lake routes. So the army moved toward Urbana to arrange for the overland transport of goods and await the arrival of the Fourth Regiment.

At this time Hull formed a small company of rangers under the command of Captain William McCulloch, and Captain Thompson Maxwell was engaged as chief guide. One of the most colorful men in Hull's army, Maxwell gained his livelihood in peacetime by driving hogs overland from the settled parts of Ohio to eager buyers in Detroit. This venerable drover, then seventy years old, had served in the French and Indian War, participated in the Boston Tea Party, and fought in the Revolution.[27]

Since the old Greenville line had been drawn eastward from Fort Recovery to Fort Laurens, then down the Tuscarawas and Cuyahoga rivers to Lake Erie, the expanse north of about 40° 30′ was Indian country. The tribes had responded to Hull's request for permission to cross this area with the army. On June 6, while Hull's army was en route, Meigs held a preliminary council at Urbana with the Indians there. The following day the army arrived and on June 8, after Meigs had reviewed the army—an event arranged to overawe the Indians—a formal treaty was concluded. The twelve chiefs representing the Wyandot, Shawnee, and Iroquois (known to frontiersmen as Mingoes) signed, authorizing the construction of a road to the Rapids of the Miami of the Lake and the erection of protective blockhouses along the road. The agreement forbade the location of any settlers along the right of way. General Hull announced to the assemblage of Indians that in forty days he would hold a general Indian council at Brownstown, south of Detroit. Some chiefs accepted his invitation to accompany his army on the march. The General felt their presence would help avoid misunderstandings with Indians on the way.

The change of route had delayed Hull's schedule of advance. But he hoped to build three blockhouses between Urbana and the Rapids and still arrive at Detroit by July 1. Captain James Manary's Rangers, one of the companies raised for federal service that spring, but not under Hull's command, had already erected a blockhouse north of modern Bellefontaine, only one mile from the Greenville Treaty line and twenty miles beyond Urbana. Hull detailed several companies to open a wagon road to the blockhouse in preparation for the early march of the army. While the army awaited the arrival of the Fourth Regiment, wagons, teams, and teamsters to transport supplies and baggage were engaged.

Toward the end of April Lieutenant-Colonel Miller, in command of the Fourth Regiment at Vincennes, had been ordered to move his regiment to Dayton, Ohio, and await further orders. Due to several recent Indian incidents in the area, the regiment's departure was delayed because Miller was reluctant to leave until other protection was provided for the inhabitants. Arrangements were made for a few regulars from other regiments to remain: Fort Harrison was to be garrisoned by Captain Zachary Taylor's company of recruits, the Seventh Regiment; the remnants of two other companies were stationed at Fort Knox; and the company of rangers raised for federal service was also available. Furthermore, an extensive militia force was called out by Governor Harrison to fill partially the vacuum created by the departing regulars.

On May 14 a stately group of regulars marched from Vincennes. Since these were regulars, their families were allowed to accompany them to the new station. The troops reached Cincinnati on June 3. Passing under an arch inscribed "To the Heroes of Tippecanoe," the regiment was escorted by an honor guard to a tavern, where a beef barbecue was served, complete with whisky and fresh bread, both highly welcome to soldiers on the march. One week later the regiment belatedly arrived at Urbana and received the accolades of their future comrades, again passing through a triumphal arch before being ceremoniously escorted to their camp site.

The exhausted condition of the regulars forced Hull to delay his departure further. To speed the eventual march, Colonel McArthur was detailed seven hundred men and ordered to advance beyond Manary's Blockhouse, to build a road, and to erect the first blockhouse in Indian country.

Meanwhile, Hull again reviewed his troops and announced new staff appointments to the Secretary of War. James Taylor was appointed quartermaster general; Lieutenant Thomas Jessup, on the rolls of the Seventh Regiment, brigade major; Robert Wallace, additional aide; and Doctor Abraham Edwards, surgeon of the Fourth and in charge of the entire medical detachment for the army. Each Ohio regiment already had its own medical department. A corp of artificers was organized, and a traveling forge acquired to assure repairs of arms. The extensive equipment required to transport the supplies of the army necessitated the formation of a separate transport section, loosely attached to Taylor's Quartermaster Department. James Thomson, L. Colwell, and William Martin were appointed respectively as wagon master, forage master, and pack horse master; [28] all had one or more assistants, in addition to the civilians under their orders.

It is impossible to state with certainty the number of wagons or teams that Hull employed on his march. Each wagon was drawn by a four-horse or ox team and, since no artillery was taken on the march, all horses were used as saddle, pack, or wagon horses.

The arrival of the Fourth Regiment precipitated the first serious friction within the North Western Army: Lieutenant-Colonel Miller, in command of the regulars, was outranked by the Ohio colonels. Miller took this situation as an affront both to himself and to his regiment. The situation was such that, in the absence of Hull, the regulars might, in effect, be under the orders of a militia officer. When appealed to by Miller, the General announced that the Lieutenant-Colonel could serve with honor until the Secretary of War could be consulted. The whole problem of rank originated when Meigs had allowed the organization of the Ohio militia volunteers under the command of full colonels rather than under one lieutenant-colonel, as authorized by Eustis. Hull's letter pointed out how this awkward situation had arisen: Meigs had acted in accordance with the constitution and laws of Ohio, which clearly authorized a full colonelcy, to be filled by election, whenever two battalions volunteered. However, at the time of the organization of the Ohio force, Eustis had offered no comment on the apparent disregard for his orders, nor did he express any concern until the protest was made. Hull, of course, had no choice but to accept the Ohio men in grade and, for that matter, Eustis himself was now just as helpless. Either deliberately evading responsibility, or perhaps only seeking to cause as little damage as possible, Eustis later shifted the problem back to Hull, stating that no official action would be taken at the time, observing, "No doubt is entertained that your Military experience will enable you to preserve harmony between the Regulars and the Militia." [29] This answer precipitated an outburst from the three Ohio colonels, who maintained that the provisions of the Ohio constitution, authorizing the rank of colonels, superseded any earlier provisions of federal militia law.

This dispute over rank illustrates the difficulties encountered before the supremacy of federal laws over state laws was clearly established. No action was ever taken to adjust the problem during the campaign, which meant that there was continued friction among Hull's highest officers and that Miller could never be delegated command functions without offending the Ohio colonels. Of course, part of the unpleasantness concerning the colonels' commissions lay in the future.

As Hull prepared to leave Urbana, he might well have paused to reflect on the successful progress of his command to date. His close co-operation with Governor Meigs had certainly aided the organization of the army, laid the groundwork for what appeared to be a period of Indian quiet, and prepared for the wilderness trek. One may hope that the old gentleman did pause to reflect, for it was almost the last time things were to run smoothly.

Notes to Chapter II

1. Properly speaking, Amherstburg was the town and Malden the fort, but the terms were used interchangeably.
2. The report may be found in *Michigan Pioneer and Historical Collection*, Vol. XXXVI, p. 235. This 40-volume series is one of the best sources of Michigan history and was published under different titles from 1877 to 1929. The entire series is usually cited only as *MPHC*.
3. Statement of Indian Annuities to be paid in 1811, The National Archives, Records of the Office of Indian Affairs Mss., Copies of Letters Sent by the Secretary of War Concerning Indian Affairs, Vol. C. Other amounts to be paid in areas affecting the Northwest were: Chicago, $750; Vincennes, $3,150; Kaskaskia, $1,000; St. Louis, $1,000. Apparently most of these were actually paid.
4. Hull to Eustis, Detroit, May 9, 1811, Clarence E. Carter (ed.), *The Territorial Papers of the United States, The Territory of Michigan, 1805–20*, Vol. X (Washington, D.C.: United States Government Printing Office, 1942), pp. 357–58. Hull believed there would be from 12,000 to 15,000 acres in the tract.
5. W. Stewart Wallace (ed.), *Documents Relating to the North West Company* (Toronto: The Champlain Society, 1934), p. 268.
6. Statement of Indian Presents Remaining in Store Houses in February, 1812, Public Archives of Canada, Indian Mss., Vol. C256.
7. William Claus (Deputy Supt. General of the Indian Dept.) to Gen. Isaac Brock, Amherstburg, June 16, 1812, William Wood (ed.), *Select British Documents of the Canadian War of 1812*, Vol. I, No. 13, of the Publications of the Champlain Society (Toronto: The Champlain Society, 1920), p. 311.

8. Public Archives of Canada, Indian Mss., Vol. C256.
9. American State Papers, *Indian Affairs*, Vol. I, p. 781. It was presented to the Senate by the President on Dec. 27.
10. Attwater to Eustis, Detroit, Jan. 21, 1812, Carter (ed.), *op. cit.*, Vol. X, p. 376.
11. Mar. 6, 1812, E. A. Cruikshank (ed.), Publications of the Canadian Archives, No. 7, *Documents Relating to the Invasion of Canada and the Surrender of Detroit in 1812* (Ottawa: Government Printing Bureau, 1913), pp. 19–23.
12. Red Hook, Jan. 2, 1812, *Ibid.*, p. 3.
13. Answers of Eustis, in writing and under oath, to questions put by Gen. Hull, James G. Forbes, *The Trial of Brig. General William Hull* (New York: Eastburn, Kirk, and Co., 1814), p. iii. Forbes was a supernumerary member of the court. Throughout the present work, references to this source refer to witnesses by their rank at the time of the campaign, not at the time of the trial.
14. Adj. Inspector Abimael Nicholl to Kingsbury, Washington, Mar. 28, 1812, The National Archives, Records of the War Dept., Office of the Sec. of War Mss., File N-Misc-1812.
15. Kingsbury to Col. Daniel Bissell, Newport, R. I., July 28, 1812. Burton Historical Collection, Kingsbury Mss.
16. Thomas Worthington Papers, Ross County Historical Society (Chillicothe, Ohio). The actual vote was 19 to 10. Since Louisiana was not admitted until April 30, there were then 17 states.
17. William Hull, *Memoirs of the Campaign of the North Western Army* (Boston: True & Greene, 1824), p. 25. Hull used the message of Madison to Congress as a basis.
18. Testimony of Gen. Peter Porter, Forbes, *op. cit.*, pp. 126–27. Porter was a New York militia officer and Chairman of the Congressional Committee on Foreign Relations. His brother, Augustus, was the army contractor for the area including Michigan.
19. William S. Hatch, *A Chapter of the War of 1812* (Cincinnati: Miami Printing and Publishing Company, 1872), p. 18. Hatch was appointed assistant quartermaster general of the North Western Army and wrote this book late in life from sketchy notes. It should be used with caution. The Census of 1810 records the population of Cincinnati Township as 2,540.
20. A certified true copy of the Militia Return of February 14, 1812, Ohio Archaeological and Historical Society, Governor's Papers, R. J. Meigs Mss.
21. *An Appeal to the People Or, an Exposition of the Official Conduct of Return Jonathan Meigs, Governor of the State of Ohio* (1812), 94 pp. Author, publisher, and place of publication unknown.
22. Signed Vouchers, Burton Historical Collection, James Taylor Papers, May, 1810–June, 1812, indicate that $6 was paid to John Hole for attendance of two privates for a week. Basic medical supplies were issued to the army from the military store at Newport amounting to $881.12 during May.
23. *The Western Spy* (Cincinnati), May 23, 1812.
24. Dillon, *op. cit.*, p. 483.
25. John C. Parish (ed.), *The Robert Lucas Journal of the War of 1812 During the Campaign Under General William Hull* (Iowa City: State Historical Society of Iowa, 1906), p. 7. Lucas, the principal messenger, had re-

signed his Ohio commission of brigadier-general to accept a regular army captaincy. He had not yet been assigned and served during this campaign as a volunteer private in his brother's company. He was a frequent adviser of the Ohio colonels and, after the war, served as governor of both Ohio and Iowa.

26. This interesting place had been an Indian town, a British trading post (Pickawillany), the site of a store owned by a Canadian named Loramie, and a fort erected by Wayne. It was at the western end of the lake in present-day Shelby county.

27. E. H. Pilcher, "Biography of Major Thompson Maxwell," *MPHC, op. cit.,* Vol. V, pp. 206–07.

28. Subsistence vouchers June–July 1812, Burton Historical Collection, James Taylor Papers.

29. Eustis to Hull, War Dept., July 2, 1812, Carter (ed.), *op. cit.,* Vol. X, p. 388.

CHAPTER III

WAR

IN THE CHANGING INTERPRETATIONS of the causes of the War of 1812, there has been fairly general agreement that there were several powerful pressures sweeping the United States toward a Declaration of War. To simplify, these forces can be divided into Eastern and Western aspirations: maritime interests (perhaps manufacturing, too) versus the Indian problem and its inextricable adjuncts, the fur trade and the availability of land for settlement.

During different periods each force has been recognized as the primary pressure. The nineteenth century granted primacy to Eastern interests, the early twentieth to Western; lately the pendulum has swung back to Eastern. But interpretation has certainly not run its full course. New studies will continue to seek to clarify the issue. Since an analysis of the causes lies outside the scope of a regional study of the war, it need be said only that seemingly all the Ohio Valley region and nearly all the Old Northwest was against England and its Indian allies.

Any government contemplating even a remote declaration of war prepares preliminary campaign plans. Confronted by British naval superiority, the United States in its preliminary plans of 1812 was essentially limited to land operations against Canada.

Canada in the early nineteenth century has been aptly compared to a tree with its tap roots at Halifax, securing much of its nourishment from Britain, and its deciduous branches in Upper Canada. One United States campaign plan suggested a simultaneous assault on Halifax by an overland force from Maine and by all available naval vessels, augmented by armed merchant marine. Such an attack might have cut off Canada's major source of supply, thus crippling the country's military potential. Of course, the campaign would have had to be expanded to include control of the St. Lawrence, but most strongholds in Canada could have been attacked at leisure or forced to surrender for want of critical supplies. This plan might well have swung New England's support for the war. It would have required the concentration of all available forces in New England. However, the West would have been left to protect itself against probable Indian attacks. The determining factor against this plan, Madison wrote Jefferson,[1] was that the most readily available and zealous men were from the settled portions of the West; it would require too long a time to move them East, and such a step would greatly increase the danger of Indian attacks.

While a land attack on Montreal would have been more feasible, it was not seriously considered.

Another plan was to attempt, from several points along the border, a piecemeal conquest of the "branches." This was approved for several reasons. For one thing, there was an overwhelming feeling that the conquest of Canada would be easy, merely a military exercise. Henry Clay did not cause this overconfidence; he merely reflected it when, on Washington's birthday in 1810, he stepped from the rostrum to address the House, saying:

> The conquest of Canada is in your power. I trust I shall not be deemed presumptuous when I state that I verily believe that the militia of Kentucky are alone competent to place Montreal and Upper Canada at your feet.[2]

Even after the war had begun, Jefferson commented that the

conquest of Canada as far as Quebec was a mere matter of marching.[3] In fact, even some Canadians in high official position feared the same thing.

Thus, by the spring of 1812, it had been decided, in case of war, to launch a three-pronged attack along the northern border from points about four hundred miles apart: Detroit, Niagara, and Lake Champlain. The army of the West, or left, was to be under Hull; the center, under Stephen Van Rensselaer, the militia general; and the North, or right, under General Henry Dearborn, nominal commander-in-chief but without authority over all the forces. The failure of the opening campaigns was not so much due to any fault in the plan as to the excessive bungling in its execution —there was no real co-operation between the armies (especially in timing attacks) and no attempt to secure naval control of the Upper Great Lakes.

On the basis of anticipated campaign requirements, Congress passed legislation to increase the size of the regular army. On January 11, 1812, the authorized strength of the regular army was increased to 35,000. Despite an enlistment bounty of sixteen dollars and a discharge bonus in the form of land to attract enlistments, the army had trouble filling the ranks; a report for May (excluding recruits for that month) showed a total enlisted strength of only 6,744.[4] This was less than six tenths of one percent of all free white males between sixteen and forty-five years reported in the Census of 1810. Most males of military age already belonged to militia organizations and preferred active service as volunteer militia on federal duty, retaining a quasi-civilian status with pay equal to that of the regulars but escaping their longer term and harsher discipline.

By Act of April 10, 1812, President Madison was authorized to place up to 100,000 militia on federal service. Quotas were assigned on the basis of each state's percentage of the total militia force. In addition, the President was authorized to accept 50,000 short-term volunteers, apart from the quota militia.

The American forces greatly outnumbered the British, which consisted of about 12,000 British or Canadian regulars and embodied (enrolled for active service) militia.[5] The British also had a larger number of sedentary, or unembodied, militia (supposed only to serve in their home district) and, of course, an indefinite number of Indian allies.

Amid political pressures primarily from the War Hawks in Congress, Madison, on June 1, sent Congress a message supporting war against Great Britain. Calhoun's House Committee on Foreign Relations soon reported out of committee a lengthy measure recommending a Declaration of War. On June 4 the House supported the measure by a vote of 79 to 49, with 13 members absent. The Senate debated the matter for some time in secret session but finally approved it, with amendments, on June 17 by a vote of 19 to 13, with two absent. The following day the House concurred in the amendments, and the President signed the measure into law.

By and large the real support for war came from representatives of the South and West. Senator Thomas Worthington of Ohio, epitomizing the minority view, wrote that he had opposed the Declaration on the ground that the country was not yet prepared for war and should remedy this deficiency first.[6] Despite such dissenting voices, on June 18, 1812, the country was at war.

On June 14, while the Senate was deliberating the Declaration of War, Hull's camp at faraway Urbana must have been the scene of frenzied activity and buzzing rumors—the long awaited march to Detroit was to begin the next day. By nightfall everything seemed in order, but the following morning when the General strolled out of his tent he was confronted by signs nailed to trees, warning him not to march until the Ohio men had been paid.

In lieu of uniforms, the Ohio soldiers had been given an advance of sixteen dollars, or a little less than half of the yearly clothing allowance to which they were entitled. Eustis had written Meigs on May 28 that he had authorized James Taylor, then Military Agent and Paymaster at Newport, Kentucky, to advance two months' pay to the Ohio soldiers. However, Taylor had joined Hull's force before the authorization had been received, and consequently the men had not received the advance. Colonel McArthur, ever sensitive to the political undercurrents among his men, had written Meigs recommending an advance. Nevertheless, Hull had received no orders to arrange a payment, and Eustis had appointed no regular paymaster for the army.

The men's desire for money is understandable: to purchase some desired luxury for the journey, to buy a present for the loved ones at home, or to drink their departure in an Urbana tavern. No mere swearing in to federal service could change the fact that the Ohio soldiers were essentially militia. Company officers, no more accustomed to army life than the men who had elected them, had not had sufficient time to improve discipline. There had been incidents of the kind one would expect from any force of that type: property damage, sleeping on guard duty, and the like. With rumors circulating about the possibilities of a pay advance, it is not surprising that the soldiers should seek to intimidate Hull.

The General, ignoring the posted signs, ordered assembly for the march. When one Ohio company refused to obey the call, Hull ordered a detachment of regulars to put down the mutiny. The businesslike approach of one of Miller's companies was sufficient inducement to the recalcitrants to obey. Granting the heat of the moment, Hull may have been guilty of only a slight overstatement when he remarked to Miller, "By G—d, Sir, your regiment is a powerful argument. Without it I could not march these volunteers to Detroit." [7]

The following day a general court-martial sentenced the three principal mutineers. Each man was to have half of his head shaved and, with his hands tied behind him and a "Tory" label fixed to his back, he was to be marched around the camp and ignominiously drummed out of the army. However the General pardoned the men before the sentence was carried out. In the interest of gaining the loyalty of the Ohio volunteers, there was little else he could do.[8]

On Monday, June 15, 1812, at 2:00 P.M., the last, and major, portion of the North Western Army left the Urbana camp on their wilderness trek to Detroit. Although McArthur's detachment of 800 men had preceded them by four days and had helped smooth their way, they moved slowly, encumbered by wagons, pack train, and cattle herd. By June 17 they had covered the twenty miles to Manary's Blockhouse, the last outpost in Ohio—and that scarcely a month old. A short five-mile march the following day and they were beyond the Greenville Line and into Indian country.

Camp was made near the Shawnee village of Solomon's Town, seventy-five miles, Hull reckoned, from the Rapids. Hull awaited the arrival of fifteen chiefs of various Indian tribes who were to accompany him through the Indian country. Captain Daniel Hughes finally joined him with the recruits for the First Infantry that he was supposed to have met in Pittsburgh. Jeremiah Munson, lately an aide of Governor Meigs, also arrived with three companies of Ohio men already attached to Cass's Regiment. Munson was promptly elected a major, filling a vacancy in the regiment. Hull's forces were now complete—2,075 according to a return at Manary's Blockhouse.[9] This included all men attached to the army, present or absent, and therefore considerably exceeded the number making the march.

On the night of June 19 the entire army was reunited at Fort McArthur, the small stockade constructed by the advance detachment on the south bank of the Scioto. Never intended as a regular fort, this unpretentious work enclosed scarcely half an acre and depended for its defense on two square, projecting blockhouses at the southeast and northwest corners, with only palisading between.[10] No artillery could be mounted, since Hull had none on the march.

Plagued previously by dry weather, the army was now subjected to nearly continuous rain that made the trail a mire. Probably after receiving a letter from Eustis dispatched on June 10 and ordering a forced march to Detroit because of "newly arisen circumstances," Hull issued general orders for June 20 calling for assembly for marching at 5:00 A.M. the following day. Part of Captain Andrew Dill's Ohio company was left as a garrison at Fort McArthur to protect any future supplies or communications and to care for the few sick left behind.

In general, Hull's army used the same procedure in marching that Harrison had used the previous fall. The nightly camp in the form of a square was enclosed by a breastwork of fallen trees, and no fires were permitted inside the lines after sundown. Mounted scouts reconnoitered for some miles in all directions. The normal order of march was: advance guard of riflemen; the major part of the army in two columns flanking the baggage and headquarters, and these columns in turn flanked by riflemen in open columns; and finally the rear guard of riflemen.

The army on the march must have made a grand sight from afar, the serpentine columns now and again disappearing from view behind a hill or perhaps just as irregularly dressing to a straight line on a level stretch. Nor did this panorama go unobserved. The Shawnee and other tribes had previously communicated with the British, offering to attack Hull's army but were dissuaded because a state of war did not then exist. But the Indians did keep a close watch on the army during the entire march, and so effectively that they were undetected.

Before leaving Fort McArthur, Findlay's Second Ohio Regiment had been detailed to proceed in advance of the main force, to build a crude road, bridging and corduroying where necessary, and to construct a blockhouse stockade. The main force left Fort McArthur on June 21. The rains continued. The trace was newly cut, the advance guard churned the mud, the first wagon made the trail a bog. Later wagons had to be nursed and cursed to move at all. After fifteen miles, Hull called a halt. He would store the heavier baggage to lighten the wagon loads.

While some of the men erected a small blockhouse, Fort Necessity (in present-day Madison Township, Hancock County), others made pack saddles and prepared fresh cartridges. Robert Lucas, one of the messengers dispatched by Hull to Detroit on May 25, rejoined the army and reported the presence of large numbers of Indians on both sides of the Detroit River and the reinforcement of the British post, Fort Malden.

With favourable weather, orders were changed to store the pack saddles at Fort Necessity and to ready the wagons with full loads for the march. The men began to trudge the thirteen-odd miles to the stockade which Findlay's Regiment was building.

Fort Findlay, a picketed structure with blockhouses at the corners and a defensive ditch in front, was located on the west side of Blanchard's Fork (the site of modern Findlay), a little less than thirty miles from Fort McArthur. The main force arrived on

June 25. The next day Hull received a message from Eustis, dated June 18, urging him to hurry to Detroit. There was no hint that war had been declared or even that it was being contemplated. Hull wrote the Secretary that he would be at the Rapids in three days, allowing time to build a blockhouse at the Portage River. He pointed out that he had left small detachments at the various blockhouses and suggested that the regular Ohio militia be ordered to relieve these men and preserve the overland communication lines so essential in case of war.

The location of Fort Findlay permitted water communication by canoe or small boat with the Rapids. Ordered to advance rapidly and faced with the necessity of crossing the Black Swamp, Hull employed friendly Indians to make canoes. Then he ordered the surplus baggage and supplies to be delivered to Indians hired to transport them to the Foot of the Rapids,[11] thus permitting discharge of some of the hired teams and wagons. Additional orders called for Cass's Regiment to move in advance of the main force, and for the remaining portion of Dill's company to garrison Fort Findlay. Some of the sick were probably also left there.

On June 27 the army moved on the final stage of their journey to the Rapids, passed the blockhouse built by Cass's men (Fort Portage), and spent the next night in the dismal midst of the Black Swamp. The following afternoon they arrived at the Rapids, pitching camp across the river from Wayne's old battleground of Fallen Timbers. The men could scarcely avoid feeling relaxed and elated; from now on they would be traveling over easier ground and sighting infrequent settlements.

At the Foot of the Rapids and across the river from the camp lay a small settlement, which in 1807 contained six American and a few French families. Two of the American settlers were relatives of General Hull; his niece and his nephew, David.[12] This village, together with another settlement down the river, comprised the Port Miami area. By 1810 a customs post to regulate Indian commerce had been established under Amos Spafford. David Hull served as captain of the small company of Michigan militia formed from the settlers along the river.

On June 30 the army crossed the river in boats, with the animals fording it. Andrew Race, a local settler, was paid four dollars for serving as a river guide.[13] The army entered Michigan Territory, and Hull issued orders for the first formal review since leaving Urbana. Hull then detailed a lieutenant of Cass's Regiment to build a small blockhouse on the north side of the river and garrison it with twenty-five men. He ordered the Fourth Regiment to precede the army on the next leg of the journey, the thirty miles to Frenchtown (now Monroe, Michigan) on the Raisin River.

On July 1 the General received an unexpected opportunity to increase the speed of his march. Captain Cyrenius Chapin of Buffalo had entered the Miami River with his schooner, the *Cayauga*. Apparently Hull did not know Chapin but understood him to be an American of good repute. The vessel was chartered for sixty dollars to make the trip to Detroit; a smaller vessel, probably an open boat, was also engaged. Although unaware of the outbreak of war, Hull cautioned Chapin to sail up the Detroit River channel on the American side of Grosse Isle, avoiding the British fort at Amherstburg.[14]

The sick of the militia were loaded in the small boat and entrusted to the care of Doctor James Reynolds of Cass's Regiment. The *Cayauga* carried a cargo of the heavier baggage, most of the army's medical supplies, the musicians' instruments, and various extra uniforms. Its heterogeneous passengers included the sick of the regulars (about thirty), four officers, three officers' wives, two enlisted men's wives, two boys, three sergeants of the regulars, some musicians to assist in caring for the sick, and possibly the Chaplain.[15]

Meanwhile, the army had resumed its march and camped some miles below the Rapids. Shortly after midnight on July 2 the peace of the camp was disturbed by the sound of a galloping horse and the challenge of a sentry. A special messenger had arrived bearing this terse message, dated June 18:

> War is declared against Great Britain. You will be on your guard—proceed to your post with all possible expedition, make such arrangements for the defence of the Country, as in your judgment may be necessary, and wait for further orders.[16]

This highly important message had been dispatched in the

52

ordinary mail from Washington, and carried to Cleveland to await the next infrequent post to Detroit. The alert Cleveland post-master, thinking something amiss, pulled it out of the Detroit pouch and dispatched a special messenger, Charles Shaler, to deliver it to Hull.[17] Although Hull had received another letter on June 26, bearing the June 18 date, this was the first notice he received of the war that had been declared more than two weeks earlier. He immediately dispatched a messenger to hail the *Cayauga* before she left the Miami River. Why did the General, ever a cautious commander, fail to dispatch messages immediately to all forts under his command (Detroit, Fort Wayne, Dearborn, and Michilimackinac) in case they, too, had been neglected by the War Department? Apparently the only message he sent to these posts was contained in the routine general orders of July 6. He may have felt that the only immediate danger to these posts was from Indian attacks, for which they were presumably on the alert at all times.

The army moved quickly to River Raisin, arriving there later on the day of July 2, and camped on the south side of the river. The few inhabitants of the town could give but little news. However, a company of cavalry arrived from Detroit with the information that Tecumseh was believed to be leading a force of 2,000 Indians in the general area, and that the cavalrymen had sighted 200 Sioux near Brownstown, displaying the British flag.[18] The next day American scouts learned from the still friendly Wyandot at Brownstown that the small boat had arrived at Detroit but the *Cayauga* had been captured.

During the night of July 1 the *Cayauga* had forged far ahead of the smaller vessel and entered the Detroit River. The larger vessel's draft rendered a passage up the American side possible but somewhat hazardous. The next day Captain Chapin felt no apprehension about sailing through the deeper channel on the east side of Grosse Isle—even though he was passing under the guns of the British at Amherstburg. Only a mile from the British fort he met an American revenue cutter, bound for the Miami Rapids, which had just passed the British fort without hindrance.[19] As the

Cayauga approached Fort Malden, a longboat from the British brig, the *General Hunter*, pulled out and its crew ordered Chapin to surrender. The Americans had no alternative: The armed brig stood by, the guns of the fort loomed over them, there were only a few able men on the *Cayauga*, the only arms were stored in the hold, and the vessel was under civilian status. In addition, a canoe bearing British reinforcements was seen approaching. The Americans surrendered to Lieutenant Charles Rolette, officer of the day on the *General Hunter*. A small party of five men quickly boarded, declared the military personnel prisoners of war, and ran up the British flag. An ironic note capped the affair—Rolette ordered the American musicians aboard to play "God Save the King." [20]

The British—or perhaps it would be more accurate to say certain individuals whose financial interests were involved—had been less remiss than the Americans about informing the military of war. Several Montreal fur merchants, who had sold the American rights of their company to John Jacob Astor but still were active in the business, had arranged for secret reports of any Congressional action regarding war to be sent from Washington by special messengers to Montreal and Queenston.[21] The fur company men at these places had quickly informed the military of the outbreak of war; General Brock, Administrator of the Government of Upper Canada, had learned of the act by June 25. Crediting the unofficial report, Brock had sent messages to his garrisons. Lieutenant-Colonel Thomas B. St. George, commanding at Fort Malden, thus had learned of the war by June 28,[22] four days before Hull received the news. British official notice followed about two weeks later.

The capture of the *Cayauga* was a severe blow to Hull. He could afford the loss of the few soldiers and the bulk of the cargo, but the medical stores were almost irreplaceable. The civilians were safe and on the following day were taken to Detroit. The sole exception was Mrs. George Gooding, who elected to remain with her husband, a lieutenant in the regulars. But the major blow was the capture of a chest, which had been mistakenly placed on board by Hull's son, containing official correspondence and complete muster rolls and records of the army. For some time to come the British knew more about Hull's army than he did—strength, character, and general campaign expectations. Fortunately, Hull and Eustis had not written any details of possible offensive campaigns.

Three other vessels were captured by the British near the western end of Lake Erie or in the Detroit River—two of them carrying rations for Hull's army. These captures were the inevitable result of the failure to inform the American forces promptly of the outbreak of war.

It is surprising that the country that had declared war should have made such ineffective use of the advantage of foreknowledge. Hull was the victim of circumstances in the affair of the *Cayauga*, an illustration of the old plague of a field commander— reliance on tardy or inaccurate information from distant headquarters. He should have received the news of the outbreak of war earlier than the enemy. Without this knowledge, the real danger, to Hull, appeared to be from Indian actions; therefore, the vessels seemed to offer an easier and safer passage for his sick than any trip through the wilderness. His action in employing the vessels was in accord with Eustis' instructions virtually ordering a forced march to Detroit. Hull can be censured only for the inclusion of official records in the cargo, and then only to the extent that any officer bears final responsibility for the errors of his subordinates.

Before the arrival of news of the *Cayauga's* capture, preparations were under way to continue the march to Detroit, some thirty-five miles from River Raisin. No garrison had to be detached from the forces, for the town was the headquarters of the Second Regiment of Michigan militia, an undermanned and dispersed force, but one capable of some resistance against small Indian raids. The town boasted a small stockade with twin projecting blockhouses and, while the whole was in a somewhat rotted state, minor repairs were being undertaken. Several small stockades were being constructed around isolated houses in the general area. However, the only piece of artillery in the region was a brass howitzer of small caliber.

The bulk of the army left River Raisin on July 3 via the River

Road, which roughly paralleled the Detroit River, and camped that night at Swan Creek, nine miles nearer their goal. Hull anxiously awaited the reports of his scouts. He had written Eustis that day that he expected to be attacked before reaching Detroit, probably at the Huron River, by a force of 1,500 Indians under Tecumseh. He had grounds for this belief. Several rumors had placed the Shawnee in the area. The country was virtually unsettled between River Raisin and the Ecorse River and, in fact, contained the area which Hull had attempted to get confirmed as a Wyandot reservation.

The Huron River was about twelve miles from River Raisin (twenty-one from Detroit) and only three miles south of Brownstown, the principal Wyandot town. An imaginary line drawn across the Detroit River from Brownstown would lie but a mile south of Grosse Isle and only a little more than that from Fort Malden. Thus, the Huron River was within easy reach of the British; and the nature of the terrain, heavily wooded and swampy, rendered an Indian attack likely, an ambush possible.

The scouts returned to camp accompanied by some of the Wyandot from Brownstown, and reported the peacefulness of the road. However, the following day, the Wyandot sent word that hostile forces were observed crossing from Fort Malden to Grosse Isle, presumably to be in a better position to launch an attack on Hull. This day, July 4, the army advanced to the Huron River and, under the cover of skirmish lines, constructed a floating bridge. The Wyandot had warned of an attack that night and indeed a British vessel was observed going up the river, but the Indians failed to appear. Eager to avoid battle at that time, Hull resorted to a subterfuge, having a civilian friend spread the rumor to Fort Malden that the Americans were collecting boats and bringing cannon from Detroit to attack the British post. Actually, this ruse had little to do with the failure of the British to attack.

Continuing their march the following day, the army heard the unmistakable noise of artillery fire and quickened their pace. They reached Spring Wells by late afternoon and camped only three miles from Detroit. The General visited the town that evening, but the army waited another day before entering. One of Hull's first acts, upon resuming his gubernatorial duties, must have been to discover the reason for the artillery fire of the previous day.

On June 28, the day he learned that war had been declared, Lieutenant-Colonel St. George, at Fort Malden, sent a detachment of Canadian militia to Sandwich, across the river and a bit below Detroit. These militia detained American ferryboats crossing to Canada,[23] giving Detroit its first intimation of war. When St. George received orders from Brock on July 1 to prepare for offensive moves, the militia were retained at Sandwich.

The citizens of Detroit were naturally aware of the danger of an Indian attack and every able-bodied man was placed on emergency duty from July 2 until the arrival of Hull's army at Spring Wells on July 5. Some of the regular militia complemented the regulars at Fort Detroit, while the rest bolstered the civilians guarding the town. On Sunday, July 5, when the British were observed building gun emplacements above Sandwich, Captain John Whistler, commanding at Fort Detroit, ordered an American battery located along the river at the lower edge of the town to open fire. Fire from these two twenty-four-pounders soon stopped the work on the enemy batteries, and was then directed against a party moving stores from the public storehouse to waiting boats, about a mile and a half from the American battery.[24] The old Huron Church, a former Indian mission, was apparently struck, and some minor damage was done to private property in Sandwich, but there was no injury to the inhabitants or, for that matter, to the soldiers. This was the artillery fire Hull's army had heard on their march.

On July 6 Hull sent Colonel Cass and Captain Hickman, under a flag of truce, to deliver a message to the commanding officer at Fort Malden. First of all, Hull stated that he had not authorized the artillery fire of the previous day, and regretted any damage done to private property.[25] He added that Cass was empowered to arrange terms for exchange of prisoners. Finally, he asked if the British intended to retain as lawful seizure the baggage captured on the *Cayauga* which belonged to officers who were not prisoners.

At Fort Malden, the Americans were received courteously but

were blindfolded before being allowed to enter. A British officer returned with the Americans to deliver the reply of the Fort Malden commander to Hull, which stated that St. George was as yet unauthorized to exchange prisoners and, in effect, that he refused to return the officers' baggage. Undoubtedly, a factor contributing to the refusal was the British custom of awarding shares in the value of any captured property to all those contributing to its capture—a practice the Americans followed only for certain naval prizes. Colonel Cass was piqued not only by St. George's actions, but also by Hull's refusal to require the blindfolding of the British officer before allowing him to enter the American lines at Spring Wells, even though it was but a temporary camp.

Perhaps Hull took time to review his present situation while awaiting Cass's return. The normal supply route via water was closed, and the Administration had not stockpiled supplies at Detroit, an area which was not self-sufficient even in peacetime. Yet Hull had left the enemy virtually astride his only supply line (overland from Ohio) eighteen miles to his rear. Some critics of Hull have felt this to be the key to the entire campaign; that is, that his failure to attack Fort Malden even before proceeding to Detroit could result only in his inevitable surrender because of his inability to provision his force. Hindsight may support this claim. But was Hull justified in the course he took, considering the knowledge he had at that time?

First of all, Hull's last orders from Eustis, dated June 18, specifically ordered him to Detroit without authorizing any voluntary offensive actions. In his *Memoirs* Hull pointed out several times that he considered it a mistake to pass Fort Malden but did not feel he could contravene his orders. However, other generals have often exceeded orders when they were convinced of the wisdom of the measure. Should Hull have done so? He could probably have crossed the river with his force in one fashion or another —on rafts, if nothing else. But the operation could have resulted in heavy casualties. The Americans had no artillery to use—on the other hand, the British had naval vessels in the area. Too, any makeshift transport would be nearly immobile; Indians in canoes could outpaddle the American troops and attack at will.

Even if he could have crossed the river with a major part of his troops, he would have been faced with an artilleryless attack on a recently repaired fort, defended, at least in part, by seasoned regulars. Attack by encirclement and slow starvation would probably have failed because the major portion of the defense, the Indians, would elude his lines. In such case, Hull's men would of necessity be stationary, but the Indians' greater mobility would allow them to attack any provision train coming to Hull's aid.

It would seem that the only kind of attack Hull might reasonably have attempted was a bayonet charge. Such a charge through enemy grapeshot would certainly have required either an extremely well-disciplined force or a fanatical one, and Hull had neither. Judging from their previous actions, Hull must have believed his senior officers divided and his militia undisciplined. He had had little chance to improve the quality of his soldiers on the vigorous wilderness march. Even later in the campaign, the Ohio colonels stated they could not answer for the conduct of their men in a proposed bayonet attack on Fort Malden.[26]

All the weaknesses of Hull's force might have been corrected in time; that is, discipline improved, provisions augmented, artillery secured—but Hull could not afford to delay his arrival at Detroit while carrying through such extensive reforms. He had been acquainted with the general campaign plan of the federal government when he was in Washington and, while he had no current information on the preparations at the other invasion points, he may have considered that a premature attack on his part could upset the effectiveness of the entire northern campaign. On the other hand, if Hull had succeeded in capturing Malden, the British might have abandoned the defense of western Upper Canada as a temporary impossibility and moved their strength eastward, seriously increasing the pressure on the American center and right. Fantastic though such a plan may seem, the British might even have allowed Hull to commit himself to an attack on Fort Malden and then, in turn, attacked and captured Fort Detroit.

As early as 1810 Hull had suggested that many of the Canadian militia might be encouraged to desert, in the event of an American invasion, provided that a proclamation were issued pledging their personal and property security.[27] Such a policy might fail if the initial contact with the enemy were bloody, for the Canadian militia might feel it had adequate reason for fighting. Also, desertion could be less easily accomplished in the actual presence of the British officers during enemy action. Thus, Hull's policy of conciliation would seem to have required an unopposed landing followed by a period of inactivity, neither of which would be possible if he were to attack Fort Malden initially. In fact, following such an attack, he would be faced with the occupation of a hostile area and the likelihood of constant Indian harrassments.

It seems that, in conformity with his orders and on the basis of information in his possession, Hull had ample reasons for proceeding directly to his post. He had no way of knowing that the British had decided to retreat eastward if the Americans crossed the river. Perhaps a more brilliant officer, a Brock for example, might have ignored his orders and successfully attacked Fort Malden; but Hull was within his rights in refusing the gamble. Certainly he had not done badly so far. He had marched his force to the relief of Detroit, averaging nearly nine and a half miles a day, including time spent constructing a road and building blockhouses. There had occurred only two incidents that could be thought to mar his record—the capture of the *Cayauga* and the failure to dislodge the British along his supply lines—and in neither was he really guilty of a basic error.

Had the Administration been dissatisfied with Hull's actions thus far, this would have been the logical time to replace him. Colonel Kingsbury, who had originally refused the command of the North Western Army because of illness, was an available replacement. With the outbreak of war, he had been ordered to a comparatively quiet command at the harbor of Newport, Rhode Island. He was familiar with the area around Detroit, and wished to return, for he wrote that he was going to apply to rejoin his troops at Detroit; he still commanded the First Regiment, and had expected to be on the Lakes before action started. This, he thought, would not be before fall. He must have been acceptable to the Administration, considering his original selection to command the army.

60

In view of Eustis' statements in his letters to Hull expressing confidence in the General's ability and discretion, the conclusion must be that the Administration not only was pleased with Hull's accomplishments to date, but was satisfied that his future career would be successful. Perhaps Kingsbury reflected the opinion of the Administration at the time, saying of Hull:

> He is (in my opinion) better calculated to command in that country than any other officer in the country, he will as Governor command all the Militia and as Indian agent will have great influence with the savages; If you recollect but a short time before I left Detroit I mentioned to you that I thought in case of alarm, Governor Hull would command in that country.[23]

Notes to Chapter III

1. Washington, Aug. 17, 1812, Gaillard Hunt (ed.), *The Writings of James Madison* (New York: G. P. Putnam's Sons, 1908), Vol. VIII, p. 211.
2. *Annals of Congress*, 11th Congress, Vol. I, p. 579.
3. Jefferson to William Duane, Monticello, Aug. 4, 1812, Paul L. Ford (ed.), *The Writings of Thomas Jefferson* (New York: G. P. Putnam's Sons, 1898), Vol. IX, p. 366.
4. Report signed by A. Y. Nicoll, Adjutant, on June 6, 1812, *Annals of Congress*, 12th Congress, 1st Session, Part II, pp. 2111–12.
5. William Wood (ed.), *Documents of the Canadian War, op. cit.,* Vol. I, p. 11.
6. Ross County Historical Society, Worthington Papers. Alexander Campbell, Ohio's other Senator was absent but their sole Representative, Jeremiah Morrow, voted yea. There were a few votes in the House to include France in the declaration as well.
7. Testimony of Lt. Josiah Bacon, Forbes, *op. cit.,* p. 124.
8. After the campaign had resulted in their capture and eventual parole, the Ohio men were paid for one year from the date they volunteered, Cass to [Secretary of War?], Washington, Feb. 13, 1817, Clements Library, Lewis Cass Papers.
9. Hull to Eustis, Camp Necessity, June 24, 1812, Henry A. S. Dearborn, *Defence of Gen. Henry Dearborn Against the Attack of Gen. William Hull* (Boston: Edgar W. Davies, 1824), p. 10.
10. Nevin O. Winter, *A History of Northwest Ohio* (Chicago: The Lewis Publishing Company, 1917), Vol. I, p. 106. It was located in present-day Buck Township, Hardin County, perhaps three miles west of Kenton.
11. Ft. Findlay, June 26, 1812, William L. Clements Library, Papers Relating to Michigan. These goods were delivered to the Rapids after Hull had left and never caught up with the army.
12. H. S. Knapp, *History of the Maumee Valley* (Toledo: Blade Mammoth Printing and Publishing House, 1872), p. 534.
13. Burton Historical Collection, James Taylor Papers.

14. Testimony of Sgt. Aaron Forbush, Forbes, *op. cit.*, p. 145.
15. There are several conflicting statements in various primary sources in regard to the passengers. Aaron Greeley, the Surveyor of Michigan, was also on board but was not connected with the army.
16. Eustis to Hull, War Dept., June 18, 1812, *MPHC*, Vol. XL, p. 396.
17. Hull, *Memoirs, op. cit.*, p. 9, stated the letter arrived by messenger of the Cleveland postmaster. Silas Farmer, *The History of Detroit and Michigan* (Detroit: Silas Farmer & Co., 1884), pp. 274–75, stated Shaler received $35.
18. Parish (ed.), *op. cit.*, p. 18. In June Tecumseh had been in the Fort Wayne area but may have arrived at Malden the first week in July.
19. *The Supporter* (Chillicothe, Ohio), Aug. 1, 1812.
20. Milo M. Quaife (ed.), *War on the Detroit—The Chronicles of Thomas Verchères de Boucherville and The Capitulation by an Ohio Volunteer.* (The Lakeside Classics, number 38) Chicago: The Lakeside Press, 1940.
21. E. A. Cruikshank, "A Sketch of the Public Life and Services of Robert Nichol," *Ontario Historical Society Papers and Records*, Vol. XIX (1922), p. 22. Nichol was the Militia QMG in Upper Canada.
22. Cruikshank, "Hull's Invasion," *Royal Society of Canada*, Vol. I, p. 232.
23. *Ibid.* Apparently the boats and men were returned on July 9.
24. Testimony of Lt. James Dalliba, Forbes, *op. cit.*, p. 83. This was about the maximum effective range for the pieces.
25. Hull to St. George, Spring Hill, July 6, 1812, *MPHC, op. cit.*, Vol. XL, p. 404.
26. Testimony of Major Jeremiah Munson, Forbes, *op. cit.*, p. 131.
27. Hull to Eustis, Detroit, Feb. 1, 1810, Carter (ed.), *op. cit.*, Vol. X, p. 306.
28. Kingsbury to Whistler, Newport, July 29, 1812, Burton Historical Collection, Jacob Kingsbury Papers.

CHAPTER IV

INVASION OF UPPER CANADA

FEW MEN IN HULL'S ARMY had ever seen Detroit before, and fewer still had any knowledge of the Canadian shore. While the General awaited further orders, the field-grade officers must have spent much of their time improving their knowledge of the military potentialities of both sides of the river.

Detroit had about one hundred and fifty houses, and a population of about eight hundred. Its inhabitants, typical of the district, earned their livelihood largely through trade; some weaving, hat manufacturing, soap and candle making, tanning, and distilling were also carried on.

Past generations of Detroiters had had cause to bless the presence of a squat businesslike fort. Fort Pontchartrain du Detroit had been built by the French in 1701 to command the river and protect the inhabitants from Indian attacks. The fort had been retained for a time under British rule, but higher ground several hundred yards to the rear rendered it vulnerable to attack by an army possessing artillery. During the Revolution the British built Fort Lernoult on the commanding ground across the Savoyard River. When the Americans took over jurisdiction of the territory, they retained the fort, renaming it Fort Detroit. The town, sur-

63

rounded by pickets, was in front of the fort, and the effectiveness of the guns of the fort in controlling river traffic was reduced by its distance from the river and by the necessity of firing over the town.

Fort Detroit measured about 100 yards on each face, besides the bastions, with four curtains of perhaps 75 yards.[1] An 11-foot parapet, 12 feet thick at the top, with the customary banquette rose from the 26-foot-wide rampart. A ditch about 6-feet deep and 12-feet wide, containing a row of 11-foot-high ribbed cedar pickets, surrounded the entire fort. Peaceful entrance was easily effected over a removable bridge and through a double-planked gate under an overhead lookout house. The fortification, enclosing less than three acres, contained the usual quarters and structures found in other forts of the time. In the early summer of 1812 work had begun on a new dirt front to be placed before the parapet, but it was still incomplete when Hull arrived. The entire work seems to have been in a fair state of repair.

There were over forty pieces of brass or iron ordnance available in the Detroit area: nine twenty-four-pounders, nine twelve-pounders, five nine-pounders, seven six-pounders, two four-pounders, one three-pounder, three 9-10 inch howitzers, one 8-inch howitzer, one 5½-inch howitzer, and three 2¾-inch howitzers.[2] At least one four-pounder and several six-pounders were used by the militia and, as will be noted subsequently, many of the others were not emplaced in the fort. There were adequate stores of ammunition for most of the pieces for normal use, except grape and canister for the twenty-four-pounders. There seem to have been at least a minimum number of soldiers to fire the emplaced pieces, for some of the First Infantry garrisoning the fort had been trained to assist the small artillery detachment.

A naval force was another matter. The *Adams*, of 150 tons and mounting fourteen guns, was the only regular naval vessel in the area but she was in dry dock at the River Rouge shipyard, and her ordnance was deposited at Fort Detroit. Actually, she was not in service in time for Hull to use during his campaign. In normal times there were several unarmed merchant vessels, under 90 tons, that operated in Detroit waters, but two had already been

64

captured by the British and the others were not in the vicinity. Clearly, Hull was entirely without naval support.

The question of the numbers of troops Hull had is a highly controversial one, as no official and complete lists are available and all contemporary accounts differ. By May, Attwater, acting under Eustis' authorization, had detached four companies from the Michigan militia for active service for a period of one year. This force, the Michigan Detached Militia commanded by Major James Witherell, had a total strength of about 300.[3] About a third were stationed in the River Raisin area. Also available to Hull were the two regular regiments of Michigan militia, vastly under strength and scattered all over the settled portions of the Territory. The Second Regiment was composed of men from the southern region, with headquarters at River Raisin. Hull had ordered its commander, Colonel John Anderson, to call out the regiment and keep the men in their own areas in scattered detachments to furnish protection against possible Indian raids. The First Regiment, from Detroit and its vicinity, was not called into service. Thus, on active duty at Detroit by July 7, there were only about 200 Michigan men, cavalry, riflemen, and infantry—all from the Detached Militia.

The Ohio volunteers and drafted militia with Hull had been reported to number 1,592 at Manary's Blockhouse,[4] but they had supplied small garrisons at each of the five posts Hull had built, and some had been captured on the *Cayauga*. It seems doubtful that more than 1,450 actually arrived at Detroit, and many were soon temporary victims of the ague, or Michigan fever.

Late in July the Fourth Regiment reported a strength of 264.[5] In addition, two small detachments of recruits for the First Infantry had accompanied Hull to Detroit. Attempts to raise a company of regulars in Michigan that spring had failed, so the only regulars previously at Fort Detroit were a small detachment of United States Artillery and a company of the First Infantry, together amounting to about 100 men. On the basis of these figures, it seems likely that Hull had a force at Detroit of about 450 regulars, 1,450 militia from Ohio, and 200 militia from Michigan—a total, allowing for some errors in the above figures, of between 2,000 and 2,200 men, largely untrained and ill-equipped.

65

Across the river from Detroit were the British, with a militia detachment at Sandwich and another force sixteen miles to the south at Fort Malden. Sandwich Township stretched from about the upper end of Hog Island (Belle Isle) south to the Riviere aux Canard, known to Americans as the Canard River. Numerous farmhouses dotted the Canadian shore from the mouth of the Thames River at Lake St. Clair southward to Sandwich. Moy House, local headquarters of the North West Fur Company, was some two miles above Sandwich. Sandwich contained some fifty log or frame houses built near the old Huron Church, a small shipyard, two small wharves, and a small government warehouse.

Amherstburg, twice as large as Sandwich, was slightly smaller than Detroit. It was the site of Fort Malden and one of the two Naval Yards in Upper Canada (the other being at Kingston). It was also a trade center, stimulated by the liberal dispensing of the Crown's bounty through the local Indian Office factotum.

Fort Malden had an ideal location, situated along the shore above the town, opposite the northern end of Bois Blanc, and within easy gun range of that island. The normally deep ship channel lay between the island and the mainland, placing ships within musket range of the fort. In case ships passed on the American side of Grosse Isle, which screened them from fire from the fort, British naval units could take over.

The fort had been planned in 1796, when the British learned they were to evacuate Detroit, and built during the following two years. Periodically strengthened and repaired, especially during the war scare of 1807–09, it had been renovated in the spring of 1812. By then it had four fraised and curtained bastions with an advanced redoubt, a surrounding ditch, and a row of fourteen-foot pickets with a framed parapet. Moreover, it was equipped with 150 loopholes on each face and protected by twenty mounted cannon. Inside were a splinter-proof barracks and a powder magazine with five-foot-thick side walls and a bombproof ceiling of logs covered with thick masonry.[6] Of course, as with most forts of the time, fires set by artillery explosions were the greatest danger to the fort.

Several companies of the Forty-first Regiment of Foot were the principal garrison at Fort Malden. Not old from the standpoint of British regiments, it had seen service in Ireland and the West Indies before coming to Canada in 1799. In early June, 1812, Fort George on the Niagara River was the official headquarters of the regiment, but its strength of 320 officers and 880 rank and file[7] was largely detached to York, Queenston, Chippewa, Fort Erie, and Fort Malden. There were probably about 300 regulars at Fort Malden,[8] besides a detachment of Royal Artillery. The senior officer of the Forty-first at Malden was Captain Adam Muir, an able professional who had been promoted from the ranks nearly twenty years earlier. Lieutenant-Colonel St. George, of the Sixty-third, commanded the fort.

Actively supporting Fort Malden was the western division of the Provincial Marine Department of Upper Canada. This consisted, in addition to minor shore installations, of the brig *Queen Charlotte,* of 180 tons, mounting (in February, 1812)[9] ten twenty-four pounders and six long guns (probably twelve-pounders), carrying a crew (in August, 1811)[10] of two officers and 27 men; the schooner *General Hunter,* of 60 tons, probably mounting six six-pounders and carrying a crew of two officers and 17 men; and the *Lady Prevost* (placed in service in July, 1812), of 80 tons, and mounting ten twelve-pound carronades. The strength of crews and armament varied as need required and supply permitted. The naval establishment was commanded by Captain George Hall, master of the *Queen Charlotte.*

In addition to the naval units, several merchant vessels were available to the British. The chief of these were two lightly armed vessels of the North West Company: the *Nancy,* of 100 tons, and the *Caledonia,* of 70. Other privately owned vessels—the *Eleanor,* of 50 tons, the *Thames,* of 80 tons, and the *Dover* (operating in the Thames River), of 20 tons—played no part in the British plans.

As if this veritable British flotilla compared to the one dry-docked American vessel were not enough, a procession of eleven bateaux, heavily laden with supplies for northern fur posts, was halted at Fort Malden to avoid possible capture at Detroit. Since learning of the Declaration of War, the British had retained their cargoes of blankets and ammunitions, and had assigned the seventy trained men to their own naval vessels. The *Nancy* was brought to Amherstburg and her brass three-pounders were used to convert at least two of the larger bateaux to efficient gunboats. The British also relied on Indians and militia to bolster their land defense. The Indians were always eager to participate in small sorties against the Americans, but, except for a small group of zealots such as Tecumseh, they were accustomed to come and go at will. The British seldom knew the exact number of Indians that were supposed to be attached to them—indeed the officers had little contact with the lesser Indians, working only with the chiefs through Canadian interpreters. Matthew Elliott, Colonel of the First Essex Militia and Deputy Superintendent of Indian Affairs for Upper Canada, wrote that he believed some 4,400 warriors were available for action in the West alone.[11] Obviously, however, all could not be assembled in one place, and a usually cautious observer believed that there were only some 400 warriors at Fort Malden on July 8.[12]

Even a small number of Indians caused concern to the British officers, for the British were obliged to furnish arms, supplies, and rations for their accompanying families, and general largess—all the while risking the Indians' withdrawal at critical times. Nevertheless, the British felt that their own weakness, compared to potential over-all American strength, necessitated the use of Indians, especially to undermine American morale.

The Canadian militia was organized more efficiently than was normally the case with the United States. Except for minor religious groups, every able-bodied Canadian male between the ages of sixteen and sixty was subject to militia service. This basic force, the Sedentary Militia, was required to attend four muster parades a year and was subject to duty for periods of eight months within its own district. The Canadian and American systems were comparable in this point except that the Americans mustered only once a year. But the Sedentary Militia formed only the mass levy of the Canadian system. The Incorporated or Embodied Militia, essentially volunteers, were subject to service anywhere in Canada for two years and were trained for six days a month until certified competent. Upper Canada did not possess Incorporated

68

Militia, but later in the war there were 4,000 in Lower Canada. In March, 1812, Upper Canada had revised its militia laws. Authorized company strength was increased from fifty to one hundred men, and a system of flank companies was inaugurated. Two flank companies were to be formed in each battalion from single men under forty, to be trained six days a month and subject to service anywhere in Upper Canada. Obviously these fifty companies were still under strength by July, but many had received some training by that time.

The number of militia actually on duty at or near Fort Malden is something of a moot point. St. George wrote Brock on July 8 that he had counted 460 militia on duty at Sandwich and that there were two flank companies totaling 140 men (of Elliott's First Essex) on duty at Fort Malden.[13] However, he mentions that both the First and Second Essex Regiments, as well as the Kent Militia, were on active service under his command. Captain M. Dixon wrote on the same day that there was a total of 850 militiamen on duty.[14] Possibly St. George either erred in his count or failed to report militia, other than flank companies, on duty at Fort Malden. The strength of the two Essex Regiments alone exceeded 600 men, and, with the flank companies and Kent Militia, should easily have reached the 850 that Dixon reported.

No real comparison of the respective armies should ignore the command of each. Hull, as the active commander of the North Western Army, was directly under the orders of Secretary Eustis. There was supposed to be an exchange of information, or at least a correlation of campaign plans, between Hull and General Henry Dearborn, the titled commander of the American army. But both generals left the correlation largely to Secretary Eustis. This crucial mistake was one that Brock was to exploit in the future.

Just as President Madison was the titular Commander-in-Chief of the American army, George III was the theoretical head of the British army. However, the King was hopelessly insane, and his eldest son, the Prince of Wales, acted as regent. In 1812 all restrictions of the regency were removed so that the Prince, later George IV, was king in all but name. The chain of command below him was amazingly haphazard. The second Earl of Liverpool, Robert B. Jenkinson, was Secretary of State for War and, following Percival's assassination in February of 1812, also served as Prime Minister. While Liverpool directed most of the war, the Duke of York, Commanding General of the Horse Guards, was the actual Commander-in-Chief. Although several attempts had been made to define the functions of the Secretary for War and the Commander-in-Chief, there was still no clear division of authority. Usually the Commander concerned himself only with the personnel of the army and with various services, such as the quartermaster. As the only representative of the military in Parliament, Lord Liverpool handled all financial matters and in general planned the over-all strategy. Nearly all orders to Canada came directly from him.

Sir George Prevost was Governor-General of Canada and Commander of all forces in North America. Below Prevost was Major-General Sir Isaac Brock, Administrator of the Government of Upper Canada. In spite of the complicated chain of command, neither Brock nor Prevost was greatly overburdened by orders or directives from higher headquarters; the real control was exerted through regulating the personnel and supplies sent to Canada. Prevost, in turn, rationed men and materiel to Brock, but the latter was usually free to use them as he wished. St. George at Malden was not only directly under Brock's orders, but Brock also assumed actual field command when possible.

Even though most British officers had purchased their commissions, they were more experienced than the Americans. Their pay was low, considering they had to allow for their commission purchase, which was usually £550 for lieutenancies in the Forty-first, and had to maintain high social standards. All British generals were honorary colonels of a regiment and received the same pay as colonels. Promotion was usually by seniority, and therefore slow. The British avoided one source of conflict that troubled the Americans by declaring that all lieutenant-colonels in the regulars outranked all militia officers.

To summarize the comparison of Hull's and St. George's forces, assuming that the figures are reasonably accurate, the British had about 325 regulars, 850 militia, and 400 Indians—a total of 1,575 for immediate service at or near Fort Malden to oppose Hull's force of over 2,000. The forces do not seem greatly disproportionate when one adds the overwhelming British naval strength. The weaknesses of Hull's army were the lack of a navy and the character of the militia. (The British feared that Hull might offset these deficiencies by using Indians.) On the British side, the weaknesses were the Indians and the militia. Hull could do little about the former. Did he possess the perspicacity to do something about the latter?

Following the Declaration of War St. George had visited the Canadian militia detachment stationed at Sandwich to impress on the men the necessity of retaining their position. However, the force was not protected by a fort and, following the American artillery fire of July 5, the men began to retreat to Fort Malden. On July 6 St. George detailed Captain Muir to lead a detachment of fifty regulars and two artillery pieces, meet the retreating militia, and return with it to Sandwich. With the American army just across the river their tenure was precarious, but St. George planned to maintain the position as long as possible.

Hull's arrival was the signal for renewed activity at Detroit. The American soldiers cleaned and repaired equipment and vainly tried to repair their arms. In March, Eustis had written Captain John Whistler, in command of Fort Detroit, ordering the emplacement of gun batteries along the river and the mounting of six twelve- and six twenty-four-pounders on carriages. Since the old carriages were too rotten for service, Whistler had ordered the construction of new ones but they were not yet completed. Hull tried to hurry the work on the traveling carriages and ordered the emplacement of five pieces along the river at Spring Wells. On July 8 the army established camp at the rear of the fort.

In his official capacity of Superintendent of Indians, Hull held a council at Detroit on July 7, and told the southern Michigan Indians of the outbreak of war, counseled neutrality, and informed them of the council to be held at Brownstown later in the month.

Hull's most pressing concern was to replace his dwindling provisions. At a council of war with his field-grade officers at his house on July 9, he reported the following rations on hand: 125,000 of flour, 70,666 of meat, 110,000 of whisky, 300,000 of soap, and 12,800 of vinegar.[15] There was little danger that his forces need be dirty or completely sober, but there was only about a two-month supply of flour and a one-month supply of meat. Detroit normally imported foodstuffs, and the only available route for provisioning was the long overland trail from Ohio. Hull therefore appointed John H. Piatt, a Cincinnati merchant who had accompanied the army to Detroit, the official contractor to supply the North Western Army north of 41° north latitude (replacing the defaulting Augustus Porter) and ordered 200,000 rations of flour and beef. Delivery of the provisions was imperiled by the proximity of the British to his supply lines, so Hull wrote Eustis informing him of the new contract and stressing the need of troops to safeguard the provision route. Hoping for more immediate protection than Eustis could order, he also wrote Meigs, warning him that the Ohio militia must temporarily maintain the overland route or cause the army to fall.

The major announcement at the council of war was the awaited orders from Eustis, who had authorized Hull to assume the offensive, saying:

> Should the force under your Command be equal to the Enterprize, consistent with the Safety of your own post you will take possession of Malden and extend your conquests as circumstances may justify. . . . an adequate force cannot soon be relied on for the Reduction of the Enemies forces below you.[16]

Several alternatives must have been obvious to Hull. He could remain at Detroit, strengthen its defenses and improve the discipline of his soldiers awaiting the commencement of activities along the Niagara frontier. This had much to be said for it, but it would likewise allow the British to increase their defenses and would not dislodge the British from his crucial communication and supply lines. He could cross the river and attack Fort Malden, and if successful would solve most of his immediate problems.

72

However, this would be an extremely hazardous operation without siege artillery, unavailable because of the lack of traveling carriages. He could withdraw to the Raisin River or the Miami Rapids, increase his provisions, and launch an attack from there. Militarily this would have been his best course, but his orders specifically forbade him to take any action inconsistent with the safety of Detroit.

The best solution, Hull believed, was to cross the major part of his army to Sandwich, dislodge the British, and establish his base there. With guns on both sides, this would permit the defense of Detroit and the control of river traffic; it would also partially aid his provision situation by capturing British stores at Sandwich, and would permit further training of his soldiers, while embarking on a piecemeal conquest of the Canadian settlements and awaiting a propitious opportunity to attack Fort Malden. After informing the council of war of his decision, he issued orders to prepare for the crossing. His letter to Eustis implied that he did not plan any rash attack on the British fort, for he wrote, "The British command the water & the savages—I do not think the force here equal to the reduction of Amherstburg—You therefore must not be too sanguine." [17]

In 1810 Hull had indicated that he believed some Canadians might be won from British allegiance by an American invasion, providing a proclamation were issued offering personal and property protection. A section of Eustis' letter of June 24 authorized such a proclamation but warned that Hull was to pledge only protection in their "persons & property & Rights." There was strong justification for Hull's belief—Joseph Watson, Hull's aide in the Michigan militia, had prepared a list of 108 people living in Canada who he felt sure would welcome an American invasion.[18] Most of these were American by birth and, as recent migrants to Canada, were settled inland from the Detroit River. It was hoped that there were others of similar mind in the Sandwich area.

The General ordered a proclamation prepared, to be distributed to the Canadians as soon as the army crossed the river. The authorship of the proclamation is in doubt. Hull never denied that he wrote it, but Cass informed Benson Lossing some fifty years later that he had written the document.[19] Certainly the basic ideas were Hull's, but the bombastic phraseology was typical of Cass in his younger days. The proclamation was printed by Theophilus Mettez,[20] probably on Father Richard's press. It was dated at Sandwich on July 13 and signed by Captain Abraham Hull for the General.

The proclamation stated that the United States, forced to arms, offered the Canadians liberty and emancipation from tyranny. It promised full protection of persons, property, and rights; and it emphasized that the Americans, while not seeking the armed assistance of the Canadians against the British, would accept it if freely given. One ominous warning was sounded by stating that no quarter would be given to any white man found fighting by the side of an Indian. The implication was clear that the Americans were entering Canada in the role of liberators, not conquerors. It is doubtful that Hull hoped to persuade many Canadians to oppose the British overtly, but his conciliation policy would be a military success if the Canadians merely deserted and if the civilians remained neutral.

Hull may have planned to cross to Canada on the night of July 10 [21] but, if so, the plan may have been thwarted by a false alarm of an Indian attack, causing an indiscriminate firing of arms and resulting in general confusion in the camp. Major Jeremiah Munson was severely wounded during the melee of untrained men. This lack of discipline by soldiers supposedly prepared to invade the enemy's country did not augur well for the American cause.

At dusk on July 11 McArthur's Regiment boarded small boats and began moving downstream, conveying the impression to the British who were presumably observing the maneuver that the army planned to cross the river well below Sandwich. After dark McArthur returned to Detroit, while two civilian spies were sent across to discover the enemy's location.[22] The army was ordered to Bloody Bridge, opposite the lower end of Hog Island, to prepare for the assault. At this point another tribulation was added to the lengthy list of Hull's unexpected misfortunes.

For several days the higher officers had delivered fervent speeches exhorting their men to cover themselves with glory in the forthcoming actions. Despite the oratory, the companies of Captains Nicholas Cunningham and David Rupe of McArthur's Regiment [23] and some seventy men of Findlay's Regiment [24] refused to cross the river. The politically experienced McArthur delivered a blistering address to his two companies and succeeded in persuading Cunningham's company to cross. Moreover, a few of Rupe's men crossed with other companies, and probably some of Findlay's did the same. Nevertheless, at least a hundred Ohio men refused to leave the United States.

This was not just a case of recalcitrant soldiers shirking combat duty—many of them were willing to fight in United States territory. The trouble was that some of them were not volunteers but were drafted militia to fill local quotas, and militiamen were subject to duty only within the United States. In theory, it was a violation of law to force militiamen to serve outside the country. Furthermore, a few had deserted the British service and hesitated to place themselves in the position, if captured, of being treated as deserters rather than as prisoners. One such soldier, Blackhall Stephens, asserting he would willingly serve in the United States, petitioned Judge Woodward for protection.

Woodward, no friend of Hull's, accepted the petition and placed Stephens under civil protection. Hull was in no position to challenge the civil authorities in a doubtful case and took no action. However, the Judge, believing he was in personal danger, wrote Eustis requesting that the General be warned not to violate civil authority. As an aftermath of this episode, Captain Rupe was court-martialed and declared unworthy to be an officer. However, his men promptly re-elected him captain, and the higher authorities did not interfere.

On the dawn of July 12 the invasion force lined the riverbank from Bloody Bridge to Detroit. There were insufficient boats to cross the army, so the first wave was composed of the Fourth Regiment on the left and Cass's Regiment on the right. The boats were to return immediately to cross the other two Ohio regiments. The First Infantry, the Michigan militia on duty, and the Ohio men who had refused to cross were left to protect Detroit. Artillerists, with lighted matches, stood by all the pieces that could be dragged

75

on the few available carriages to the riverbank. Captain Samuel Dyson, commanding the United States Artillery stationed at Fort Detroit, was to direct the fire of the three six-pounders accompanying the expedition.

The first wave moved across the river, landed, and met nothing! The regiments formed and began a cautious advance toward Sandwich. Scouts soon reported that the British had withdrawn and most of the civilians were hiding in the woods.

On July 10 St. George had ordered that all livestock be moved from Sandwich to Amherstburg. The following day Colonel Jacques (James) Baby of the Kent Militia notified him that, in view of the obvious preparations the Americans were making to cross in force, he was following the unanimous advice of all officers present and withdrawing his men to Fort Malden. Baby had ample reason for the withdrawal; his force was insufficient to repel an invasion, and an American crossing below Sandwich would cut him off from Fort Malden. St. George had planned to order the withdrawal, mainly because the militiamen were proving difficult to control at a distance and he felt they would respond better when confronted by the larger numbers of regulars at Fort Malden. Therefore, Hull's landing was unopposed, and McArthur's ruse wasted.

With the Americans in possession of Sandwich, a detachment of regulars was ordered to seize a quantity of unground wheat and flour from a local mill. A few British cavalrymen were seen in the distance herding livestock, and Captain John Robison's company was ordered to pursue them.[25] Most of the soldiers began establishing camp on the old Indian Reserve at Sandwich. Hull's headquarters was located in a new brick home, not completely finished inside, ironically belonging to Colonel James Baby. Some of the soldiers were told to deliver copies of the proclamation to the few remaining civilians in town, for circulation among the people in hiding.

While waiting to observe the effect of his conciliatory policy, Hull could fortify his camp, seize all the British provisions he could find, extend his protection to Canadian militiamen who sought it, and gradually expand his area of conquest. He obtained information about British movements when Robison's company returned to camp with three prisoners. The next day, July 13, Captain Henry Ulry's company was detailed to proceed to Turkey Creek, spread copies of the proclamation, and ascertain if any British forces were in the vicinity. Ulry's men learned that a large body of men had lain in ambush at Turkey Creek the previous evening, but all signs indicated that the group had left for Fort Malden. By July 14 the American camp was protected by breastworks on three sides and by artillery emplaced along the river side. It appeared to be safe from all but a general attack.

The day of the invasion, the King's Commissary had surrendered the keys of the public warehouse with its store of 80 barrels of flour and other supplies valued at $10,000. There were also supplies at Moy House, belonging to the North West Company, but Hull felt it necessary to write to Eustis as to whether they were to be treated as inviolable private property. However, the army had learned of some public provisions in the area of the Thames River, and the following day Hull ordered a detachment of Captain James Sloan's light cavalry to go there and seize the goods. Sloan's men left late in the afternoon, soon sending back word that a party of Indians had been sighted. Ordered to take immediate action, McArthur quickly assembled some 115 of his men, impressed Robison's company, who were waiting to be dismissed after bringing in their prisoners, and, without even stopping for rations, marched to join the cavalry in pursuit of the Indians.[26]

McArthur marched until dark, slept until dawn, released Robison's company, and continued his pursuit. Forced to arrange for food (although the men must have found something to eat at that time of the year in at least semisettled country), McArthur halted at Belle River (more than twenty miles from Sandwich) and purchased provisions. After a short break the march was continued for several miles until the troops arrived at the Ruscomb River in time to see three canoe-loads of Indians pull from the shore. McArthur and the cavalry galloped ahead and succeeded in capturing one canoe containing a squaw and some children. McArthur released these captives, consoling himself by capturing the horses abandoned by the Indians.

77

Orders from Hull arrived, brought by Captain Richard Smyth, a member of the Michigan Detached Militia selected to cross to Canada because of his knowledge of the area. The General's orders were to continue to the Thames area, secure provisions, and spread copies of the proclamation that Smyth had been given. Camp that night, July 14, was on the north side of the Thames River. A Canadian militia corporal's guard was captured at that place, guarding the home of Isaac Hull,[27] a younger brother of the General and the father of the Michigan Militia Captain, David Hull. The militia were disarmed and sent home, and the expedition continued up the Thames the next day.

McArthur's job was merely a question of locating the supplies, since the Kent Militia, which had had their depots along the river, had been ordered to duty at Fort Malden. Systematically they proceeded to Captain Richard Pattinson's, Captain George Jacob's trading store, Thomas McCrae's, and Isaac Dolsen's, and located flour, whisky, salt, guns, and other military stores. Camp was located that night at Matthew Dolsen's stable (Dover), where a quantity of blankets was obtained. The next morning, July 16, the force rapidly moved to John McGregor's mills (now Chatham), secured flour, and prepared for their return. Major Denny was assigned a few men to convoy the boats, captured at various places and loaded with the supplies, back to Detroit; the rest of the force pushed on toward Sandwich, arriving there late the following day.

The expedition was a decided success—100 barrels of flour, 20 barrels of salt, 5 bales of blankets, 3 barrels of whisky, and some arms and ammunition were eventually delivered to Detroit or Sandwich.[28] McArthur had accomplished his other objective of making friends for the army. Some of the hand guns seized may have been the private property of militia officers, but, if so, this was a reasonable retaliation for the British seizure of officers' property on the *Cayauga*. By no means the least important result was that three Canadians—Ebenezer Allan, Andrew Westbrook, and Simon Z. Watson [29]—returned with McArthur to offer their services to Hull, who promptly authorized Watson to form a Canadian cavalry unit.

Hull's July 19 letter to Eustis assumed an optimism long absent from his communications. He reported that the Canadian militia was deserting in large numbers and that preparations were being made for an attack on Fort Malden, possibly within a week. The *Adams* had been taken from dry dock and was at Detroit being armed; she could be used on the Upper Lakes without danger from the British navy. Furthermore, a large Indian council was in session at Brownstown, and the General felt sure that the Indians would adhere to their pledge of neutrality. The only adverse section of the report concerned the unfortunate friction over his colonels' commissions (which had flared up again as a result of events at the Canard River).

Hull was soon able to confirm his expectations: He addressed a proclamation to the Indian council pledging that his government would respect the Indians' land and rights, providing they remained neutral. Representatives of the Ottawa, Chippewa, Potawatomi, Wyandot, the Six Nations, and smaller bands all pledged neutrality and agreed to attend the general council to be held in August at Piqua. Only Tecumseh, Marpot, and a number of their followers remained at Fort Malden.

On July 16 the Americans heard that a British force had crossed to the north side of the Canard River. Cass was authorized to reconnoiter, but not to cross the Canard nor attack the enemy if met at the river.[30] Cass assembled a mixed force, consisting of Captain Josiah Snelling's company of regulars, five companies of Ohio infantry and a troop of cavalry, and Captain William McCulloch's small detachment of Ohio rangers (accompanied by Robert Lucas). Lieutenant-Colonel Miller volunteered to accompany the force.

Colonel Cass moved his party down the road, forded Turkey Creek, and was only a mile or two from the bridge over the Canard when his advance cavalry sent word that that bridge was intact and that only about fifty of the enemy were in sight. The Colonel decided to attack the inferior force and win possession of the bridge. He ordered some of the riflemen to advance along the road, avoid being seen by the enemy, and conceal themselves as close to the bridge as possible. The main body was to make a circuit to the east, cross the river well above the enemy, and proceed down the south bank to flank the British guard. The advance of the main

79

body escaped the notice of the British. But the movement of Cass's force was sighted at long range, and the British opened fire. Surprised by the sudden fire and by the realization that the British had a larger body than reported,[31] Cass's men were thrown into a temporary state of confusion. However, the American riflemen on the north side of the bridge opened fire, and the British withdrew. The Americans now gave chase; the British twice formed and withdrew. At this point Cass ordered a halt because it was getting dark and his men were within three miles of Fort Malden.

Cass returned his men to the bridge, left Robison's company to guard it, and withdrew the rest of his force about a mile to camp for the night. Lieutenant J. Clemow, of the British Forty-first, had neglected to inform two picket guards of his retreat. These two privates bravely withstood the American attack until, severely wounded, they were forced to surrender. These were the first real battle casualties of the campaign (probably of the war). Private Hancock died that night, but Private Dean was later taken as a prisoner to Sandwich.

Cass sent a message to Hull, telling him of the action and, recognizing that he had exceeded his orders, requested permission to hold the bridge. On July 17 the rest of the Fourth Regiment arrived, bringing a small artillery piece and Hull's answer. The General mentioned that he had had no news of McArthur (actually then on his way back from the Thames) and that it would be at least a week before the heavy artillery could be mounted on carriages. He wisely pointed out that the bridge was over twelve miles from the American camp but only five from Fort Malden and that the British could easily pass Cass's force by land or water and cut them off from the main camp. However—and this was the rub to Cass—he was content to leave the decision to Cass *and* Miller.

When the guards on the bridge reported the arrival of an enemy force in the area, Cass moved his entire force to the south side. In view of the fact that two boatloads of British were sighted going up the Detroit River, and that he no longer had absolute authority, Cass held an officers' council. All officers, except Cass and Snelling, voted to return to Sandwich, since Hull did not plan to bring the entire army to their support.[32]

80

By his attack Cass had unwittingly precipitated a delicate situation. Captain Return Brown, of the Fourth Regiment, had been ordered by Hull to bear a message to St. George. Protected by a flag of truce, he had reached a point about two miles from Fort Malden at the time of the attack on the bridge. (Hull later apologized for this unintentional breach of military etiquette on the grounds that Cass had not been expected to attack.) The General's note requested the return of his private papers and the restoration of all personal property captured on the *Cayauga*.[33] St. George answered that his officers had no time to sort the captured papers, that he still had received no instructions from his government concerning the disputed property, and that he regretted Hull's use of the words "retaliation and avenge." [34]

What had been accomplished by the fracas at the bridge? Certainly Cass knew that Hull planned no immediate attack on Fort Malden and that the bridge was a long distance from camp. Probably he had expected Hull to bring his entire force to that area and then prepare for the attack on the fort. The effect on Hull's conciliation policy may have been negligible, but such a move would have been militarily foolhardy, for without the defense of heavy artillery the troops would have been exceedingly vulnerable to fire from the British naval vessels. The Sandwich camp was on more favorable terrain and, since it was at least partially protected by the guns of Fort Detroit, the effect of the British naval strength was minimized.

It seems difficult to believe that the British were really caught off guard at the bridge. They could easily have torn up the bridge, stationed a larger guard, and anchored a regular naval vessel or the gunboats in a covering position. If the bridge was, indeed, their first real perimeter of defense, then they were negligent in their duty; but perhaps they *wanted* an American force to pass that point and fall into a previously prepared ambush. St. George wrote on July 15 that he hoped the enemy would move by land because "The Canard is so strong a position that I think (with the assistance of the Indians) I can annoy them much before they can get to this by that Road." [35] This does not sound like a man who would pin his faith on a small picket guard.

81

It is difficult to avoid the conclusion that Cass was overzealous and would have tried to hold the bridge had he had sole authority to make the decision. He must have reached sympathetic ears when he returned to camp because the three Ohio colonels addressed a joint letter to Eustis regarding the validity of their commissions.[36] They threatened to resign their commissions and disband their regiments if lowered in grade to lieutenant-colonels; and they even pointed out that they would still outrank all similar grade officers in the army, using the dubious argument that they held generals' commissions in the Ohio militia. While the letter stated that the signers felt Miller to be a good officer, it is obvious that the Canard affair had deeply rankled Cass. Newspapers throughout much of the country received exaggerated accounts of the action, and Cass became known as "the Hero of the Tarontee," the Indian name for the river. The only good from the action was that the men had gained some experience under enemy fire and that two prisoners had been taken.

On the evening of July 17 Colonel Findlay led a small patrol to the Canard and returned the following day to report the bridge torn up and the *Queen Charlotte* anchored at the mouth of the river. On July 18 Captain Snelling left on patrol, and on the following day McArthur was dispatched with a force of over 150 to relieve Snelling. This was to be just another reconnaissance; McArthur was specifically ordered not to go within reach of the *Queen Charlotte's* guns nor to attempt to cross the river.[37] McArthur relieved Snelling's force about a mile north of the bridge and, with his adjutant and a few riflemen, left his main force to observe the bridge more closely. He discovered that the planking had been taken up but that the stringers were intact and that an artillery battery was emplaced. Some Indians were observed crossing on the stringers of the bridge, and the riflemen opened fire. As McArthur moved down the north side to observe the brig, he was fired on from a concealed gunboat and he thereupon ordered the Americans to return to the main body of troops a mile away. Later in the day, while the men were receiving their customary ration of whisky, McArthur and his surgeon, advancing toward the bridge, were fired on by the Indians. The whole American force

82

rushed forward and forced the enemy back across the bridge. McArthur, with two men wounded, began his return to Sandwich, having already sent a communication to Hull, informing him that he was short of ammunition.

Thus far, McArthur had carried out his orders, but three miles down the road he encountered Cass bringing ammunition, a six-pounder, and a reinforcement of 150 men. Cass insisted on returning to the Canard to fire on the British.[38] They succeeded in drawing fire from the *Queen Charlotte,* contrary to orders, and then withdrew to camp for the night. The next morning, July 20, McArthur and Cass approached the bridge and noted that the British still had artillery protection. Cass and Major William Trimble insisted that the men be brought up to fire at the British. McArthur, though he strongly disapproved this needless exposure of the men, foolishly agreed.[39] The American six-pounder fired three rounds; the British nine-pounders and the *Queen Charlotte* returned the fire. This satisfied Cass, and the entire force returned to Sandwich.

There can be no doubt that Hull's orders to avoid the fire of the *Queen Charlotte* had been disobeyed; McArthur himself admitted in a letter to a friend that they had been fired on by her.[40] There could have been no real purpose to this last affair at the bridge— except to justify a juvenile whim of Cass's. Hull certainly had good reason to question the faith he might henceforth place in even his senior officers. He should have taken strong disciplinary action, but he did not, and the worst was yet to come.

Notes to Chapter IV

1. The dimensions of the fort are taken from the testimony of Lt. Dalliba (U.S. Artillery), Forbes, *op. cit.,* p. 81.
2. List of Brass and Iron Ordnance taken at Detroit, Lt. Felix Troughton to Maj.-Gen. Glasgon (C.O. Royal Artillery in Canada), Amherstburg, Apr. 1, 1813, *MPHC, op. cit.,* Vol. XXV, p. 433. Most of the smaller pieces were brass and the list includes the guns of the *Adams.*
3. Morning Report, Michigan Detached Militia, June 28, 1812, Burton Historical Collection, B. F. H. Witherell Papers.

4. Hull to Eustis, Camp Necessity, June 24, 1812, Henry A. S. Dearborn, *op. cit.*, p. 10.
5. Morning Report, July 28, 1812 (signed by Adjutant John Eastman), Burton Historical Collection, B. F. H. Witherell Papers.
6. A sketch of the fort may be seen in *MPHC, op. cit.*, Vol. XXV, p. 235. A report of the condition of the fort in 1808 may be found in J. Grant to Brock, Amherstburg, Feb. 1, 1808, Dept. of Public Records and Archives of Ontario, F. B. Tupper Papers. Its 1812 condition is described in Capt. M. C. Dixon (Royal Engineers) to Lt.-Col. R. H. Bruyeres, Ft. Amherstburg, July 8, 1812, Wood (ed.), *Documents of the Canadian War, op. cit.*, Vol. I, pp. 350–51.
7. David A. N. Lomax, *A History of the Services of the 41st (the Welch) Regiment* (Devonport: Hiorns & Miller, 1899), p. 49.
8. Dixon to Bruyeres, Ft. Amherstburg, July 8, 1812, Wood (ed.), *Documents of the Canadian War, op. cit.*, Vol. I, p. 351. The figure probably included officers and artillerymen.
9. The guns of the *General Hunter* and *Queen Charlotte* were reported in the Report on Marine in Upper Canada signed by Capt. A. Gray on Feb. 24, 1812, *Ibid.*, p. 254.
10. The strength of the crews were as of Aug. 30, 1811, in the Report of the Proposed Establishment for 1812 signed by A. H. Pye, *Ibid.*, p. 246.
11. Elliott to Wm. Claus, Amherstburg, Dec. 9, 1811, Esarey (ed.), *op. cit.*, Vol. I, p. 661.
12. Capt. Dixon to Lt.-Col. Bruyeres, Ft. Amherstburg, July 8, 1812, Wood (ed.), *Documents of the Canadian War, op. cit.*, Vol. I, p. 350.
13. E. A. Cruikshank (ed.), *Documents Relating to the Invasion of Canada, op. cit.*, p. 46.
14. Dixon to Bruyeres, Ft. Amherstburg, *Ibid.*, p. 49.
15. Report submitted to council of war at Detroit on July 9 and admitted as evidence at Hull's trial, Forbes, *op. cit.*, p. 154.
16. War Dept., June 24, 1812, *MPHC, op. cit.*, Vol. XL, p. 397.
17. Detroit, July 9, 1812, *Ibid.*, p. 406. Hull acknowledged receipt of Eustis' orders of June 24.
18. Report dated July 10, 1812, Burton Historical Collection, B. F. H. Witherell Papers, 1796–1924.
19. Cass to Lossing, Detroit, May 17, 1862, Burton Historical Collection, Benson Lossing Papers. Mrs. Sarah A. Clarke, Hull's daughter, wrote Lossing (Philadelphia, Mar. 8, 1863) that Cass had never mentioned this before Hull's death and she believed Hull had written it himself.
20. Mettez was paid $14 for printing 14 quires, July 11, 1812, Burton Historical Collection, James Taylor Papers. The proclamation is printed in many places, among which are: *Annals of Congress*, 12th Congress, Vol. I, p. 1397, and *MPHC, op. cit.*, Vol. XL, pp. 409–11.
21. Lucas stated this as a fact and his journal is usually reliable, but Hull never mentioned the postponement in his letters or *Memoirs*. See Parish (ed.), *op. cit.*, p. 27.
22. Francis Gubby and Isadore Pettier were paid $10 for "Secret Service" on the evening before the army crossed the river. Receipt dated July 15 in Burton Historical Collection, James Taylor Papers.
23. Parish (ed.), *op. cit.*, p. 27. *Roster of Ohio Soldiers in the War of 1812* lists these companies' strength, when sworn into federal service, as 3 officers and 56 men and 3 officers and 55 men, respectively.
24. Van Horne to Maj.-Gen. John Gano (Ohio Militia), Sandwich, July 28,

1812, "Selections from the Gano Papers, I," *The Quarterly Publication of the Historical and Philosophical Society of Ohio* (1920), Vol. XV, p. 80.
25. Diary of Capt. John Robison, Burton Historical Collection, Ms. Photostat (original in private possession), p. 8. The value seems very high. *Roster of Ohio Soldiers in the War of 1812*, p. 57, lists a Capt. John Robinson, clearly the same man, but the diary spells it Robison. Robison served in Findlay's Regiment.
26. McArthur's Testimony, Forbes, *op. cit.*, p. 53. There are several partial accounts of the Thames expedition, the most complete being in Quaife (ed.), *War on the Detroit, op. cit.* However this account is chiefly based on Lucas' journal, and Lucas was not on this expedition. The account is in error as to the dates of the events.
27. Isaac Hull, the uncle of the famous Commodore of the same name, was born in 1760 and moved to Canada in 1804, staying there until after the war. He then moved to Maumee, Ohio, and still later to Monroe, Mich., where he died in 1829.
28. Contemporary accounts in newspapers and other sources differ widely as to the amount of captured stores. The figures quoted are from an Extract of McArthur to Morris, Sandwich, July 24, 1812, *Poulson's American Daily Advertiser* (Philadelphia), Aug. 20, 1812.
29. Fred C. Hamil, "Ebenezer Allan in Canada," *Ontario Historical Society Papers and Records* (1944), Vol. XXXVI, p. 91. All three of these men figured in later events.
30. Hull to Prevost, Montreal, Sept. 8, 1812, Wood (ed.), *Documents of the Canadian War, op. cit.*, Vol. I, p. 519.
31. Parish (ed.), *op. cit.*, p. 33. Robert Lucas believed the British force to be 150 whites and 50 Indians; Cass thought it nearly twice that large.
32. Parish (ed.), *op. cit.*, p. 35.
33. Hull to St. George, Sandwich, July 16, 1812, Cruikshank (ed.), *Documents Relating to the Invasion of Canada, op. cit.*, p. 70.
34. St. George to Hull, July 16, 1812, *Ibid.*, p. 71.
35. St. George to Brock, Amherstburg, Wood (ed.), *Documents of the Canadian War, op. cit.*, Vol. I, p. 370.
36. Sandwich, July 18, 1812, National Archives, Records of the War Dept., Office of the Sec. of War Mss., M-341 (6).
37. Parish (ed.), *op. cit.*, pp. 36 and 39.
38. *Ibid.*, p. 39.
39. *Ibid.*, p. 40.
40. McArthur to Morris, Canada, July 24, 1812, Cruikshank (ed.), *Documents Relating to the Invasion of Canada, op. cit.*, p. 105.

CHAPTER V

A PROBLEM IN LOGISTICS

ON JULY 21 GENERAL HULL crossed to Detroit to determine the progress of preparations for the assault on Fort Malden. To avoid friction among his colonels, he took Lieutenant-Colonel Miller with him. The disappointing news that the gun carriages would not be ready for another two weeks was offset by an audacious plan for the capture of the *Queen Charlotte*. Captain Brevoort, of the Second Infantry and also the master of the *Adams*, suggested that artillery be mounted on a raft and floated downstream on a dark night to the side of the *Queen Charlotte*, and the vessel be captured by hand-to-hand fighting, supported by artillery fire.[1] If absolute secrecy could be maintained, this plan might be successful. So Hull decided to attempt the operation when he attacked Fort Malden.

McArthur, left in command at Sandwich, had been ordered to discover if a road suitable for artillery could be constructed across the Canard far above the regular bridge. His rangers reported such a route impractical.

Late on July 24 McArthur got a report from Canadian citizens that a group of Indians were observed to the north of the Canard River. He ordered a detachment under Major James Denny to set an ambush, by proceeding to the vicinity, dividing his force into two parts, and catching the Indians between. Denny's 117 men and a few of Captain McCulloch's rangers set out that evening and reached the vicinity of the Canard River by 3:00 A.M. the next day. The exhausted troops lay down to rest, but were disturbed by a boatload of British soldiers passing down the Detroit River. Soon they discovered a suspicious-looking Frenchman sneaking down the road. This man, Captain Laurent Bondy, of the First Essex, disclaimed any knowledge of the boat, insisting that he was merely returning home to cut his wheat. Denny sent him to Detroit under guard and moved his force to various positions in an effort to discover the enemy. In the early afternoon the men lay down to rest, having taken the routine precaution of posting guards.

The guards failed to see a group of Indians approaching the camp from the woods. However, Denny suddenly noticed the Indians and shouted to his men. There may have been only 22 Menomini Indians,[2] but most of the inexperienced Americans felt they were confronted by a superior force and fled in confusion toward Sandwich, heedless of Denny's commands to stand firm.[3] Denny had no choice but to withdraw with the remnant of his force and carry on a running fight with the pursuing Indians.

Meanwhile, Robison's rifle company, sent by McArthur to check a report of an American killed on the road to Malden, discovered the body of Avery Powers, a ranger who had left Denny's force because of illness. On hearing gunfire, the company rushed to Denny's aid, joining forces near Turkey Creek. The Americans then returned to Sandwich. Denny probably lost the following: four killed (including Powers), one wounded, and one taken prisoner; the Indians, a minimum of one killed and one wounded.

The ambush had backfired—this time through no rash action of Hull's colonels but because of the failure of some of the Ohio men to do their duty in the face of the enemy. Furthermore, Captain McCulloch scalped the slain Indian, an act which caused the Indians to renege on their promise to the British to forego such conduct. (Denny was later vindicated in a court-martial which he requested.)

Some time before Denny's action, Hull, seeking ways to increase his provisions, had sent a detachment under Captain Robert Forsyth to the area of Baldoon. This Highland Scotch settlement, consisting of some thousand acres several miles up the Sydenham River, had been founded in 1804 by the agents of the Earl of Selkirk (Thomas Douglas).[4] Forsyth returned on July 27 with some wool and 900 Merino sheep, which were taken to a pasture near Detroit. Although receipts were probably given for the sheep, they were private property, and the conduct of Forsyth's men caused some ill-feeling.

By July 25, in response to Hull's proclamation, most of the Canadians who desired to do so had placed themselves under Hull's protection. There are no official records of the militia who were granted protection (the register was turned over to the British after the surrender of Detroit). But there may have been 500 in this category. Joseph Watson, Hull's aide, testified that he had enrolled 367.[5]

Perhaps the best evidence of the success of Hull's policy is the fact that Brock felt compelled to issue his own proclamation to the Canadian people. This proclamation, dated at Fort George on July 22,[6] pointed out that the Canadians owed their prosperity to the maritime might of Britain, that they would lose British protection if attached to the United States and would run the grave risk of again becoming a part of France. Brock pledged no peace without British retention of Canada and stated that Hull's threat of no quarter to whites fighting by the side of Indians would, if carried out, be considered murder.

Crude though these claims were by modern standards of propaganda—French control, for example, would have been welcomed by most French Canadians—they could be effective if supported by positive actions. Brock, therefore, had to win some American territory or regain his own—or risk the complete loss of his militia and the Indians. An able subordinate contributed to the solution of this problem by the early capture of a key American position, Michilimackinac.

Fort Michilimackinac was located on a high limestone bluff,

overlooking the harbor, on the southeastern end of Mackinac Island. The fort was a typical log structure with wooden pickets, designed to afford protection only from Indian attacks; its heaviest guns, nine-pounders, could not begin to command the water passage from Lake Huron to Lake Michigan. A large hill, less than a mile away, rose to a much greater height than the fort, but nothing was done to prevent an enemy from emplacing artillery there. Even the spring which furnished the water supply for the garrison was not commanded by the fort's guns. In early July the garrison of 61 officers and men,[7] commanded by Lieutenant Porter Hanks of the regular artillery, was unaware that war had been declared.

The nearest British post was on St. Joseph Island, more than forty miles to the northeast. On June 25 the garrison under Captain Charles Roberts consisted of 46 officers and men of the Tenth Royal Veteran Battalion.[8] On July 8 Roberts received a message from Brock, notifying him of the outbreak of war and ordering him to take such measures as he could. The Captain immediately assembled a force to attack Fort Michilimackinac but deferred action due to later orders instructing him not to take the offensive until authorized to do so. On July 15 another message arrived from Brock, dated July 4, ordering Roberts to act at his discretion. Believing his post indefensible in the event of a large-scale American attack, and having been authorized to use fur company men and Indians to augment his own force, Roberts reverted to his offensive plans.

He hastily gathered all available men: most of his own garrison; at least 180 and perhaps as many as 230 Canadians, mainly local residents or *engagees* of the North West Fur Company; and nearly 400 Indians. The Canadians were led by Lewis Crawford and Toussaint Pothier. The Indians were led jointly by Robert Dickson (the most influential, although only semiofficial, agent of the British among the Indians of the Upper Mississippi), who had recently arrived with some 120 Sioux, Menominee, and Winnebago, and by John Askin, Junior, the Storekeeper and Interpreter at the post, who had assembled a force of over 280 Chippewa and Ottawa. Two of the garrison's six-pounders were loaded on the *Caledonia*, a North West Company vessel of 70 tons armed with four guns, which had arrived at St. Joseph a few days before and remained at Robert's request. With some of the men aboard the *Caledonia* and the rest in canoes, they set off about 10 :00 A.M. on July 16.

At Michilimackinac, Lieutenant Hanks had received an indirect warning of the attack plan from an Indian. Inclined to credit the report, he sent a militia captain, Michael Dousman, to St. Joseph. Dousman was captured by the invading force some distance from the island and was taken back to Mackinac Island.

About 3 :00 A.M. on July 17, the British landed far to the north of the fort. Roberts ordered some of his men to drag a six-pounder up the height commanding the fort. After promising not to contact the fort, Dousman was released to warn the civilians in the village to move quickly to the western part of the island. On seeing the civilians in the process of moving, a Doctor Day (probably Sylvester Day, Garrison Surgeon's Mate) notified Hanks of the danger, and the latter took what steps he could to defend his post.

With the gun emplaced and the whole force in position, the British sent a demand to Hanks to surrender—the first definite news the latter had received that his country was at war. Hopelessly outnumbered by at least ten to one and menaced by artillery he could not reach, Hanks had no choice but to surrender. Even had Hanks been notified earlier of the outbreak of war, little could have been done to save Michilimackinac. Only a large permanent garrison and intelligent peacetime preparation could have saved the fort from such a bloodless conquest.

The Articles of Capitulation granted the honors of war to the Americans; provided for the parole of the soldiers contingent on their not serving further until exchanged; and recognized private property rights, but required all civilians not taking an oath of allegiance to the king to depart within a month.[9] The two merchant vessels in the harbor, the *Selina* under Captain Daniel Dobbins and the *Mary* under Captain Ruff, were included in the private property pledge and their crews granted the same terms as the garrison. Two vessels arriving later, the *Freegoodwill* and the *Erie,* were accorded similar protection.

A rich haul, this—island, fort, Indian factory, seven pieces of ordnance, arms, ammunition, equipment of all kinds, 700 packs of furs, and a considerable store of provisions (the first division of prize money amounted to £10 a share). There was some protest about the furs seized from the Indian factory, but Hanks could do little in the face of Roberts' insistence that it was public property.

When asked if his garrison included any British subjects, Hanks replied no. Roberts then produced his own list of three deserters and twenty British subjects,[10] and retained them at Mackinac Island. The rest of Hanks's meager company departed on July 26 on the *Selina* and the *Mary*. On August 2 they reached Detroit, where they learned that Hull had been apprised of their capture by two Chippewa Indians some five days earlier. The soldiers disembarked, and the vessels, apparently destined for Cleveland, were held at Detroit lest they be seized and retained by the British at Malden.

The real significance of the fall of Fort Michilimackinac was the direct effect it had on the Indian situation and the indirect effect on Hull's invasion. Now the Indians of the north fairly flocked to Mackinac Island to demonstrate their friendship for the British, hoping to obtain a share of the captured goods. Matthew Irwin, factor at Fort Dearborn, who was captured on a vessel at Mackinac, later wrote that there were soon 1,460 Indians (including women and children) at Mackinac Island.[11] Unable to provision such a horde of Indians, Roberts sought to induce them to go to Amherstburg. However, the first news of Hull's invasion arrived, and most of the Indians returned home to await events.

Since the Indians were dominated by the North West and South West companies, most of them could have been persuaded to join an expedition to relieve Fort Malden—especially when the news came that Hull had not immediately swept all the British defenses before him. There is no question that the fur companies were willing to support the British; they already had, and had good economic reasons to continue doing so. In fact, a number of North West Company men had left Fort William, on northern Lake Superior, on the long journey to Mackinac and arrived a few days after the surrender. But one thing acted in Hull's favor: The fur company *engagees* were very eager to reach their distant winter quarters before the early fall storms. They were not willing to

91

risk the loss of a season's trade—advancing for this the practical and patriotic reason that the Indians needed their goods to avoid starving. Even without the men of the far north, a considerable force of Canadians and Indians could be gathered at any time—a force that, Hull feared, might amount to 3,000.

Still trying to win the Indians' friendship or at least their neutrality, the Americans, at President Madison's request, had called for a general council at Piqua on August 1. All tribes of the Northwest were invited, especially those of Ohio and the territories of Michigan, Indiana, and Illinois. Because of a food shortage, the council was postponed until August 15, when the new corn crop would be ready. There was but little time for the Americans to counteract the loss of prestige occasioned by the fall of Mackinac. What better way than by Hull's capturing Fort Malden?

Before making any plans for an attack, Hull sent word to Fort Dearborn, ordering the abandonment of that post and the removal of the garrison to Fort Wayne or Fort Detroit. On July 29 he wrote Eustis asking for reinforcements of 2,000 men from the militia quotas of Kentucky and Ohio. The same day he addressed an urgent appeal to the governors of those states to call out 1,500 and 500 men, respectively, organize and equip them, and be ready to dispatch them as soon as authorized by the Secretary of War.

In a separate action, McArthur and Cass wrote to Meigs asking for reinforcements of 300 men for their own regiments. Their situation was probably not unlike that of Findlay's Regiment, which originally had over 500 men but on July 28—because of sickness, men left behind along the route to Detroit, and the 70 remaining in Detroit—had an effective force of well below 400.[12]

Hull was now ready to return to his problem of attacking Fort Malden. The army had transported six-pounders to the Canard River; however, these would be ineffective as siege weapons when opposed by the twenty-four-pounders mounted at the fort. Not only were the traveling carriages for Hull's twenty-four-pounders still not ready, but Captain Dyson, his senior artillery officer, believed that heavy artillery (the twenty-four-pounders weighed nearly 5,000 pounds) could not be transported over the marshy sections of the road to Fort Malden.[13] Hull, therefore, decided to continue building rafts, planning to float his guns past these sections despite the danger of attack by enemy naval units.

A severe setback came to Hull on August 2, when the Wyandot Indians of the Brownstown area, whose loyalty Hull did not doubt, joined the British. Colonel Henry Procter, who had taken command of Fort Malden on July 26, sent a force of some 100 regulars and some Indians to help protect the Wyandots as they moved to Fort Malden.[14] The defection of the highly respected Wyandot influenced other vacillating tribes and removed the last friendly group along the vital road to River Raisin.

Meantime the British had their own problems: Disaffection had spread beyond the area directly controlled by Hull. Ebenezer Allan, Andrew Westbrook, and Simon Z. Watson, the Canadians who had offered their services to Hull, had returned to Delaware Township with a small cavalry force recruited in Canada, spread Hull's proclamation, and succeeded in getting the inhabitants of Delaware and Westminster townships to petition Hull for protection.[15] The local militia captain, Daniel Springer, informed Lieutenant-Colonel Henry Bostwick (Oxford Militia) of the action. Bostwick led an arresting party and, failing to find Allan or his closest associates, arrested two of Westbrooks's hired men. Allan and Westbrook were subsequently seized, but the latter escaped and fled to Detroit.

These partisans had all been former residents of the United States, but the same was true of most of the loyal people of the area. Brock may have magnified the importance of a few disaffected people, for he wrote, "My situation is most critical, not from anything the enemy can do, but from the disposition of the people—the population, believe me is essentially bad." [16]

Brock felt powerless to deal with the militia situation; his provincial legislature refused to take any effective action, and his advisers believed that if he applied martial law to the entire province the whole militia would disperse. He did transfer a detachment of 50 of the Forty-first to Moravian Town on the Thames River. The dual purpose of this force, commanded by Captain Peter

Chambers, was to stamp out the disaffection in the Thames area and, being strengthened by a considerable number of militia and Indians, to relieve the pressure on Fort Malden by creating a strong diversion on Hull's flank. However, only some 50 Indians appeared willing to march, although Brock had expected 400 from the Grand River area.

Two hundred militiamen were requisitioned on a quota basis from the Norfolk, Oxford, and Middlesex regiments and ordered to march to the Thames area under the command of Major George Salmon of the Second Norfolk. Unexpectedly, many of these groups, influenced by the general disaffection, refused to march, ostensibly because they would not leave their homes while the Grand River Indians might turn hostile. The flank companies of the First Oxford and a few other militia—perhaps a total of nearly a hundred in all—did join Chambers. Major Chambers, major by local rank only, moved his force to Delaware on July 31 because of its central location and of his expectation that Simon Watson would soon return to the area with a raiding party. By August 4 Hull, over a hundred miles away, learned of Chambers' force but assumed that it was at the authorized strength.

A constant problem to Hull was his provision shortage. The regular contractor, Augustus Porter, arrived at Detroit with the news that he had 400 barrels of provisions in small boats skirting the southern shore of Lake Erie. While these provisions might eventually be landed in Ohio and transported overland, Porter's agent at Detroit (who had charge of all provisions purchased from any source) reported on July 28 that there were on hand only 70,000 rations of flour and 21,000 of salted meat.[17] With the sheep from Baldoon and the various rations already delivered to Sandwich, Hull probably had more than the twenty-day supply reported. Nevertheless, he was gratified to learn that some of the rations ordered from John Piatt had arrived at the Miami Rapids.

Piatt's agents in Ohio had hurriedly gathered the first portion of the rations and notified Governor Meigs on July 18 that the provisions were being held at Urbana, awaiting escort to Detroit. A public meeting at Chillicothe the following day produced a number of volunteers; a company was formed and sworn into federal service; and Captain Henry Brush, a local attorney, was elected to command. The company of 69 men [18] left Chillicothe on July 20, arriving at Urbana four days later.

On the following day Brush's men left Urbana, escorting 300 cattle and 70 pack horses, with each horse carrying 200 pounds of flour. Some twenty men of the Fourth Regiment, under a sergeant, joined Brush. These regulars were some of the sick that had been left previously at various places and had gradually assembled at Urbana to await an opportunity to rejoin their regiment. On August 3 Brush arrived at the Rapids and, in accordance with Hull's orders, moved his provisions into the small blockhouse. Here he awaited a reinforcement of two companies, from Sandusky and Cleveland, before continuing to Detroit.

He would need this escort, as well as one from Hull's army, if he were to deliver the provisions to Detroit, for British Indians had maintained a blockade of the road from River Raisin to Detroit since the end of July. In one incident they had killed two American messengers only a short distance north of River Raisin and had captured their dispatches. On August 4 the Indians again intercepted the mail. After a few of the settlers were killed in isolated areas around River Raisin, the rest moved into larger groups for protection. The available local militia did what they could but, with the defection of the Wyandot, adequate protection for messengers could be obtained only from the main army.

On August 4 Hull ordered Major Van Horne of Findlay's Regiment to lead a large force across the Detroit River, proceed with the mail to River Raisin by a back trail,[19] and, by-passing Brownstown, escort Brush's force and provisions to Detroit. Although authorized to take all the riflemen of the Ohio soldiers,[20] Van Horne took only 150 of his own battalion, crossed the river in the early evening, picked up a few mounted men and some of the Ohio militia in Detroit, and camped for the night at the Ecorse River.

At daybreak Van Horne searched for the back trail, but to no avail. Moreover, the inhabitants told him that they knew of none, warning him that, unless the sun shone brightly, he would be in danger of getting lost in the heavily wooded swamp. (Such a back trail did exist, and Hull was negligent in not supplying a guide.) Van Horne sent a message to Hull informing him that he was taking the regular road. Without waiting for other orders, he assembled his men, and the force marched down the river road, despite the scouts' reports that Indians had been watching their camp the previous night.

A short distance beyond Monguagon the road forked to pass an Indian cornfield, and two men of the advance (Captain McCulloch and Van Horne's Negro waiter), who had taken the left trail were fired on by a small party of Indians and killed.[21] The main force rushed over from the right trail, but the Indians escaped. While the detachment halted to carry the bodies to a deserted Indian hut, a Frenchman appeared and warned that a large force of Indians and British were preparing an ambush at Brownstown. The Americans, who had had so many false reports, paid little attention.

Van Horne did adopt a definite marching order—two columns (with the mounted escort for the mail between them) and advance and rear guards. The force moved to Brownstown Creek and, since it was fordable for only a few yards, the columns were forced to move closer together. The opposite side of the creek was covered with thick bushes. When nothing out of the ordinary was observed, Van Horne decided to keep his normal intervals and begin the crossing. Although his force had been fired on and he had been warned of an ambush, he did not take the routine precaution of sending across scouts.

During the inevitable confusion preparatory to crossing, the Americans were fired on from an Indian ambush some fifty yards away. Most of Captain G. W. Barreres' mounted men in the left column stood firm and returned the fire, but many of Van Horne's men ran. The Indians, led by Tecumseh, fired again, and Van Horne ordered his men to retreat to better ground to form a firing line, but the officers could not get their men to stop running long enough to do so. Even the mounted men fled.[22] The Indians pursued the force only a short distance, but the retreat was in such disorder that a full firing line could not be formed even after the Indians ceased firing.

Van Horne thought the Indians had a force of 150 or 200 and believed, since they were in ambush, they possessed a great advantage over his men. However, Richardson, the young Canadian volunteer with the Forty-first, although not present at the engagement, stated there were only 24 Indians, plus Matthew Elliott's son dressed as an Indian, in Tecumseh's force.[23] Most secondary writers accept Richardson's figure, although there are some discrepancies in his account. It does seem that the Americans should have been able to distinguish between 25 and 200 muskets firing from concealment. The smaller figure seems more likely since, had the Indians had a large force, they would have continued the pursuit. A British force was moving to support Tecumseh but arrived after the action was over.

Van Horne reached the Ecorse River with most of his men. Some, who had never stopped running, arrived in Detroit before him—if not brave, they were at least in good physical condition. The Major loaded his wounded in a canoe and continued his retreat, meeting reinforcements under Captain Snelling at Spring Wells. The entire force reached Detroit by evening.

The Ohio men had heavy losses in the Battle of Brownstown. Captains Robert Gilchrist, William McCulloch, and Henry Ulry, Lieutenant Jacob Pentz (of Samuel Stewart's company), Ensigns Edward Roby (of Robison's company) and Andrew Ellison (of Spencer's company), and 10 enlisted men were killed, and Captain Jacob Boerstler (in command of the rear guard) was mortally wounded. Beside these 17 casualties, there were a number of wounded—Van Horne reported 12—and two men were taken prisoners and then murdered by the Indians to avenge the death of Chief Logan, an interpreter and the only Indian killed.

Not only had Van Horne failed to reach his objective, but the Indians had captured the mail abandoned by the fleeing escort. Apart from the fact that the Major had committed two cardinal errors—in taking the river road and in failing to scout dangerous terrain—his conduct had been satisfactory. Had his men performed their duty, the passage would have been forced—another evidence of the untrained character of part of Hull's army.

Nor was that all that happened on August 5. Twenty mounted

97

men, escorting the mail from River Raisin, were attacked near Swan Creek. The mail was captured, and most of the escort killed. The Indians had had a busy day. The British once more had possession of American mail, this time both to and from Detroit, and knew as much about Hull's position as he did.

Since about mid-July Hull had been hoping that operations along the Niagara front would commence. In letters to Eustis on July 19, 21, and August 4, he indicated that he felt such operations essential to avoid his own defeat.

To silence the grumbling of his army over the delay in the attack on Fort Malden, Hull had called a council of war four days before the Brownstown battle. He had told his officers of a fierce bayonet charge he had led during the Revolution leading to the capture of Stony Point, a fort on the Hudson. Fort Malden, he believed, was equal in strength to Stony Point. Did his officers feel, he had asked, that they could answer for the conduct of their men in a similar assault, but without the aid of artillery? As the General must have expected, Miller had stated that he could answer for his men, but the normally overzealous Ohio officers could not guarantee the conduct of their soldiers.[24]

Certainly the Brownstown affair should have indicated the wisdom of postponing the attack until the necessary artillery became available. The day after Brownstown, Hull again assembled his field-grade and senior artillery officers. Encouraged by the prospect of the recently constructed floating batteries, the officers voted for an immediate attack on Fort Malden. The measure was opposed only by the artillery officers,[25] probably because they regarded the plans for their guns as inadequate. Hull believed he had only two immediate alternatives: to retreat or to attack Fort Malden. Although not bound by his officers' decision, Hull bowed to the general will.

The general orders of August 7 provided for preparations necessary for the attack. However, before action could be taken, the plan was abandoned when Hull received word that British regulars from the Niagara region were en route to Fort Malden and no attempt was being made to stop them.[26] In the face of these reinforcements and the prospect of an early arrival of fur men and Indians from the north at Fort Malden, the attack became too great a gamble. Instead, Hull proposed that the army retreat to the Raisin River or the Miami, reform their severed supply lines and await reinforcements. Militarily the plan had much merit, but the Ohio officers threatened that their men would leave Hull if any retreat were made. The earlier weeks of the campaign, when Hull had neither won the admiration of the Ohio men nor sufficiently established control over them, were now beginning to tell. Perhaps the Ohio officers failed to realize that even if the fort were captured, Hull would have to destroy it or split his force; in either case, his supply lines would still be vulnerable to raids by the Indians or by British naval units.

General Hull decided to cross the bulk of his force to Detroit and attempt to reopen his supply lines. He asked McArthur to command a garrison at Fort Hope, but the Colonel refused to do so unless ordered, on the ground that he believed the position untenable. Perhaps, too, he felt the command unworthy of his rank. Major James Denny, of McArthur's Regiment, was ordered to occupy the position. Denny's garrison, consisting of Captain Joel Cook's regulars, nearly 150 Ohio men, and a small artillery detachment, was ordered to hold to "the last extremity." However, the force was authorized to retreat if, in the absence of aid from Detroit, it was attacked by artillery.

Hull could scarcely have arrived in Detroit before he received an anxious note from Denny stating that, while the regulars were performing their duty, the Ohio men were nearly in revolt.[27] The General was unable to replace the recalcitrant soldiers with the more dependable regulars, for he planned to use all that were available to open his supply and communications line, a project that the Ohio men had already unsuccessfully attempted.

The General ordered Miller to assemble a force of 600 and force a passage down the river road to escort Brush's force and provisions to Detroit. Miller took two hastily composed detachments of the First Infantry, under Lieutenant Dixon Stansbury and Ensign Robert McCabe, and all the remaining effectives of the Fourth

99

Regiment. Besides these 280 regulars,[28] he assembled a picked company from each of the Ohio regiments, Sloan's cavalry, Captain Antoine Dequindre's company of Michigan Detached Militia, most of Captain Richard Smyth's troop of Michigan cavalry, and an artillery detachment under Lieutenant John Eastman and Second Lieutenant James Dalliba (armed with a six-pounder and a howitzer). Several officers volunteered to accompany the force and were assigned duties: Majors Van Horne and Morrison; Captains A. Hull, Brevoort, and Daniel Baker (First Infantry); and Lieutenant William Whistler (First Infantry). The total force was actually over 600.

Miller paraded his force in Detroit, addressed a few remarks to the men, and began the march. The expedition camped across the Rouge River the night of August 8 and resumed the march at daybreak, with Captain Snelling commanding the advance guard.

The British and Indians were maintaining a constant surveillance of the river road. On August 7, believing the Americans were preparing to attempt to bring the provisions and mail to Detroit, the British crossed a large detachment of regulars, Canadians, and Indians, under the experienced command of Captain Adam Muir. The force erected brush shelters near Brownstown and awaited the reports of the Indian scouts. Nothing had happened by the morning of August 9, and the British were preparing to leave when the scouts brought word of a large party of Americans some eight miles away. Because the Americans were proceeding cautiously, they were not expected to arrive at Brownstown much before night. So Muir decided to move his detachment to Monguagon and engage the Americans that day.

The Americans were not much more than a mile away when the British force of about 350 moved to a ravine near Monguagon, hastily dragged what logs they could into a defensive position, and settled down to ambush the enemy. Tecumseh's Indians were dispersed in a cornfield and in the woods on the British left flank. Just about the time the American advance was sighted, 60 British regulars arrived—probably bringing the total force to more than 400.[29] About 4:00 P.M. Snelling's advance guard came into view, was fired on, and the Battle of Monguagon was on.

100

For the first time in the campaign the American advance guard held its position, while the men in the main body shed their knapsacks and rushed to the battle line to return the British fire. The British observed movement in the woods on their right and, believing the Americans were attempting to flank them, fired. Actually, they were firing on their own men—Indians who had unexpectedly shifted from the left. The enraged Indians, as might be expected, returned the British fire. While this internal fight was going on, Muir ordered the bugler to sound the signal for a bayonet charge. However, the recently arrived regulars had not been informed of the signal and thought it an order to retreat. When some of the regulars began withdrawing, the rest of Muir's thoroughly confused force followed suit.

Since the retreating British and Indians were taking separate courses, Miller ordered his men to pursue the Indians. The British thus withdrew some distance and reformed their line without opposition. Suddenly Muir, who had been wounded, heard musket fire and, believing the Americans might cut off his retreat, ordered his men to their boats. The British sailed to Fort Malden, confident that the Indians could elude pursuit in the dense woods.

The Americans pursued the Indians for more than two miles, lost contact, and returned to a cleared area south of the battleground to protect the wounded. Since Miller was afraid to let his men go into the woods to recover their provision knapsacks, cast off at the first sign of battle, he sent the intrepid Snelling to inform Hull of the battle and ask for provisions and reinforcements. Then Miller assembled his men, delivered the customary oration, and, at the start of a very heavy rain, ordered the wounded moved into some old Indian huts. The tentless and nearly foodless camp faced an almost sleepless night in a downpour.

On the following day, August 10, a day's rations were brought to the camp, when McArthur arrived with 100 men and twelve boats and bateaux. He granted permission for a few of his men to remain with Miller, loaded the wounded into the boats, and began the return trip in the afternoon. After rowing a short distance up river, his men noticed the *General Hunter* leaving the Canadian shore. The ship had probably been alerted by the British lookouts on Grosse Isle, who must have seen McArthur's down-river passage. The Americans frantically pulled to shore and, in direct disobedience of McArthur's orders, ran into the woods, deserting their wounded comrades.[30]

Disgusted at this action, McArthur lured the men back to the boats by promising to let them fill their canteens from a cask of whisky. Aided by this stimulant, and perhaps regretting their impulse to abandon the wounded, the men resumed their passage up the river until the *General Hunter* anchored some distance ahead of them. This time McArthur ordered them to pull to shore and remove the wounded to the shelter of the woods.

Before McArthur had left Detroit, Colonel Gabriel Godfroy,[31] of the Michigan militia, believing that a return trip by water would be impossible, had offered to gather some wagons to transport the wounded back to Detroit. Now, finding Godfroy right, McArthur sent for the wagons, only to find that Godfroy had not waited for such word, but had started out and was only a short distance away. The wounded were moved by boat to a place where the wagons could approach, and reloaded into the wagons for the rest of the journey.

The *General Hunter*, probably unaware that there were wounded in the wagons, fired several shots at the Americans, but without effect. A British gunboat at the mouth of the Ecorse made no attempt to fire, and the Americans proceeded toward Detroit, encountering Cass near the Rouge River. Cass's men hurried to the scene but found McArthur's abandoned boats gone. They had been captured by the guard boats of the *General Hunter* and the *Queen Charlotte*.[32] Believing the British would capture the boats, McArthur had left two British soldiers considered too severely wounded to move to Detroit by wagon.

On the day after the battle, Cass had sent a message to Hull requesting permission to relieve Miller, who was ill. Instead of waiting for a reply, he moved his detachment toward Monguagon, camping that night a few miles from Miller's force. With no answer from Hull by the next morning, August 11, he returned to Detroit.

Although Miller should have been able to continue his march the day after the battle—his scouts had reported no sign of Indians beyond Brownstown and he had been relieved of the wounded—he remained stationary. True, his men were tired from the long march, the previous day's battle, and the lack of sleep. Considering the men's condition, Miller decided to delay the march until the next day.

But on the following day Miller still made no move to march. Instead he sent a request to Hull for two days' rations. In view of the rations originally given to the force, the provisions brought by McArthur, and the hogs, corn, and potatoes the men rounded up in the vicinity, it is difficult to believe that the force did not have a day's makeshift ration on August 11. Moreover, considering his distance from River Raisin, Miller could have reached there as quickly as rations could be delivered from Detroit.

Perhaps he thought that he would have to march to the Rapids to meet Brush's provision force, not knowing that Brush was now at River Raisin. Suffering from a recurrent attack of fever, he may not have been thinking clearly. But he must have feared another attack on his force, especially an ambush farther down the road. It was evident that he was leaving the decision to Hull—if the rations were sent, he would be forced to march.

For his part, Hull had little alternative, not knowing why Miller made no advance. Realizing that Miller was endangering his command and accomplishing nothing by remaining in a position known to the British, the General ordered him to return. Miller received the order on or before the morning of August 12, promptly struck camp, and reached Detroit late that afternoon.

There had been heavy casualties in the Battle of Monguagon. Hull reported his losses for the regulars as 10 men killed, 6 officers and 45 men wounded; and for the Ohio and Michigan troops, 8 killed and 13 wounded—a total of 18 killed and 64 wounded.[33] Procter reported the British losses for the regulars as 3 killed, 13 wounded, and 2 missing (the Americans had taken 4 prisoners, but the British had regained the 2 badly wounded men); militia, 1 killed and 2 wounded; and Indians, 2 killed and 6 wounded—a

103

total of 6 killed, 21 wounded, and 2 prisoners.[34] However, Procter admitted he did not know the total Indian force in the battle and, since some of the Indians remained on the American side of the river, he was probably in error as to their casualties. Since Miller's force had pursued the retreating Indians and exchanged fire for some two miles, it would seem that the Indians must have suffered higher casualties than Procter reported. In his report of the battle, Hull informed Eustis that the Americans had discovered 40 dead Indians on the field, and a resident of Detroit reported that he had personally seen 40 scalps brought in by Miller's men.[35] Most contemporary British accounts gave the British casualties at an even lower figure than Procter's. There seems to have been a deliberate attempt to minimize British losses, especially of the Indians, throughout the campaign.

Miller, Snelling, and Baker were subsequently brevetted for the battle. The Americans had, indeed, won a partial victory: They had dented but not broken the British blockade. Yet they had nullified their success by retaining the field for at least thirty-six hours without attempting to advance. With a third of his effective force, and the best third at that, Hull had been unable to force a passage to River Raisin. His position, obviously, was hopeless without outside aid.

Hull was now convinced that he must withdraw to his fortified enclosure, avoid further engagements with the enemy, and wait for help. On August 8 he had received word, in answer to his request, that reinforcements were on the way. A letter from Eustis informed him that he had directed Meigs to furnish troops to guard the provision lines and had ordered General James Winchester to assemble a force of 1,500 recruits and volunteers from Kentucky and march to Detroit.

Hull's completely defensive state of mind is best illustrated by the fact that, on August 11, he ordered Fort Hope at Sandwich abandoned and destroyed. It is difficult to find a logical reason for this withdrawal from Canada. His garrison had been in no immediate danger and could easily have retreated had the situation required it. On the other hand, the retreat lessened his control of

104

that section of the Detroit River, took the last of his men from Canada, and left the Canadians who had applied for protection the dubious choice of moving to Detroit or throwing themselves on the mercy of the British. Perhaps he believed that the British, if left alone, would reciprocate—but, if so, he reckoned without Brock who was, even then, building a trap.

As early as July 29 Brock had ordered a hundred picked militia from York to Long Point (on Lake Erie), where he expected to collect a detachment to reinforce Amherstburg. A few days later he received word from Prevost that he was sending two companies of the Royal Newfoundland and all the separate detachments still in Lower Canada whose regiments were already in the upper province. Previously hard-pressed to maintain his communication lines with Lower Canada, Brock finally was able to concentrate on the events in the West. He adjourned the Assembly until September and left on August 5 for Fort Erie and Long Point.

Two days later he held an Indian council at a Mohawk village on the Grand River and was promised that at least 60 warriors would follow him to Fort Malden. He had already sent 60 regulars to Amherstburg on August 8 (probably from the Forty-first but possibly from the Royal Newfoundland), and now ordered Chambers' force, still at Delaware, there.

On August 8 Brock set sail from Port Dover, planning to skirt the northern shore of Lake Erie on the two-hundred-mile trip to Amherstburg. His ten boats, loaded with 300 militia and 40 men of the Forty-first, arrived at Amherstburg just before midnight on August 13.

There, probably, the two most brilliant soldiers of the campaign met for the first time—Brock and Tecumseh. The two generals— Tecumseh had been, or shortly was to be, given the rank of a brigadier [36]—were mutually impressed. The Shawnee had no high opinion of Procter—later regarded him with utter contempt—but his legendary remark on meeting Brock was the laconic observation, "There is a man." Tecumseh promised to assemble his men later in the day, and departed.

Brock had arrived at Fort Malden with major reinforcements,

the Indians were gathering, and the trap was being prepared.

Still another trap, of quite a different kind, was being readied for Hull—an event that might be called the Cass Conspiracy, for Cass played a prominent part in it. On August 12 a round robin had been circulated to the Ohio colonels "requesting the arrest or displacement of the General, and developing the command on the eldest of the colonels, McArthur." [37] A day or two later, probably another round robin was circulated among residents of Detroit and the Ohio men, stating, "We signers hereto, agree to seize General Hull and depose him from command, and to defend the fort at all hazards." [38] Prominent among the eighty signatures were the names of Lewis Cass and Gabriel Godfroy. The full details of the plot have never been uncovered.

It is apparent that the Ohio men had not taken to heart Governor Meigs's enjoinder, on the occasion of Hull's assumption of command on May 25, "Subordination is the soul of discipline: order, safety, and victory are its results." [39] Insubordination of long duration was about to play a prominent part in defeat.

Notes to Chapter V

1. Milo M. Quaife (ed.), "Two Girls of Old Detroit," *Burton Historical Collection Leaflet*, Vol. VIII (May, 1930), No. 5, p. 72. The account is by the daughter of Brevoort, who, although born in 1812, heard members of her family discussing this later.
2. Alexander C. Casselman (ed.), *Richardson's War of 1812* (Toronto: Historical Publishing Co., 1902), p. 22. Richardson, a schoolboy of sixteen, the son of a British physician, was a volunteer with the Forty-first. Years later, as a famous writer, he wrote this account of his experience in journal form.
3. Parish (ed.), *op. cit.*, p. 43.
4. For an account of Baldoon see, Fred C. Hamil, *The Valley of the Lower Thames 1640 to 1850* (Toronto: University of Toronto Press, 1951), pp. 46–56.
5. Forbes, *op. cit.*, p. 151. Other estimates are even higher.
6. Printed in Cruikshank (ed.), *Documents Relating to the Invasion of Canada, op. cit.*, pp. 81–83.
7. Capt. Charles Roberts to Glegg, Ft. Michilimackinac, July 29, 1812, Wood (ed.), *Documents of the Canadian War, op. cit.*, Vol. I, p. 442. Some writers call the fort "Fort Mackinac" to distinguish it from the older

fort on the mainland, but all the participants styled it Fort Michili-mackinac.

8. General Return 10th R.V.B., Public Archives of Canada, Royal Veteran Battalions, 1807–14, Mss. Vol. C789.
9. Capitulation of July 17, 1812, Wood (ed.), *Documents of the Canadian War, op. cit.,* Vol. I, p. 435.
10. Roberts to Hanks, Ft. Michilimackinac, July 22, 1812, *MPHC, op. cit.,* Vol. XL, pp. 443–44.
11. Irwin to Mason, George Town, Oct. 16, 1812, Carter (ed.), *op. cit.,* Vol. X, p. 413.
12. Van Horne to Gano, Sandwich, July 28, 1812, "Gano Papers," *Historical and Philosophical Society,* Vol. XV, p. 80.
13. Testimony of Dyson, Forbes, *op. cit.,* p. 133.
14. Procter to Brock, Amherstburg, Aug. 11, 1812, Wood (ed.), *Documents of the Canadian War, op. cit.,* Vol. I, p. 456. Procter was born in 1763, began service in the Forty-third Foot in 1789, and, by 1810, was the colonel of the Forty-first.
15. Capt. Daniel Springer to Brock, Delaware, July 23, 1812, Cruikshank (ed.), *Documents Relating to the Invasion of Canada, op. cit.,* p. 86.
16. Brock to Baynes, York, July 29, 1812, *Ibid.,* pp. 106–07.
17. Forbes, *op. cit.,* p. 155.
18. Samuel Williams, "Two Western Campaigns in the War of 1812" in Ohio Valley Historical Series' *Miscellanies* (Cincinnati: Robert Clarke & Co., 1871), p. 13, stated 95 men volunteered but the muster roll in the Appendix lists 69 men. Williams served on the expedition.
19. Cass and McArthur testimony, Forbes, *op. cit.,* pp. 30 and 56.
20. Van Horne testimony, *Ibid.,* p. 72.
21. Parish (ed.), *op. cit.,* pp. 47–48. A major was authorized two waiters—possibly Van Horne had brought this man with him from home. Lucas was in advance on the right fork.
22. Van Horne testimony, Forbes, *op. cit.,* p. 69.
23. Casselman (ed.), *op. cit.,* p. 27.
24. Munson testimony, Forbes, *op. cit.,* p. 131.
25. Quaife (ed.), *War on the Detroit, op. cit.,* p. 275.
26. "Defense of Hull," *MPHC, op. cit.,* Vol. XL, p. 616. Miller testified that he had seen these letters. Probably Simon Watson had returned from the Thames to confirm the information.
27. Denny to Hull, Ft. Hope, Aug. 8, 1812, Burton Historical Collection, Hull Papers.
28. Miller testimony, Forbes, *op. cit.,* p. 115.
29. As usual, all sorts of estimates of strength are available—several contemporary Canadian or British sources placed the force even larger—Richardson stated there were 190 whites; Procter, 150 whites (and an undetermined number of Indians); Verchères, 215 whites and 200 Indians; Lomax's semiofficial history (not contemporary) stated there were 135 whites and 325 Indians. Hull believed they had 400 whites, besides the Indians. Many writers call this the Battle of Brownstown, but it is less confusing to reserve that name for the August 5 affair.
30. Quaife (ed.), *War on the Detroit, op. cit.,* p. 284.
31. Godfroy was born in Detroit in 1758 and had a trading post along the Huron River, at present-day Ypsilanti.
32. Return of Prizes, Cruikshank (ed.), *Documents Relating to the Invasion of Canada, op. cit.,* p. 232. The British had also captured, on August 1, a

large raft, designed for a floating battery, which had apparently broken loose from its mooring and floated down the river.

33. Hull to Eustis, Detroit, Aug. 13, 1812, Cruikshank (ed.), *Documents Relating to the Invasion of Canada, op. cit.*, p. 141. The numerous contemporary estimates of casualties are substantially in agreement.
34. Procter to Brock, Amherstburg, Aug. 11, 1812, Wood (ed.), *Documents of the Canadian War, op. cit.*, Vol. I, p. 457.
35. *The Albany Register*, Sept. 1, 1812.
36. Today it is becoming more apparent that Tecumseh was never an official general, but participants in the war considered him one.
37. Hatch, *op. cit.*, p. 40.
38. Talcott E. Wing (ed.), *History of Monroe County Michigan* (New York: Munsell & Company, 1890), p. 91. Wing states that a signer, Charles Larned, gave the document to his son in 1833 who, after the last survivor had died, turned it over to B. F. H. Witherell, then President of the Detroit Historical Society. Wing could not locate the document in 1890, and the present writer has found no trace of it.
39. *MPHC, op. cit.*, Vol. XL, p. 381.

CHAPTER VI

THE SURRENDER OF DETROIT

WHEREAS GENERAL HULL had hesitated and vacillated in his plans for an attack on Fort Malden, General Brock was to act boldly and decisively against Detroit. Taking advantage of Hull's withdrawal from Canada, he issued general orders praising the faithful members of his army on their somewhat unexpected success. He offered reinstatement without punishment to those previously considered deserters. He promoted several of his senior captains to majors, with local rank only, thus creating three non-Indian brigades: the first, under St. George, consisting of the Kent and Essex militias and the recently arrived detachment from the Royal Newfoundland; the second, under Major Chambers, of the militia from the east and Chambers' own detachment of regulars; and the third, under Major Joseph Tallon, of the rest of the Forty-first at the post.

The same day, August 14, he addressed the assemblage of Indians—possibly as many as 1,000.[1] Meeting later with the most important chiefs, he secured their approval of a major demonstration against Hull's force, even to an outright attack on Fort Detroit.

Procter, under the direct orders of Brock, would command

the British force, and Tecumseh would lead the Indians. Procter, like Hull, performed adequately as a subordinate but always in a routine fashion. There was a Brock to more than compensate for Procter's lack of brilliance; but, unfortunately, this was not so in the case of Hull.

On August 14, when the artillery left for Sandwich, the British began their move against Detroit. The main force followed the next morning, leaving only a token guard at Malden. The force crossed the newly repaired bridge over the Canard River, with the Indians ranging the woods on the right and gunboats patrolling the shore on the left. The *Queen Charlotte* and *General Hunter* sailed in deeper water transporting ammunition and heavy equipment and standing by to augment the land artillery. The main force stopped short of Sandwich, but the artillery had already been rolled above the town and emplacements ordered for an eighteen-pounder, two twelve-pounders, and two 5½-inch mortars. Brock planned to cross to Detroit on the following day.

On the American side of the river, the progress was less than satisfactory. Brush's provision train at River Raisin still awaited an army escort to Detroit. Brush, acting as commander of his original force and of a company of Ohio volunteers, which had joined him on August 9, had ordered a trench dug, with a breastwork of logs on the outside edge, around the River Raisin stockade. The post was not a strong one, but with a small howitzer mounted in one of the blockhouses, the men were confident they could withstand an artilleryless attack.

However, the British made no attempt to attack River Raisin. Possibly they realized that as long as Brush remained there, Hull would send successive detachments to his aid, thus weakening his own garrison. Probably they were concentrating on easier goals. The force at River Raisin, a total of 194 men,[2] was not a small one: There were three small companies of Ohio men (Captains Brush, Rowland, and Campbell), Sergeant Story's detachment of the Fourth Regiment, and Lieutenant Couch with 22 rangers from Manary's Blockhouse. Also there were Captain Hubert LeCroix's company of the Michigan Detached militia, part of another company of the same organization, and most of Lieutenant-Colonel John Anderson's Second Michigan Militia. Anderson, however, was committed to defend River Raisin, and could not risk his post by accompanying Brush to Detroit.

After the Battle of Monguagon, Hull had notified Brush that the escort party was returning to Detroit and ordered him to remain at River Raisin, but added in a postscript:

> If consulting with col. Anderson and capt. Jobart, the bearer of this, and from all the information you can obtain, it should be the opinion you can come an upper road crossing the river Huron at Godfrey's trading establishment, you are authorized to proceed that route, in which case you will give me an immediate notice. No person must know this excepting colonel Anderson, capt. Jobart and yourself. Take captain Jobart for a guide, and if he recommends other guides with him, they shall be paid. Capt. LeCroix, with his company, will proceed on with you.[3]

Aware of the plight of Hull's army, Brush replied that he would attempt the journey. His message reached Detroit on the morning of August 14,[4] and by noon Hull had ordered McArthur and Cass to assemble 400 picked men to meet him. Late that afternoon he discovered that about 350 men had been chosen but no attempt had been made to begin the march. In answer to Hull's demand for an explanation, McArthur said that Quartermaster James Taylor had not furnished provisions. Obviously this was a flimsy excuse for, had McArthur desired to march, he would have soon enough notified Hull of Taylor's slackness.

Indeed, the real cause of the delay was that Cass and McArthur had set in motion a plot to depose Hull and were reluctant to march from Detroit. Two days earlier they, along with Taylor, had addressed an urgent plea to Meigs, asking him to come to Detroit with reinforcements of 2,000; in a postscript, probably written on August 13 or 14, they had reported that the British were opposite Detroit and that the General was talking of a capitulation.[5] Perhaps Cass and McArthur had planned to delay Hull's deposition in the hope that Meigs would appear and now, believing that their hand was forced, had decided to act that night. Cass later boasted that only the sending of McArthur and himself on detachment prevented the plot from being carried out.[6]

Although apparently Hull was aware of the plot against him, there was little he could do even had he known the details—arrest of the ringleaders would have precipitated the mutiny. Outwardly accepting the explanation of the delay, he ordered McArthur to march immediately, assuring him that provisions would follow. The detachment was to take the back trail to the Huron River and, if Brush were not there, was to continue to River Raisin and escort the provision train to Detroit. There would be no question of finding the back trail this time, for Colonel Godfroy was ordered to serve as the chief guide. The force finally left Detroit about sunset and camped that night only a little more than two miles from the fort.

At Fort Detroit, on August 15, Lieutenant-Colonel Miller was presiding at a court-martial which Lieutenant Hanks had requested for a review of his action in surrendering Fort Michilimackinac. The proceedings were interrupted when an alert sentry noticed a small boat, carrying a flag of truce, leave the Canadian shore. Miller immediately adjourned the court (no one was very interested anyway, for exoneration was a foregone conclusion), and Captains Snelling and Fuller hurried to the landing to meet the boat. Lieutenant-Colonel John Macdonell and Major John Glegg landed, were blindfolded, and escorted to a near-by house to await Hull's answer to a communication from Brock. Brock's message stated:

> The force at my disposal authorises me to require the immediate surrender of fort Detroit. It is far from my intention to join in a war of extermination, but you must be aware, that the numerous body of Indians who have attached themselves to my troops, will be beyond controul the moment the contest commences. You will find me disposed to enter into such conditions as will satisfy the most scrupulous sense of honour. Lieut-colonel M'Donnell and major Glegg are fully authorised to conclude any arrangement that you may lead to prevent the unnecessary effusion of blood.[7]

Certainly Brock did not expect Hull to surrender at that time, but he did expect the threat of an Indian massacre to prey on Hull's already overburdened mind. Besides, he was playing for time so that his men could complete the emplacement of guns above Sandwich without having to dodge American shells.

Hull delayed his reply for several hours in the hope of hearing from Colonel McArthur. Too, he wanted time to complete last-minute defensive arrangements, such as shifting the uppermost river battery to the more favorable position in Judge Woodward's garden, on the high ground in the center of town. Finally, he drafted his reply to Brock, saying, in the most significant paragraph:

> I have received your letter of this date. I have no other reply to make, than to inform you, that I am prepared to meet any force which may be at your disposal, and any consequences which may result from any exertion of it you may think proper to make.[8]

Abruptly at 4:00 P.M., barely an hour after Hull's reply had been delivered, the British shore batteries in Canada and the guns of the *Queen Charlotte* and *General Hunter* bombarded Detroit. The Americans, who had not attempted to hinder the placement of the British guns before or after the truce, returned the fire from their two river batteries and the twenty-four-pounders recently emplaced in the town. During the next several hours while the brisk fire continued, the guns of the fort, because of their location, remained silent. Each side was primarily interested in silencing the other's batteries. The theoretical advantage lay with the more numerous British guns, but the actual results proved inconclusive. No damage was done to either side's artillery, and only one man was wounded on each side. Obviously, unless the British gunners made a series of lucky shots at long range, the only threat to Fort Detroit would be an invasion.

The logical place for the British to attempt a crossing was at a point below Detroit, beyond range of the American guns, and where the river was the narrowest. Undoubtedly, this would be Spring Wells. If Hull were to oppose the British crossing, a large force would have to be detached for service well beyond sight of the fort. This would split Hull's force into three groups—McArthur's detachment, those at Spring Wells, and those at the fort; the

Spring Wells detachment would have to be commanded by a regular captain or a militia field-officer, since Miller was too ill for field command. Past events had demonstrated the futility of using separate detachments to engage the enemy. Moreover, Hull believed the Indians would attack the fort that night. In view of all these reasons, he decided not to oppose a British crossing, if made beyond range of the Detroit guns; but, late that afternoon, he did order Snelling to lead a small detachment to Spring Wells to report on any attempted night crossing by the British.

After reaching Spring Wells, Snelling sent a note back to Hull requesting that a twenty-four-pounder be emplaced at Spring Wells and that he be authorized to hinder a British crossing. Captain Dyson, the senior artillery officer at Detroit, stated that in his opinion so heavy a gun could not be transported over a bridge en route to Spring Wells, but offered to try. Hull might have allowed Dyson to make the attempt had he but known one vital fact—that McArthur and Cass were only a short distance from Detroit.

On August 15 McArthur and Cass had resumed their march toward River Raisin, their mounted men having been sent ahead to contact Captain Brush. The detachment moved slowly, and sullenly at that, because they had not eaten the evening before. The provisions Hull had promised, although dispatched from Detroit, had not arrived. Either its escort had taken the wrong trail or a conspirator in the deposition plot, as Hull later believed,[9] had deliberately misdirected it.

Late in the afternoon the mounted men returned to inform McArthur and Cass that they had discovered no sign of Brush at Godfroy's trading post, the rendezvous. And with good reason, for Brush had never left River Raisin. Perhaps he had notified Hull he would move and had then changed his mind—he did write to a friend, on August 14, that he would have left for Detroit had he had 400 men.[10] Perhaps he had learned of the deposition plot and had decided to aid the conspirators by remaining at River Raisin.

In any event, when the two colonels learned Brush was not at

114

the rendezvous and since the provisions had not arrived from Detroit, they immediately began their return march. Just before dark, a messenger from Hull, brought them urgent orders to return.[11]

The colonels sent Brush a messenger (who apparently never reached him) and marched until late that night, before camping within three miles of Detroit. They probably arrived there long after the artillery fire had ceased, and may not have known of it, but they committed an unpardonable error: They failed to notify Hull of their presence [12]—a fact neither ever denied. There could be no justification for this negligence: It was a serious neglect of duty, complete incompetence, or deliberate intent. Hull had every reason to believe the colonels were a great distance from Detroit. It was a costly mistake, for the General was unaware of it and could not plan accordingly.

Brock, in possession of many American letters, knew Hull's desperate position. Moreover, having detached troops from the Niagara area, he ran a grave risk that American offensive operations might begin in that region if he held his eastern men overlong at Fort Malden. In spite of the contrary advice of his officers, especially Procter,[13] Brock determined to attack Detroit and issued orders for his soldiers to be ready to cross the river at 3:00 A.M. on August 16.

Hull had carefully encircled the fort and town on all but the river side as a defense against an expected Indian attack on the night of August 15. Findlay's Regiment was situated behind an incomplete row of pickets below the fort and town; the remnants of McArthur's and Cass's regiments, augmented by the Michigan Detached Militia and a recently formed company of teamsters, were in the rear of the fort; and the First Michigan Militia, under Colonel Elijah Brush, was located above the fort and town. All the regulars (other than those on parole from Mackinac Island) were assigned posts in the fort or at the various batteries. Snelling's small detachment at Spring Wells was under strict orders to return to the fort before dawn. The reserves consisted of soldiers slightly wounded or ill, who were lying at ease in their blankets at the rear of the fort. Most of the women and children had been moved to a stone root cellar in a near-by orchard but a few stayed behind to prepare powder bags.

At dawn on Sunday, August 16, the British recommenced the bombardment of Detroit. Their target was the fort, the fire was heavy, and several casualties were inflicted on the garrison. Apparently a soldier was killed on the parade ground; another shot killed an ensign of the Fourth Regiment and a paroled soldier; and still another killed Lieutenant Hanks and Doctor James Reynolds and severely wounded Doctor Hosea Blood (of the Fourth Regiment). Although the American artillerists were more effective than on the previous day, Hull at 10:00 A.M. ordered Dyson to cease firing.[14] He had learned of events which caused him to ask for terms.

Shortly after dawn three brigades of British soldiers, preceded by Indians, had crossed the river and landed at Spring Wells, meeting not the slightest American resistance. Originally Brock had believed that concentrated artillery fire from Canada might panic Hull into leaving the fort to engage the British force in the open.[15] But after his scouts learned that a large detachment— 500, they thought—had recently left Detroit and was still absent, Brock determined to send his soldiers to storm the fort while the Indians attacked the town.

The British formed in close order and advanced on Detroit. Less than a mile from the outpost of Findlay's Regiment, Brock ordered his men to break formation and prepare their cold breakfasts, while he and his aides reconnoitered. His Indians had slipped through the woods behind Detroit and even then were entering the opposite, or upper, part of town.

Hull, aware of the British position, had ordered two twenty-four-pounders, shotted with grape, placed amidst Findlay's men west of the fort. His men had been prepared to repel only an Indian attack. In the event of an assault by soldiers with artillery (Brock had landed with three six-pounders and three three-pounders), his thinly spread and unprotected perimeter would be in danger of engulfment by the enemy. Besides, such an assault would hamper the use of most of his artillery from the fort. By this time Hull realized he had only three alternatives: to leave only a skeleton guard in the fort and meet Brock in the open; to gather all his men into the fort and attempt to defend it; or to surrender.[16]

Hull knew he did not have enough troops to justify meeting Brock in the open. If he called all his men inside, he would seriously overcrowd the fort and present an inviting target for the British artillerists. As the old General steeled his heart to do what his head told him he must do—surrender—he received the news that the Indians were entering the outskirts of the town. Another shock came when his old friend, Colonel Brush, reported that the regular Michigan militia had deserted their vital posts.[17] (Two companies had already gone over to the enemy.) His chief fears were for the helpless civilians, now all in the root shelter, for he tragically exclaimed to Lieutenant Jessup, "My God! what shall I do with these women and children?" [18]

With the safety of the noncombatants in mind—and Hull was in the difficult position of bearing responsibility for them as both General and Governor—there could be but one choice: He ordered his son to hoist a flag of truce. Captain Hull started to hoist the signal on the flagpole, unaware that it would be a sign of complete surrender, but was persuaded to raise it on a bastion. The Captain then crossed the river with a communication, addressed to Brock, stating, "I propose a cessation of hostilities for one hour to open negociations [*sic*] for the surrender of Detroit." [19] Probably the General had already decided to surrender, but the truce was not irrevocable. If McArthur and Cass were on their way back (preferably with Brush's men, making a total of over 800), he could resume the fight, perhaps persuading Brock to pass the defenseless civilians through his lines.

Although they had heard the artillery fire, Colonels McArthur and Cass, camped only three miles from Detroit on the morning of August 16, made no attempt to communicate with Hull. Instead, they sent some mounted men to investigate, who returned with the information, told them by a Frenchman, that Detroit had already surrendered.[20] On the strength of this rumor, the colonels retreated a few miles up the Rouge River and allowed their men to kill, roast, and eat an ox before considering any other action. On first hearing the artillery, the colonels should have sent a messenger to slip into the fort or at least to bring adequate information to enable them to aid in its defense. With proper timing, their force could have created havoc in the rear of the British had the latter actually stormed the fort. Short of surrender, the colonels had taken the worst possible action. Their only excuse could have been the acute hunger of the men, a far from sufficient explanation considering the situation. Cass is reported to have broken his sword when he later learned of the surrender—and well he might have: It must have been of little value in cutting roast ox.

On learning that his perimeter was broken by the desertion of the Michigan militia (the Detached Militia had held their ground), Hull issued orders to call his troops into the fort. In conveying these orders to Findlay's battery, Snelling arrived in time to receive a flag sent by Brock to inquire the purpose of the communique sent to Canada. Informed of Hull's request for terms Brock's aides, Lieutenant-Colonel Macdonell, Attorney-General of Upper Canada, and Major Glegg, an experienced regular, were then detailed to treat with the Americans.

In the belief that McArthur was at River Raisin, and after consultation with Miller, Hull had determined to capitulate. The terms [21] provided that all soldiers (except the Michigan militia, who had never joined the federal army) were to be prisoners of war; that private persons and property would be respected but all public property and records were forfeit. To protect the McArthur-Cass and the Brush detachments from the Indians, Hull received permission to include them in the surrender.

The British refused to grant the customary honors of war to the defeated garrison. Perhaps this was due to Hull's rejection of Brock's original offer, but in any event the Americans were in no position to protest. The terms were signed by Macdonell and Glegg for the British and by Miller and Elijah Brush (representing the separate Michigan militia) for the Americans, and were then approved by both generals. Supplementary articles author-

118

ized all men to return to their homes (except the regulars), with the provision that they were not to serve again until exchanged.

Contrary to the terms, a small British honor guard was marched into the fort before the Americans had evacuated but was quickly withdrawn before any unpleasant incidents occurred. Then the Americans stacked their arms and dejectedly filed out of the fort. Shortly after noon on Sunday, August 16, 1812, the British entered, lowered the American flag, and—while a salute was fired from a recaptured cannon (first taken from the British in the Revolution) and the band triumphantly played "God Save the King"—hoisted the Union Jack. After an absence of sixteen years, the British flag again waved over Detroit.

Following the surrender, Hull and most of the regulars were placed on board ships and taken to Montreal to be held until regularly exchanged. A few of the married officers, accompanied by their wives, were paroled at Newark. At Detroit, the British retained any whom they deemed deserters from the British service, but even these were eventually taken to Montreal. The Ohio men were given lake transport behind the Indians' lines and released on parole to make their way home overland as best they could.

Meanwhile, after the fort had been surrendered, McArthur and Cass had finally taken some action. They had sent Captain John Mansfield to the fort under a flag of truce. Shortly after Mansfield's departure, a British officer, Captain William Elliott, reached McArthur and Cass with Hull's orders to return to the fort. The colonels, seething in their mistaken interpretation of Hull's surrender and vowing vengeance, returned to Detroit and laid down their arms.

Elliott continued to River Raisin to obtain Brush's surrender, arriving there early the following afternoon. When presented with Hull's orders, confirmed by McArthur, to come to Detroit, Brush declared the orders had been forged and had Elliott locked up. Even after later evidence arrived (possibly from McArthur's messenger) indicating that the orders were genuine, Brush left Elliott confined and hurriedly departed for Ohio, with his men, wagons, and cattle.

This was yet another example of an Ohio officer who openly ignored orders. Only by Hull's foresight had the orders been delivered by a British officer rather than by an Indian scalping knife. The fact that Brush had escaped made little difference, for his men were officially listed as paroled prisoners.

On August 18 Lieutenant-Colonel Anderson released Elliott, apologized for Brush's conduct, and surrendered the Second Regiment of Michigan militia. (Eventually the blockhouse was destroyed, and the Indians plundered some of the inhabitants' houses.)

On August 21 Major Chambers took an Indian force to the Miami Rapids, accepted the surrender of that garrison, confiscated the property, and burned the blockhouse. The British made no immediate attempt to take the posts on Hull's road below the Miami River, which were not included in the surrender.

Paramount in the highly controversial problem of justifying Hull's surrender is the question of the respective size of the contending forces. The official American records, turned over to the British, were lost when the ship carrying them to eastern headquarters was sunk. Contemporary estimates differ widely, but some reasonable calculation may be attempted.

The official British list for the transport of the prisoners indicates that 582 regulars and 1,606 Ohio troops were captured at Detroit.[22] The total of 2,188 included the Michilimackinac garrison, the *Cayauga* contingent, those at River Raisin and the Rapids, but did not include any Michigan men and made no allowance for sick or absent soldiers. On one copy of Nichol's report, Hull made the following subtractions: wagoners, 82; boatmen, 60; artificers, 50; sick (and wounded), 430; Michilimackinac prisoners, 70; absent (at River Raisin), 120; McArthur-Cass detachment, 400— a total of 1,212 not available for combat duty at Detroit—leaving a total of 976 effectives in addition to the Michigan men.[23] Actually some of the sick and the wagoners were being counted on for defensive purposes and probably Hull's figures are inaccurate, but the errors seem to balance out.

A study of the Morning Report of the Michigan Detached

Militia for August 15 [24] reveals that about 150 effectives were present at Detroit. The regular Michigan militia seem to have been about the same number, possibly somewhat larger.

Certainly Hull's figure of 800 effectives on the day of surrender was too low. Lieutenant Thomas Jessup, Acting Adjutant General of Hull's army, later stated that there were over 1,000 effectives,[25] and Cass reported the force at 1,066 besides the regular Michigan militia.[26] Perhaps Cass was not far off in estimating that, after the desertion of the Michigan militia, Hull's effective force was less than 1,100.

Brock wrote Prevost that his British force consisted of 330 regulars, 400 militia, and 600 Indians, a total (not including officers) of 1,330.[27] However, the Official Prize Pay List records 117 officers, 131 noncommissioned officers, and 1,112 privates—a total (*not including Indians*) of 1,360.[28] The conditions for eligibility to share in the prize required actual presence at Detroit or active support (the garrison at Fort Malden was ineligible). Certainly Brock had reported only the number actually at Detroit for the surrender. He could not have included the Provincial Marine on the vessels, reported by the Prize List as 133, or the men at the batteries on the Canadian shore. Adjutant-General Edward Baynes signed Prevost's Orders of August 25 announcing the capture of Detroit by 700 regulars and militia and 400 Indians.[29] This further minimizing of Brock's figures (for it was based on his report) only confirms the prevailing British tendency. There is no reason to doubt the accuracy of the Prize Pay Lists, and the great discrepancy between that report and Brock's may indicate the existence of a sizable reserve at or near Sandwich. Before the invasion Brock had indicated to his commissariat that field rations were to be provided for 2,000.[30]

It seems an inescapable conclusion that Brock's forces were larger than Hull's, probably nearly twice as large. Hull may have been unaware of the real size of the British force, but had reason to believe that the number of regulars in sight of the fort was larger than it was because many of Brock's militia were dressed as redcoats, the uniform of the British regulars.

There were still other factors that influenced the surrender.

121

Hull had no immediate prospect of reinforcements, or even of a diversion along the Niagara front. Besides, there was a great danger that, if a siege of the fort lasted for a considerable time, the Indians of the north would flock to the British standard. Indeed by August 22, John Askin, Jr., did arrive with 270 Indians;[31] by September 10, according to the later testimony of Lieutenant John Eastman (detained at Detroit to conclude the Fourth Regiment's affairs), some 1,200 Indians had arrived there.[32]

In addition, there was a shortage of provisions at Detroit. There was an abnormal shortage of foodstuffs in the surrounding countryside—a siege would have diminished the chance of gathering even these meager supplies. The only public provisions that Hull could expect for some time were with Captain Brush, and his last possible attempt to secure those had failed.

Hull did have sufficient ammunition for his small guns, but only 1,300 round, 20 grape, and 12 case shots were on hand for the twenty-four-pounders.[33] Apparently he lacked the canisters to load more regular grape or case for his largest guns—a fact which would have hampered repelling a storm of the fort, although the guns could have been loaded in less effective fashion. However, he had only 5,625 pounds of powder,[34] enough for only a few days' fire since each discharge of artillery piece required half as much powder as the weight of the projectile.

Then, too, there were several less statistical factors that influenced Hull. Brock's warning that he would be unable to restrain his Indian warriors after the action commenced was not all bluff. Charles Askin, a British participant well acquainted with Indians, wrote in his journal that most of the Canadians hoped Hull would surrender, "for the sake of the poor Women & Children who we knew would not be spared by the Indians should an action once commence."[35] Even after the surrender, while there were no actual murders, there was considerable plundering of houses and stealing of horses by the Indians.

Hull—faced by a superior and growing force, shortage of provisions, inadequate gunpowder, and the prospect of a general Indian massacre—had some justification in surrendering on August 16.

Through indecision and delays, the Secretary of War and the Administration had contributed to the failure of the opening campaign of the war. They should have built a navy on the Great Lakes; discouraged Hull from moving until forces were ready at the other invasion prongs; adequately provisioned Detroit before the war started; promptly informed Hull of the outbreak of war; given him more latitude in the earlier phases of the campaign; and resolved the internal conflict of rank involving Lieutenant-Colonel Miller. Even further, they probably should have concentrated their opening campaign against Lower Canada rather than attempt a balanced attack on the whole of Canada.

Hull, of course, had made his own crucial mistakes: He had never gained complete control of the Ohio men and had done little to change their undisciplined character; he had assumed too much of the routine administrative duties of his army; he should have been more decisive in giving orders and insisting on their performance; he should have arranged stronger safeguards for Canadians who had applied for his protection (at the least, he should have seen to the destruction of the lists before turning his records over to the British) ; and he should have vigorously opposed the British artillery installation on August 14. He was not a physical coward; his experience in the Revolution proved that. However, he was an older man in 1812, and a more cautious one. Certainly he was a general of at least average ability.

It is interesting to note what the two highest ranking officers with the best knowledge of Michigan Territory, both writing without the rancor engendered by the later political magnification of Hull's defeat, said of Hull's campaign. General Wilkinson, writing to Governor David Holmes of Louisiana, stated:

> Hulls misfortunes grew out of too much precipitancy too much confidence and too little foresight—I knew Him a good officer, but he has forgot his trade—for indeed nothing can be so easily forgotten & with such difficulty acquired as a Knowledge of the art of War—which depends almost entirely on practice.[36]

Colonel Kingsbury wrote that Hull's surrender was "the want of reinforcement of Three Thousand men at least,—with six months provision and regular Troops in lieu of Militia, and his pieces all mounted with a plenty of Cannon shot." [37]

It was Hull's misfortune to command the opening campaign of the war. He surrendered for the sake of humanity, but lost his good name because of the Administration, weighing the fact that a large segment of the American population was openly opposed to the war, required a scapegoat to bear its responsibility for the disastrous blow to American arms and pride.

While en route to Montreal, Hull was permitted to dispatch his official account to Eustis, in which he summarized his overwhelming difficulties but attached no blame to his subordinates. To the contrary, McArthur and Cass—politicians always—refused to share the responsibility for the disaster. They profited by the feeling against Hull excited by the Administration—Hull was dishonored, but the forces under him were completely exonerated.

Notes to Chapter VI

1. Ferdinand B. Tupper, *Life and Correspondence of Maj.-Gen. Sir Isaac Brock, K. B.* (London: Simpkin, Marshall & Co., 1845), p. 228. The figure seems high but Tupper, a nephew of Brock, quoted an eyewitness, Capt. John Glegg.
2. Couch to Meigs, River Raisin, Aug. 11, 1812, *Independent Chronicle of Boston*, Aug. 31, 1812, cited by Cruikshank, "Hull's Invasion," *Royal Society of Canada*, 3rd Series, Vol. I, p. 288, note 1.
3. Hull to Brush, Detroit, Aug. 11, 1812, article dated at Chillicothe, Aug. 25, in *National Intelligencer*, Sept. 3, 1812. Jobart may have been the Capt. J. Jobean that Robert Kaene, Gen. Hall's messenger to Hull, hired to deliver his message from River Raisin.
4. Cass testimony, Forbes, *op. cit.*, p. 24. Lt.-Col. Anderson seems to have arrived in Detroit that day and probably carried the message.
5. Cruikshank (ed.), *Documents Relating to the Invasion of Canada*, *op. cit.*, pp. 137–38.
6. Cass to Eustis, Washington, Sept. 10, 1812, *MPHC*, *op. cit.*, Vol. XL, p. 480.
7. Wood (ed.), *Documents of the Canadian War*, *op. cit.*, Vol. I, p. 461.
8. *Ibid.*
9. "Defense of Hull," *MPHC*, *op. cit.*, Vol. XL, p. 685.
10. Brush to J. Couch, River Raisin, *National Intelligencer*, Sept. 3, 1812.
11. McArthur testimony, Forbes, *op. cit.*, p. 60.
12. Hull, *Memoirs, op. cit.*, p. 120.
13. Brock to his brothers, Lake Ontario, Sept. 3, 1812, Tupper, *op. cit.*, p. 267.

14. Testimony of Lt. Dalliba, Forbes, *op. cit.*, p. 83. Some indication of the volume of fire is revealed by his testimony that 200 rounds were fired by the twenty-four-pounders during the campaign. Probably nearly all these were fired on August 15 or 16.
15. Brock to Prevost, Detroit, Aug. 17, 1812, Wood (ed.), *Documents of the Canadian War, op. cit.*, Vol. I, p. 467.
16. Hull to Eustis, Ft. George, Aug. 26, 1812, *MPHC, op. cit.*, Vol. XL, p. 466.
17. Testimony of Lt. Jessup, Forbes, *op. cit.*, p. 95.
18. *Ibid.*, p. 91.
19. Hull to Brock, Aug. 16, 1812, Burton Historical Collection, C. M. Burton Papers, Detroit-History, War of 1812.
20. Testimony of Cass, Forbes, *op. cit.*, p. 60.
21. Capitulation terms, Camp at Detroit, Aug. 16, 1812, Wood (ed.), *Documents of the Canadian War, op. cit.*, Vol. I, pp. 470–71.
22. Return signed by Lt.-Col. Robert Nichol, Detroit, Aug. 26, 1812, *Ibid.*, p. 497.
23. Burton Historical Collection, Wm. Hull Papers.
24. Report signed by Adjutant Josiah Brady, Burton Historical Collection, Wm. Woodbridge Papers.
25. Jessup testimony, Forbes, *op. cit.*, p. 94.
26. Cass to Eustis, Washington, Sept. 10, 1812, *MPHC, op. cit.*, Vol. XL, p. 482.
27. Detroit, Aug. 17, 1812, Wood (ed.), *Documents of the Canadian War, op. cit.*, Vol. I, p. 467.
28. *Ibid.*, p. 474.
29. *Ibid.*, p. 493.
30. District general orders, Ft. Amherstburg, Aug. 15, 1812, *Ibid.*, p. 462.
31. Casselman (ed.), *op. cit.*, p. 82.
32. Forbes, *op. cit.*, p. 100.
33. Undated report, signed by Lt. Felix Troughton of the British Artillery, Wood (ed.), *Documents of the Canadian War, op. cit.*, Vol. I, p. 496.
34. *Ibid.*
35. Cruikshank (ed.), *Documents Relating to the Invasion of Canada, op. cit.*, p. 243.
36. New Orleans, Sept. 14, 1812, Chicago Historical Society Mss.
37. Kingsbury to Maj. Stoddard, Newport, Sept. 7, 1812, Burton Historical Collection, Jacob Kingsbury Papers.

CHAPTER VII

THE SECOND NORTH WESTERN ARMY

AFTER HULL'S SURRENDER, the Northwest found itself in the midst of war—without an army and with its main post lost to the British. Before the President was to appoint a new commander on September 17, Harrison—the hero of Tippecanoe—was to assemble a force that was to be recognized as the second North Western Army. And the Indians, in many instances with Harrison's foe, Tecumseh, as the mastermind, were to threaten or raid a number of frontier settlements and posts in Illinois, Ohio, and Indiana.

Besides Detroit, Hull had command of Fort Dearborn [1] and Fort Wayne. But in July, Hull had ordered the company at Dearborn to evacuate and move to Fort Detroit or Fort Wayne. In the slow delivery of messages at this time, these orders were not to arrive until about a month later.

Since early 1812 the region around Fort Dearborn had been subjected to a wave of Indian incidents. The garrison of the First Infantry was commanded by Captain Nathan Heald. The most influential person was John Kinzie, the Indian factor. For the most part supplies were brought to the garrison by lake vessels, making the long voyage via the Straits of Mackinac.

The news of the outbreak of war, arriving about July 10, increased the uneasiness. In early August a friendly Potawatomi chief, Winnimeg, arrived with Hull's orders: Heald was to distribute the property at Dearborn as he saw fit, evacuate the post, and proceed by land to Fort Wayne or Detroit.[2] Heald had little choice but to comply: Hull could not spare reinforcements and, with the British in control of the Lakes, the garrison could not expect any additional supplies or provisions.

Within a week, and before the orders could be carried out, a large number of hostile Indians gathered near Dearborn. To obtain Indian assurance for a peaceful departure, Heald decided to distribute the public property of the fort and factory among the Indians. Captain Wells, Indian Subagent and Interpreter at Fort Wayne, and an experienced Indian fighter and guide, arrived with twenty-five Miami while preparations were being made to leave the fort. The goods were distributed—except for all extra arms, ammunition, and liquor, which were dumped into a near-by well or the canal. Even though the Indians considered this a breach of agreement, the Americans probably could have departed in peace from the fort early on August 14. But some time that day a red wampum belt reached the local Potawatomi from Main Poc, who was with Tecumseh in Canada. Telling of American reversals in the Detroit area and the loss of Michilimackinac, Main Poc called on the Indians to attack Fort Dearborn.[3] Piqued by Heald's withholding of the arms and liquor and spurred by Main Poc's plea, the Potawatomi and a few members of the other tribes planned an attack.

Even if Heald had known of the Indians' decision, his ability to defend his post had passed with the destruction of the extra arms and ammunition. At midmorning of August 15 (the day Brock commenced his attack on Detroit), a group of 54 regulars, 12 militia, 9 women, 18 children, and the guard of Miami with Wells in the van, marched out of Fort Dearborn.[4] Skirting the shores of Lake Michigan, they encountered a force of 400 Potawatomi on a sand dune less than two miles from the fort, and Heald ordered his regulars to storm their position. The Miami guard remained out of the fight, which proved to be short but

127

fierce; Heald surrendered after the Potawatomi chief, Black Bird, promised to spare the lives of the survivors. Heald reported the American losses as 26 regulars, all the militia (including Wells), two women, and 12 children; the rest were taken prisoners. Most of the prisoners later escaped or were ransomed at the request of the British.

The British had neither ordered nor had had previous knowledge of the massacre. In fact, Brock, to prevent such a thing happening, had requested Captain Roberts to obtain the surrender of Fort Dearborn, but his request had arrived too late.[5]

Forts Dearborn and Michilimackinac, while not involved in the campaign plans, had been under Hull's orders and had fallen. Only Fort Wayne in the Old Northwest remained in American control by August 16. Attempts to influence the Indians at the Piqua Council were doomed to fail.

The Piqua Council, to which all Indians of the Northwest had been invited, began on August 15. There were only a few Indians in attendance, mostly Shawnee and Delaware, with a scattering from other tribes. The Potawatomi were conspicuously absent. The Americans could give no ammunition and few personal presents—far from enough to overcome the effect of the American reversals. While the meetings were still in session, the Indians learned of the surrender of Detroit. The council broke up, with the Americans losing their last bid for the Indians' neutrality. Now forced to abandon any offensive moves, the Americans concentrated on the defense of the frontier.

In the spring of 1812, the governors of Indiana, Illinois, and Ohio had taken what steps they could against numerous Indian raids. Although there were reported to be over two thousand Indians residing in the Ohio region,[6] mainly Shawnee and Ottawa, the threat there was less serious, for the population was larger and more concentrated. The situation was much more acute in the sparsely populated territories of Indiana and Illinois, especially since the withdrawal from Vincennes of the Fourth Regiment. Governors Harrison and Edwards held local Indian councils, but put small faith in the promises they received.

The danger in Indiana, Harrison believed, came from the Tippecanoe area, again populated by unfriendly Indians. In the belief that he could trust the Delaware, Harrison encouraged those living close to the settled parts to move to designated areas if they wished to remain neutral or if they felt too weak to resist hostile forces which might pass through their lands. Besides, he feared the average militiaman would make little attempt to distinguish between Indian friend and foe.

For his part, Governor Edwards believed that Peoria was the focal point of the Illinois hostiles, and therefore urged that the government support the Fox Indians in a war they had commenced against the Peoria Winnebago, many of whom were followers of the Prophet.

Both governors ordered mounted militia to patrol north of the main settlements. They also encouraged and later required isolated settlements to build community blockhouses and to maintain their own security patrols. Many settlers began to leave the threatened areas, and in so doing decreased the strength of the frontiers.

By early summer Colonel William Russell was in active command of the few regulars left in Indiana and of the various companies of United States rangers throughout the Northwest. His rangers were on constant patrol to give notice of any Indian movement toward the settlements, and Russell planned to assist in establishing a post at Peoria. Such defensive measures probably deterred the Indians to some extent. However, the frontiers were generally quiet in the summer of 1812 because the Indians were waiting to see what progress Hull would make and also because they had had poor crops the year before and, faced by starvation, were forced to rely on hunting to maintain their families. A raid on Tippecanoe from Vincennes during this lull, Harrison urged, would force the recall of warriors with Tecumseh, and thus relieve some of the pressure on Hull. If there were to be an offensive, Eustis had already authorized Harrison to command in Indiana and Illinois and to draw on Kentucky for militia if needed.

In southern Illinois, between the Mississippi and Kaskaskia rivers—both favorite invasion routes of the Indians—Colonel

Russell established a ranger camp and headquarters, called Camp Edwards. In August he had two ranger companies and as many as four companies of Illinois militia stationed there.

About the time that Hull was withdrawing from Canada, Harrison was in Kentucky arranging for some militia to reinforce Vincennes. He wrote Eustis his suggested plans for frontier defense, a project in which he was soon to become deeply involved.

He pointed out that in the past two basic plans of operations had been used against the Indians: either raids on the areas of greatest concentration closest to settlements or the establishment of fortified posts at strategic places in advance of the frontier.[7] He recommended the erection of a series of posts along the Illinois River and a major reinforcement of Fort Wayne. These were necessary steps, he explained in an astute summary, because the American position at Detroit was hopeless (even if Hull received reinforcements). He pointed out that the building of the forts would require a force of 5,000 to ensure protection against the almost certain large-scale Indian attacks. He added that provision difficulties might force a postponement of the new posts for the current season. But at least a fort could be established at Peoria and a raid on Tippecanoe undertaken by mounted troops before winter.

In answer to Hull's July request for reinforcements, Eustis had appointed Brigadier-General James Winchester to gather and lead a force to Detroit. Winchester was a rather unfortunate choice. He had risen to the rank of captain in the Revolution, but had led an inactive life until his appointment, in March 1812, to the rank of brigadier-general at the age of sixty. Though he had moved to Tennessee, he, like Hull, remained essentially eastern in thought and manners. He failed to understand the Westerners' enthusiasm for a fight, along with their reluctance to submit to the discipline necessary to win.

In August Winchester was assembling a force in Kentucky. Recruits for a new regiment of regulars, the Seventeenth Infantry, were being sworn in and receiving rudimentary training under

130

their commander, Colonel Samuel Wells, a veteran of the Post Revolutionary Army and many Indian fights, including Tippecanoe. Winchester was empowered to add a thousand Kentucky militia to this force and march them to Detroit by regiments or in a group. However, the situation was too risky for him to order the more experienced Wells to proceed ahead of the militia. In any event, Winchester's command of the reinforcements for Detroit was soon to be challenged by an even stronger man than Wells—General Harrison, with the help of the Governor of Kentucky, Isaac Shelby.

Believing Harrison to be the most effective commander in the militia in the West, Shelby (with the concurrence of the former Kentucky Governor, Charles Scott, and other influential leaders such as Henry Clay) appointed him a major-general in the Kentucky militia by brevet. Harrison was now armed with the authority of three divisions of government: as Governor of Indiana he commanded its militia; he was a major-general in the Kentucky militia; and Eustis had authorized him to command any offensive operations in Indiana and Illinois.

En route from Frankfort, Kentucky, to Cincinnati, Harrison learned of Hull's defeat. After his arrival in Cincinnati on August 28, he relieved Brigadier-General John Payne in command of the Kentucky men that Winchester had moved there, consisting of three regiments (Lieutenant-Colonels John Scott, John Allen, and William Lewis), plus a number of rather unorganized volunteers. He persuaded Winchester to let him assume active command of the total force, including Wells's regulars, while Winchester devoted his time to the less honored task of recruiting.[8] Thus, Harrison had a force of over 2,100 men at Cincinnati, and expected three infantry regiments, a mounted rifle regiment, and several troops of dragoons to arrive in September.[9] He had no artillery, but remedied this by immediately requesting some from the Pittsburgh arsenal.

When he received word that Fort Wayne was surrounded by hostile Indians, he determined to march to its relief and then decide on his later strategy. In a letter to Eustis he summarized

131

his position by pointing out that the situation justified departure from normal procedure, saying, "It appeared to me Sir, necessary that some one should undertake the general direction of affairs here and I have done it." [10]

The original Fort Wayne had been built in 1794 in a strategic location, on the south bank of the Miami (or Maumee), within sight of the St. Mary's and St. Joseph rivers (which form the Maumee), and not far from the Eel and Wabash rivers. By 1812 the post had been reduced in size and was garrisoned by only seventy men of the First Infantry. The commander, Captain James Rhea, was reputed to be a somewhat inferior soldier even when sober. The fort was the location of the most important Indian office on the frontier, but the chief agent, Benjamin F. Stickney, was neither feared nor respected.

Among the Indians around Fort Wayne were the Miami, who since the death in July of their great chief, Little Turtle, a faithful friend of the Americans, had turned hostile. When other tribes came to the Fort Wayne region promising British co-operation, the Miami agreed to join in an attack on the fort. Unknown to the Indians, the British were restricted from aiding their Indian allies because an armistice had been signed precluding British participation.

Action along the Niagara and Lake Champlain fronts, the eastern prongs of the planned American offensive, had been restricted to sporadic firing across the boundaries, and preparations for larger operations were proceeding slowly. The British had not desired the war with the Americans (although they had not been adverse to furnish provocation for it), and had not discarded the possibility of an early armistice.

At the start of the war the British Minister, Augustus J. Foster, had left Washington for Halifax, where he learned that on June 23 his government had repealed the Orders in Council, which had imposed various trade restrictions and which had been a primary consideration in the American decision for war.

Foster immediately communicated the information to Prevost,

who determined to make a final effort to halt the war, or at least to increase the strong opposition of New England to the conflict. Prevost sent his Adjutant-General, Colonel Edward Baynes, to General Henry Dearborn's headquarters at Greenbush (near Albany, New York) to arrange an armistice, pending notification of the government at Washington of the development. Dearborn agreed to the request, and on August 9 both governments pledged to act only on the defensive until four days following the arrival at Montreal of any termination notice from President Madison. Hull, not under Dearborn's command, did not come under the agreement, but was to be allowed to do so if he desired.

Later, Dearborn defended his agreeing to the armistice on the ground that he was in no position to assume the offensive in the near future. Actually he had little to gain by signing, because he must have known that the British were not planning an immediate offensive and he had no supplies to forward to other posts during the armistice period. The agreement relaxed pressure on the British and ensured them greater safety in their detachment of men and supplies to the West, a project Dearborn knew they had already begun. He had been urged repeatedly by Eustis to create a diversion to take the pressure off Hull and, while he could not do this, he certainly should not have aided the British in increasing the pressure. His proper conduct would have been to refuse the armistice and pass the information to Washington for final decision.

That part of Brock's command not in contact with Hull came under the agreement, but Brock was free to capture Detroit during the armistice. Had immediate notice of the agreement been sent to Hull, it might have arrived in time to permit him to avail himself of the terms. But Dearborn, not aware of the need for haste, imitated the stupidity of Eustis' Declaration of War message, and merely sent Hull a letter to be forwarded by various post commanders as they saw fit. The message did not arrive at Detroit until September.[11]

Prevost was elated at the complete success of his plan, writing:

A suspension of hostilities therefore on a considerable portion of the extremely extensive line of Frontier which I have to defend has enabled me rapidly to strengthen the Flank attacked. The decided superiority I have obtained on the Lakes in consequence of the precautionary measures adopted during the last winter has permitted me to move without interruption, independently of the arrangement, both Troops & supplies of every description towards Amherstburg, whilst those for Genl. Hull having several hundred miles of wilderness to pass before they can reach Detroit, are exposed, to be harassed and destroyed by the Indians.

... In the mean time from a partial suspension of hostilities I am enabled to improve & augment my resources against an Invasion, whilst the Enemy distracted by Party broils & intrigues are obliged to remain supine & to witness the daily diminution of the Force they had so much difficulty in collecting.[12]

President Madison was too deeply committed to end the war on the settlement of only one grievance. He ordered that immediate notice be given to the British, and the armistice expired on September 8. He realized how disadvantageous was the position Dearborn had created, writing to Jefferson, "Nothing could be gained by us, whilst arrangements & reinforcements adverse to Hull might be decisive." [13]

Before the surrender of Detroit, Brock had no knowledge of the armistice and was quite disturbed to hear of it later—for, with Hull gone, he believed the armistice agreement binding in the West as well. He feared that if the Indians learned of the agreement they would believe that the British were deserting them to form a separate peace. Procter was instructed to conceal the armistice from the Indians, while allowing them to engage in planning offensives, but to restrain the British from action. Therefore, at first, Procter was unable to aid in the attack on Fort Wayne and probably did not know it had already begun.

Despite the many hostile-looking Indians who had arrived near Fort Wayne at the end of August, the garrison was not greatly alarmed until an attack, which was ineffective, was made on the sentinels on the night of September 5. On the following day no Indians were in sight, but when a small party of soldiers passed out of the gates of the fort, they were fired on by concealed Indians and two were killed.[14] The Indians attacked in force that night, but without success. Abandoning hope of a frontal assault, they shaped two logs to resemble artillery at a distance and, under a flag of truce, informed the garrison that the British had sent siege weapons and that if the Americans refused to surrender at once they would all be massacred when hundreds of additional Indians arrived the next day.[15]

William Oliver, who had delivered Captain James Rhea's message requesting help from Harrison, had slipped back into the fort with word that reinforcements were on their way, thus enabling Rhea to ignore the Indian surrender request. Having failed in their ruse, the Indians made only one other serious attack, on September 10, which was easily repelled by the garrison.

Harrison had started most of his force on the road to Piqua on August 29 and on the following day he joined them near Lebanon. He probably pushed ahead of most of his men and reached Piqua on September 1—at least he appears to have been there the next day to receive a message from Eustis dated August 22. This notified him of his appointment as a brigadier-general (not yet confirmed by the Senate) and assigned him to the defense of the areas of Indiana and Illinois, in co-operation with Hull and Governor Benjamin Howard of Missouri Territory.[16]

Harrison was clearly in the wrong place at the wrong time to accept the commission immediately. He had been trading on his Kentucky command and, if he accepted the federal appointment, would be inferior to Winchester and under his orders, in the absence of any statement to the contrary from Eustis. Harrison took the best course open: He proceeded to Piqua, planning to remain there until Winchester appeared and enabled him to turn over his command and decide about the federal offer.

However, he learned from four Shawnee that the hostile Indians were still in the vicinity of Fort Wayne. Therefore, he ordered Allen's Kentucky riflemen, three companies from other regiments, and William Garrard's troop of cavalry to proceed the next day toward St. Mary's, on the route to Fort Wayne. Never one to let administrative protocol stand in his way, he wrote Eustis that he had delayed acceptance of the commission in case the fall of

135

Detroit should change the plans. At the same time he seized the opportunity to make a none-too-subtle plea for the command of all the forces in the West. He wrote that the West should have a unified command, that Winchester did not know the country and the country did not know him. He clinched his argument by observing that the backwoods people "never will perform anything brilliant under a stranger." [17]

He did not completely lose sight of his other responsibility, the security of his own state, for in the same letter he told of his call (by getting Governor Meigs to issue a proclamation on September 2) for a force of mounted thirty-day volunteers to assemble at Dayton on September 15. These he expected to use in a raid against Tippecanoe and the villages near the source of the Illinois River.

Late on September 4 Harrison received word (actually the report was untrue) that a British detachment had left the Detroit area on August 18 to attack Fort Wayne, Fort Harrison, and the town of Vincennes.[18] He did not know the size of the British party but he believed it completely changed the picture. He now had ample excuse to act on his own initiative and when a load of cartridges arrived from Cincinnati on September 6—only the shortage of ammunition had prevented him from moving sooner—began a forced march with the remainder of his men, sending word to Winchester either to join him or bring up reinforcements.

Within two days Harrison reached the area where Allen's advance was engaged in building blockhouses (at the first, or Girty's, crossing of the St. Mary's River, later to become Fort Barbee). He was joined by Major Richard M. Johnson, then a popular Congressman from Kentucky and later the Vice-President of the United States, leading a troop of mounted volunteers. By now there must have been over 2,200 men, and Harrison confidently pushed them toward Fort Wayne. Within two more days they were at the Second Crossing of the St. Mary's, and Harrison issued to the untrained force such orders for battle formations as he could. A number of Ohio militia, probably 600 men under a Colonel Adams, had been at this place for several days but had made no

136

attempt to advance to Fort Wayne. Since they were not under his command, Harrison made no objection when some returned home, but he took the rest, some four hundred, with him.

The night of September 11 was spent seventeen miles from Fort Wayne. Harrison wrote Eustis that, while he had had no word from the fort since September 3, he expected to be forced to fight his way and should reach there the next day. A party of scouts had seen Indians that day, had even killed one; and Harrison sent several scouts out that night to attempt to reach Fort Wayne, ascertain the situation, and return under cover of darkness.[19]

On September 12 the army continued the march, being especially cautious in crossing a swamp five miles from the fort. As it turned out, this was needless, for the Indians, on learning of Harrison's approach, had quietly left the area. Harrison's men filed into the fort without opposition. The garrison had suffered few casualties, but the outbuildings, including the Indian factory, the few crops in the area, and all the livestock had been destroyed. Fort Wayne had been saved, but Harrison learned later that it had not been the only object of Indian attacks.

On September 3 a few marauding Shawnee, led by Missilimetaw, a councilor of Tecumseh,[20] had killed two men hunting bee trees near Pigeon Roost, a small Indiana settlement. They then ran amuck in the settlement killing well over twenty persons, mostly children, and burning all the houses of the area. Members of one family escaped that night and spread the alarm. The next day 150 mounted militiamen assembled to chase the retreating Indians, but without success.

Another settlement, Fort Madison, near St. Louis, was hit by a large party of Winnebago on September 5, but successfully beat off the three-day attack.

Of more direct concern to Harrison was the attack on Fort Harrison. Captain Zachary Taylor's report[21] clearly summarized the events: After retreat had been sounded on September 3, the men of the garrison heard the report of four muskets outside the fort. Fearing an Indian trap in the growing darkness, they did not investigate but the next day discovered the bodies of two settlers. Later that day a delegation of Indians from Prophet's Town arrived, stating that an official representative would arrive the following day to make a formal request for food for the starving Indians. Taylor was not taken in by this old trick, designed to allay suspicions and relax vigilance. Even though many of his men were officially listed on the sick report, he made sure that his sentries were especially alert on the night of September 4.

Before midnight the Indians crept up to a corner blockhouse (whose lower story contained provisions), reached into several small holes, and started a fire. The guard in the upper story discovered the fire and turned out the entire garrison. With the men forced to maintain the defensive against the advancing Indians, the fire began to get out of control. Several men courageously exposed themselves to the Indians' muskets and succeeded in pulling off the roof to prevent the further spread of the fire. A temporary breastwork was constructed; and the entire garrison, free to concentrate on the enemy, forced their retreat in a few hours.

The gap in the wall was repaired by the following night. The Indians made no further assault, but continued to surround the fort. On September 10 Taylor attempted to send word of his plight to Vincennes, but the messengers were forced to return. Three nights later two men did succeed in escaping and delivered Taylor's letter.

At Vincennes a force of over a thousand rangers, Indiana and Kentucky militia and citizen volunteers were assembled by Colonel Russell, who had recently arrived there. Russell reached Fort Harrison on September 16, without encountering any Indians. However, part of his provision train had been attacked and captured the previous day, and most of the men in the small escort had been killed. With the Indians gone, Russell left one small regiment of Kentucky men at Fort Harrison and led the rest back to Vincennes.

Taylor's men had suffered two killed and two wounded. Also two deserters had fled from the fort during the fire; one was killed by the Indians, but the other returned with only an arm broken. In addition, two civilians had been killed and all the livestock captured. Nevertheless, Taylor's defense had been spirited, and Madison gratefully promoted him to major by brevet, thus starting his spectacular rise to the presidency.

Apparently the British were not behind the series of Indian raids in early September; yet the raids were too well co-ordinated to be the result of chance—Pigeon Roost, September 3; Fort Harrison, September 4; Fort Madison, September 5; Fort Wayne, September 6. Tecumseh was certainly the mastermind, taking advantage of the confusion following Hull's defeat to press the attack in other quarters. Dearborn's armistice, causing the absence of any British artillery in the raids, may have prevented heavier American losses.

The day after his arrival at Fort Wayne, Harrison discovered the identity of the ringleaders of the attack. He decided to split his force into three parts and attack the villages of the offenders. The first detachment, commanded by Colonel Wells, consisted of his regulars, Scott's Kentucky Regiment, Johnson's mounted men, and perhaps a hundred Ohio militia under Colonel James Dunlap. (The rest of the Ohio men who had not withdrawn at St. Mary's had done so as soon as Fort Wayne was relieved).[22] This group was ordered to destroy the Potawatomi villages, usually known as Five Medal's Towns, on the Elkhart River (east of modern Ligonier). The second unit, under General Payne, consisting of Lewis' and Allen's Kentucky regiments and Garrard's cavalry, was ordered to move against the Miami villages at the fork of the Wabash River some thirty miles away. The rest of the army garrisoned the fort.

Both attacking forces left on September 14, arrived safely at their targets, discovered them deserted, burned the towns, destroyed the crops, and returned to Fort Wayne on September 18. Wells had been ordered to destroy Little Turtle's main village, about twenty miles northwest of the fort, but had been unable to do so because the Ohio men insisted on returning home.[23] So Lieutenant-Colonel James Simrall, who had arrived on September 17 with four troops of Kentucky dragoons, and his men were assigned to this task, and they promptly destroyed the village except for the small buildings that the government had constructed for the personal use of Little Turtle.

On September 18, while the soldiers were still engaged in the raids, General Winchester arrived at Fort Wayne. The popular Harrison relinquished command to the unpopular Winchester on the following day, after vainly trying to smooth the exchange by a diplomatic address to the assembled men. In spite of the pressure of his past march, Harrison had had to devote considerable time to ensuring that provision trains and wagons converged on the area. He informed Winchester that he had arranged for orders from three contractors: John Piatt (who had already delivered a quantity of rations originally ordered by Hull but now consumed by Harrison's men) ; Thomas Buford, the Kentucky commissariat, ordered to deliver 300,000 rations to St. Mary's; and the regular army contractor for the region south of 41° north latitude, ordered to deposit 100,000 rations at the same place and smaller amounts at Piqua and Dayton.[24]

Harrison turned over all Wells's regulars, the three Kentucky regiments under Payne, and Garrard's dragoons, but he retained control of Johnson's and Simrall's mounted men and all other Kentucky soldiers who were en route. He departed for St. Mary's and, arriving there by September 21, found a letter from Eustis, dated September 1, ordering him first to secure the frontiers and then join Winchester, or co-operate with him, in regaining Michigan.[25] Eustis' letter indicated the seriousness with which the Administration viewed the situation. It reported that 1,500 men each, from the militia quotas of Pennsylvania and Virginia, had been ordered to the region, and it indicated that an attempt would be made to gain control of the Lakes.

Encouraged by these moves, Harrison abandoned his plans to raid Tippecanoe and the Illinois River area. Instead, he decided to lead an all-mounted force along an old trail from Fort Wayne to the St. Joseph River in Michigan, cross the Territory to the Raisin River, and attempt a surprise attack on Detroit.[26] He then had 1,100 men and mounts; and he awaited the arrival of 700 more. These were the volunteers he had requested, and they were organizing at Dayton before starting the expedition. The delay would be necessary anyway, he wisely explained, because his ability to hold Detroit, once captured, would depend on Winchester's arrival with the main force at least as far as the Rapids, preferably farther.

On September 22 General Winchester, leaving a slightly larger garrison than normal at Fort Wayne, proceeded with the rest of his force down the north bank of the Miami. He expected to go as far as old Fort Defiance and either await reinforcements there or continue to the Rapids. His march was rather slow because he expected to encounter Indians at any time. However, he met no Indians until September 25, when he had covered nearly thirty miles of the fifty-mile journey. At this point his advance scouts suffered their first casualties from a party of Indians who were in advance of a British force en route to Fort Wayne.

Toward the end of August, Colonel Procter, at Detroit, had acknowledged Brock's orders to suspend hostilities and had journeyed to the Miami Rapids to familiarize himself with the terrain and also to determine if, as reported, Wells was advancing his Kentucky force. Returning to Detroit by the second week in September, Procter wrote that he believed the "back" Indians were besieging Fort Wayne but that he had taken measures to restrain them,[27] presumably from committing another massacre, since he believed the armistice still in effect. He certainly could not have been very much surprised when, a few days later, he received a request for aid from the Indians at Fort Wayne.

Procter was undoubtedly happy to employ, in an area away from his own headquarters, the large number of Indians who had gathered at Detroit following its capture. On September 14, perhaps still unaware that the armistice had expired, he ordered a detachment of 150 regulars, 100 militiamen, and 800 Indians, under the command of Major Muir, to proceed to Fort Wayne.[28] Transporting his three artillery pieces and heavy equipment by boat up the Miami to the site of Fort Defiance, Muir disembarked there to continue the journey by land. On September 25 a party of seven Indian scouts from Muir's force suddenly came upon five of Winchester's scouts, seated around a campfire. Pretending to be friendly, the Indians learned of the advancing American army before murdering the American scouts, who were probably unaware of the nearness of Muir's forces.[29]

On learning of the advance of the American army along the north bank of the Miami River, Muir, on the south bank, abandoned his trip to Fort Wayne and prepared to engage the Americans. Meanwhile, Garrard's mounted men, in advance of the main American force, had discovered the scouts' bodies and, in fact, had had a slight skirmish with Indians. This caused the main force in the rear, although unaware of the presence of British soldiers, to halt the march, form battle lines, and erect a high, strong breastwork around their premature camp.

Realizing that the Americans might continue on the north side and cut off his retreat, Muir withdrew to the site of Fort Defiance. The next morning he learned that the Americans were advancing and received information about the size of their force from a captured American. Muir selected a site for the British and Indians to make a stand, but the Indians refused to fight at that site. Muir rejected the one they selected because it offered insufficient room for effective use of artillery.[30] Believing the disagreement was due to the Indians' misunderstanding of the use of artillery, Muir loaded his guns on board a vessel and ordered it to return to Detroit. Then he got a promise from the Indians to join in an attack the next day, unhampered by artillery.

Although Muir had cause to believe that most of his Indians would leave—some already had—he moved his force to the east side of the Tiffin River about three miles above Fort Defiance, where he expected to engage the Americans. Another prisoner stated that Winchester not only had 3,000 men but that a force of the same size was expected to join him at any time. Muir then received reports from his own scouts that, while they had not seen such a relief force, they believed it possible. Since he thought he could count on only 600 (only 350 Indians seem to have been left), he decided to abandon his ambush plans and return to Detroit.

The various alarms had slowed Winchester's progress, and it was the end of September before his main force arrived at the

142

site of old Fort Defiance. There he paused to await provisions, information, and reinforcements before marching to the Rapids.

Meanwhile, Harrison, who had been planning a surprise raid on Detroit, wrote Winchester a letter informing him that he had declined the appointment of brigadier-general, but making it clear that he believed his Kentucky commission superior to Winchester's. He added that the three expected Kentucky regiments had arrived and that he was placing two of them—those of Lieutenant-Colonel Joshua Barbee and William Jennings—under Winchester's command but was retaining that of Robert Pogue and the mounted men.

The letters between Eustis, Harrison, and Winchester concerning the command of the army had created a great deal of confusion. Madison had nearly appointed his trusted friend, James Monroe, to the command, but the latter had finally advised against it. The problem was resolved on September 17 when the President appointed Harrison to command the extensive forces to be known as the North Western Army.[31] The letter, which Harrison received at Piqua on September 24, added that the purpose of his force, expected to number 10,000 men, was to protect the frontier, recapture Detroit, and move against Upper Canada. Eustis wrote that he was arranging for artillery to be sent from Pittsburgh, with the first shipment being accompanied by Captain Charles Gratiot, trained at West Point and an experienced officer of the Corps of Engineers; and that Major James V. Ball, a veteran officer of dragoons now assigned to the newly created United States Second Light Dragoons, would report for duty immediately. Harrison was authorized to appoint his own staff officers and draw on the Pittsburgh contractor, Ebenezer Denny, for provisions. Eustis, perhaps profiting by Hull's experience, offered no detailed instructions to Harrison, stating merely, "Exercise your own discretion and act in all cases according to your own judgment."

Units for Harrison's command were still appearing. He learned that Brigadier-General Edward W. Tupper was at Urbana with 1,200 mounted men of the Ohio militia quota and that Colonel James Findlay, who had served under Hull, was not far from St.

Mary's with 350 mounted men. Findlay was not to join Harrison's army officially—that would be a violation of his parole—but he could perform militia duty in operations against frontier Indians. He was ordered to destroy some Ottawa towns on Blanchard's Fork of the Auglaize (at modern Ottawa) because the absent inhabitants had aided the British against Hull and their villages lay close to the road being constructed to Fort Defiance.

General Harrison was now ready to outline his general campaign plans to Eustis. His planned deployment envisioned three main columns, each separately supplied but striving to converge on the Rapids of the Miami.[32] Winchester's force at Fort Defiance formed the left. Preceded by a mounted expedition from Fort Wayne against the Indians between the Rapids and River Raisin, it was to advance down the river. Tupper's 1,200 men, plus those at St. Mary's not assigned to Winchester, were to form the center, garrison the posts along Hull's old trail, and act chiefly as a general supply column. The right, consisting of the Virginia and Pennsylvania units plus various militia, was to form at Upper Sandusky to guard the later advance of the artillery on the crucial more than sixty-mile journey to the Rapids. Each of these columns was to protect its own route by establishing blockhouse forts and, when all had arrived at the Rapids and had well over a million rations on deposit there, they would advance to Detroit.

In summary, the left column would be mainly used for observation and offensive probing, the center for stockpiling supplies for future use, and the right to conduct artillery. Their widespread locations would go far to protect the entire frontier.

Harrison moved to St. Mary's at the end of September to oversee the completion of the fort being built by Barbee's men. Within a few days he received a message from Winchester informing him he had encountered Indians in force. Shortly afterward Meigs reported that he had received information that a British force had left Fort Malden to attack Fort Wayne. Harrison immediately ordered a march of most of his 3,000 men at St. Mary's toward Winchester's position.

At the temporary camp constructed by Jenning's road crew, Harrison received a later message informing him that the enemy had left Winchester's area. The following morning, October 2, he ordered Barbee's men back to finish their fort at St. Mary's, Jenning's to build a fort at their camp, and Pogue's to construct a road from Jenning's camp to Fort Defiance. His mounted men— General Tupper's, and Lieutenant-Colonel R. M. Johnson's commands (Harrison had recently formed a regiment of the Kentucky mounted men at St. Mary's, and they had elected Johnson their colonel)—were detailed to accompany Harrison in his march to Fort Defiance.

That night Harrison and his relief force had moved to within several miles of Fort Defiance, and he quietly slipped into Winchester's camp. There he discovered that the men were close to mutiny. The following morning, instead of reveille, he had the general alarm sounded. When the men assembled, he dramatically stepped among them to be introduced by Winchester as their new commander. This ended all thoughts of mutiny.

That day Harrison picked a site for a new fort on the Auglaize, a short distance above old Fort Defiance. On the following day he wrote orders for Winchester to take command of the left wing of the new army, but urged him to advance his force to the Rapids as soon as possible to secure the several hundred acres of corn known to be there—an easy way of reducing part of his supply problem.

Harrison departed to arrange the assembling of the right wing of his army. Never would he be happier: In command of an army four times the size of Hull's, he believed Detroit and most of Upper Canada lay within his power.

Notes to Chapter VII

1. Around the turn of the century the American government had decided to build a fortification near the southern end of Lake Michigan. After local Potawatomi had refused permission to locate the post at the mouth of the St. Joseph River, the site had been changed to a point just south of the mouth of the Chicago River. This post, Fort Dearborn, had been completed by 1804.
2. Heald to Eustis, Pittsburgh, Oct. 23, 1812, Cruikshank (ed.), *Documents Relating to the Invasion of Canada, op. cit.*, p. 225.

3. Thomas Forsyth to Gov. Howard (Missouri), Peoria, Sept. 7, 1812, Carter (ed.), *op. cit.*, Vol. XVI, p. 262. Forsyth was a half-brother of Kinzie and arrived at Chicago on Aug. 16.
4. The figures are from A. B. Woodward to Procter, Oct. 8, 1812, *MPHC, op. cit.*, Vol. XV, p. 160.
5. R. H. Sheaffe to Procter, York, Sept. 1, 1812, Wood (ed.), *Documents of the Canadian War, op. cit.*, Vol. I, p. 516.
6. *The Supporter*, Mar. 1, 1812, citing report of John Johnson, Indian Agent at Fort Wayne.
7. Harrison to Eustis, Lexington, Aug. 10, 1812, Cruikshank (ed.), *Documents Relating to the Invasion of Canada, op. cit.*, p. 132.
8. Cleaves, *op. cit.*, p. 117.
9. Harrison to Eustis, Cincinnati, Aug. 28, 1812, Esarey (ed.), *op. cit.*, Vol. II, p. 99.
10. Cincinnati, Aug. 29, 1812, *Ibid.*, p. 104.
11. Procter to Brock, Detroit, Sept. 9, 1812, Wood (ed.), *Documents of the Canadian War, op. cit.*, Vol. I, p. 520.
12. Prevost to Bathurst, Montreal, Aug. 24, 1812, *Ibid.*, pp. 491–92.
13. Washington, Aug. 17, 1812, Hunt (ed.), *op. cit.*, Vol. VIII, p. 213.
14. Lossing, *op. cit.*, p. 314.
15. *Ibid.*
16. National Archives, Military Book 6.
17. Harrison to Eustis, Piqua, Sept. 3, 1812, Esarey (ed.), *op. cit.*, Vol. II, p. 110.
18. Harrison to Eustis, Piqua, Sept. 5, 1812, *Ibid.*, p. 117.
19. Milo M. Quaife (ed.), "A Diary of the War of 1812," *Mississippi Valley Historical Review*, Vol. I (1914), p. 275. The anonymous author was a scout in Wells's regulars.
20. Robert B. McAfee, *The History of the Late War in the Western Country* (Bowling Green: Historical Publications Co., 1919), p. 406. This is a reprint of McAfee's original work published in 1816. He stated Missilimetaw was captured later in the month near River Raisin by a scouting party sent by Major Johnson.
21. Fort Harrison, Sept. 10, 1812, Esarey (ed.), *op. cit.*, Vol. II, pp. 124–34.
22. Harrison to Eustis, St. Mary's, Sept. 21, 1812, *Ibid.*, pp. 143–44.
23. Quaife (ed.), "A Diary of the War of 1812," *op. cit.*, p. 276.
24. Harrison to Winchester, Fort Wayne, Sept. 19, 1812, Esarey (ed.), *op. cit.*, Vol. II, p. 140.
25. Eustis to Harrison, *Ibid.*, p. 105.
26. Harrison to Eustis, St. Mary's, Sept. 21, 1812, *Ibid.*, p. 145.
27. Procter to Brock, Sept. 9, 1812, Wood (ed.), *Documents of the Canadian War, op. cit.*, Vol. I, p. 521.
28. Extract of Journal of Charles Askin, *Ibid.*, p. 545.
29. Casselman (ed.), *op. cit.*, p. 94.
30. Muir to Procter, Above Fort Miami, Sept. 30, 1812, *Ibid.*, p. 296.
31. Eustis to Harrison, War Dept., Sept. 17, 1812, Horace S. Knapp, *History of the Maumee Valley Commencing with its Occupation by the French in 1680* (Toledo: Blade Mammoth Printing and Publishing House, 1872), pp. 139–40.
32. Piqua, Sept. 27, 1812, Esarey (ed.), *op. cit.*, Vol. II, pp. 156–58.

CHAPTER VIII

FRONTIER ACTIONS AND
THE BATTLE OF RIVER RAISIN

WHILE THE SECOND North Western Army prepared for a major engagement against the British, several independent expeditions were made against hostile Indian villages in Illinois and Indiana territories.

Shortly after Harrison's appointment in August to the rank of major-general of the Kentucky militia, Governor Shelby had ordered Brigadier-General Samuel Hopkins to command large militia reinforcements to Vincennes. During the tense period following the capture of Detroit, some of Hopkins' men had been diverted to Harrison. Governor Shelby's call for a short-term volunteer force of mounted riflemen to make up the deficiency had met with an overwhelming response, and Hopkins and his detachment had left for Vincennes. By late September Hopkins' camp at Busseron consisted of five loosely organized regiments.

After he assumed command of the North Western Army, Harrison appointed Hopkins to command all troops in Indiana and Illinois. In a move against hostile Indians in the Illinois Territory, Hopkins ordered Colonel Russell at Vincennes to advance a ranger force to meet a militia group in Illinois and join him at Peoria in

147

an expedition against the Kickapoo and Peoria tribes along the Illinois River.

By the night of October 14, Hopkins had marched 2,000 mounted Kentucky riflemen to Fort Harrison, where ten days' rations were issued, and then the force crossed the Wabash and camped a few miles above the fort. Thus far it had been a routine march, but the morale of the men was low as they headed deep into Indian country. Many had already deserted, although desertion may be too harsh a term. (The force was made up almost entirely of volunteers: They had not entered formal federal service and were not even a normal militia organization.) The desertions naturally did not improve the morale of the men who remained, even though Hopkins, feeling the deserters were potential troublemakers, was undoubtedly relieved to see them go.

Leaving camp the following morning, Hopkins proceeded for four days on a course more north than northwest,[1] despite the fact that Peoria was northwest of Fort Harrison. The troops had averaged about thirty miles a day but had not yet reached their goal. The chief guides, Touissant Dubois and Joseph Baron, both of whom had served as experienced Indian guides for Harrison, admitted they were lost.[2] However, on the fifth day, they discovered signs that led them to believe an Indian village lay within ten miles, and the force spent the rest of the day searching for it.

Since the men had already consumed most of their ten days' rations, they would have to find their goal soon or make a hasty return to Fort Harrison. That night a prairie fire, unmistakable evidence of the nearness of Indians, was discovered. The camp was saved by a backfire, but the next morning the men were determined on a retreat. Hopkins, who had lost all control of his force, pleaded in vain for five hundred men to continue the march, but the men even refused to let him lead the disorganized retreat. Believing that an Indian attack would come from the rear, Hopkins stationed himself there to protect his men on the return to Fort Harrison. At the fort on October 25 he authorized the immediate discharge of his men. Colonel Russell, whom he had ordered to Peoria from Vincennes, would have to fend for himself.

148

Colonel Russell had left Vincennes with detachments from three of his ranger companies and, at Camp Russell, had joined Governor Edwards, leading a small militia force. As they prepared to move to Peoria, Edwards assumed theoretical authority, but Russell retained the practical command.[3]

The small force, a reported total of only 360 privates, left Camp Russell on October 17 or 18, reached the vicinity of Peoria and, having heard nothing from Hopkins, by-passed the stronghold. Twenty miles north of Peoria, they attacked a Kickapoo village. Most of the Indians fled, the village was destroyed, and some canoes and horses were captured. Edwards, perhaps overly optimistic, believed twenty Indians had been killed, while none of the Americans had been killed and only four wounded.[4] With all hope of Hopkins' arrival gone, Edwards and Russell returned southward—the combined expedition a failure.

Undaunted, Hopkins at Fort Harrison was determined to try another expedition against hostile frontier Indians, this time at Prophet's Town. Early in November he directed a force of over 1,200 men to assemble at the fort: three regiments of Kentucky infantry, Taylor's company of regulars, a company of United States rangers, and a company of scouts. Delayed by heavy rainfall and swollen streams, the expedition finally approached Prophet's Town on November 19—only to find that it and the near-by villages had been recently vacated.

Hopkins' men burned Prophet's Town and its forty huts, as well as two other near-by villages, one a Winnebago and the other a Kickapoo. No Indians had been seen, but on November 21 a small party was attacked on Wild Cat Creek and a Kentuckian was killed.

On the following day a force of sixty mounted men left the main camp at Prophet's Town to recover and bury the body of their slain comrade. The detachment, led by two Kentucky lieutenant-colonels, Miller and Wilcox, moved up Wild Cat Creek, came across a lone Indian, gave chase, and rode into an ambush. The Americans had discovered the Indians' hiding place but paid a heavy price for the knowledge—sixteen killed and three wounded.

A heavy snowfall, continuing for two days, delayed the main

149

force's pursuit of the Indians, and when they reached the site of the ambush on November 24, the Indians had withdrawn. Hopkins had planned to spend another week in the field, but the adverse weather and the lack of winter clothing for his Kentucky men forced his return to Fort Harrison.

The second expedition had been of some success; and, with the advent of cold weather, the Indian danger lessened. On his return to Fort Harrison, Hopkins, an elderly man, resigned his command, his long military career at an end.

The next series of expeditions were more directly connected with the main army. Before he had left Fort Defiance on October 4, Harrison had ordered General Tupper and his mounted men to proceed as far as the Rapids, perhaps as far as River Raisin, sweeping all the Indians before him. In making the arrangements for his march, Tupper discovered that the commissary could issue no flour and that it had supplied cattle for the meat rations. He ordered his men to butcher the animals and prepare an eight-day supply of jerked beef. His plans to start on November 5 had to be abandoned when he discovered that hard rains had rendered most of the musket cartridges useless.

While Tupper pondered this problem, a ranger was killed by Indians just across the river from Winchester's main camp at Fort Defiance. Tupper ordered pursuit, but his men were delayed because they had to recover their mounts which had been taken to grazing land a mile away. Finally they dashed across the river, devoid of any organization, and broke into small groups. One group observed the enemy at a distance but, being outnumbered, returned to camp. Winchester then ordered Tupper to pursue the Indians before undertaking the expedition to the Rapids. Tupper pointed out that the chase might be a long one and might render his force ineffective for the main operation; that they lacked ammunition; and that they should, in any case, await the scouts' report on the size of the hostile band before deciding on a pursuit.[5]

The following morning, on learning that the Indians numbered only forty and were headed in the direction of Lake Michigan, Winchester again ordered Tupper to pursue them. Even though

150

this would involve a long detour on the march to the Rapids and Winchester could not furnish any cartridges, Tupper prepared to carry out his orders. Winchester wanted only volunteers to make the trip to the Rapids, and four hundred of Tupper's men applied; Lieutenant-Colonel John Allen received Winchester's permission to accompany the force.

Winchester, who had apparently never approved of Tupper's appointment to command the expedition and who was probably disgusted with the delay in getting started, abruptly ordered Allen to replace Tupper. However, the Ohio men refused to march except under Tupper's command,[6] despite Allen's attempt to smooth things over by suggesting two expeditions to the Rapids—his own taking a direct route, and Tupper's making a wide circle to the south via Tawa (Ottawa) towns, as Harrison had suggested, with the two forces joining above the Rapids. Because each force would have been smaller than minimum safety required, Tupper rejected this plan.

Deciding to proceed to the Rapids, Tupper moved his men to Tawa, on Blanchard's Fork. On October 9, when he ordered the march to the Rapids, only two hundred men were willing to continue—too small a force to risk an attack and too large to be used as a scouting party. Therefore, Tupper moved the entire force to Urbana and discharged those who had faithfully performed their duty.

Winchester, busy with his own problems, planned no immediate move of his entire command to the Rapids to secure the corn there, and made no attempt to send a sizable detachment to accomplish Tupper's thwarted mission. He did send out routine scouting parties, with orders not to engage the enemy, and also preferred charges against Tupper and requested that Harrison order his arrest.

Toward the end of October Tupper moved his reorganized command to McArthur's Blockhouse and ordered his scouts to the Rapids to capture a prisoner for questioning. The scouts returned on November 9 with a captive, Captain Thomas Clark, who informed Tupper that a British expedition of 50 regulars and 500 Indians had been sent to the Rapids to gather corn.[7] Perhaps this

151

was deliberate misinformation, for Colonel Elliott, who arrived at the Rapids the day of Clark's capture, wrote that there were only 250 Indians present and that the British had moved them there, not to gather corn, but because they were short of provisions and this was the easiest way of maintaining the force.[8] Having no reason to doubt his information, Tupper passed it on to Winchester, and left the following morning with 604 enlisted men, mainly infantry, carrying five days' rations and equipped with a light fieldpiece, which they were soon forced to abandon.

On November 14 Tupper halted five miles from the Rapids. After learning that the British were on the north side of the Rapids, he notified Winchester of his position. He avoided enemy patrols by waiting until sunset to move to a ford more than two miles above the British position. Dramatically he gathered his men, informed them that there could be no retreat if they crossed the river, and won their consent to a dawn attack.

If Tupper had visions of emulating Washington's crossing of the Delaware and his routing of the Hessians, he was sadly disappointed. He had no boats, and the first men crossed the deep ford through the frigid water with such difficulty that he was forced to abandon his attack. His few horses could not cross the entire command before dawn would bring certain discovery, and the only shallow ford was directly in front of the British camp. Tupper recalled the few who had crossed and let them dry out as best they could without fires.

The next morning he tried to entice the British to cross by exposing his scouts on the south bank opposite the enemy camp. A few British troops did cross, but they returned before coming in range of Tupper's main body in concealment. Then all the Americans showed themselves—and with results. A few British soldiers boarded boats, downstream, and the other regulars and Indians opened fire across the river with rifles, muskets, and a small fieldpiece.

Suddenly a group of yelling Indians rushed up the bank of the river. Tupper ordered his men to push back the few who had crossed at the shallow ford and then marched his men up the south side to meet those who had crossed at the deep ford. By the time

152

these were forced back, it was near sundown and Tupper withdrew his force. With his supplies exhausted, he returned to McArthur's Blockhouse. Only two men within his lines had been wounded but, as usual, there were casualties in a group of men who, contrary to orders, had left the lines during the march up the river to get some corn and a stray hog or two—four of these men were killed.[9]

Tupper had atoned for his earlier failure—the British had left the area. If he had not defeated the British, at least he had done more than Winchester, who had made no move to carry out Harrison's orders to secure the corn at the Rapids.

Meanwhile, Harrison had not abandoned his plans to chastise the hostile Indians in northern Indiana. In his belief, there were only two groups of Indian villages large enough to serve as rallying points or to house dangerous concentrations of warriors for the winter—one on the St. Joseph River in Michigan and the other along the Mississinewa River in Indiana. His first expedition against White Pigeon's Town, on the St. Joseph River in Michigan, ended in failure. Colonel Allen Trimble, of the Ohio militia, set out with a 500-man force to raid the village. But when the detachment reached Fort Wayne, half of the men refused to go further; the rest, while they did destroy two small villages, were unable to kill or capture any Indians.

The villages along the Mississinewa River presented the greater threat because they lay along the supply route to Winchester's command. These villages were occupied by three divisions of the Miami (the regular Miami, the Eel River Miami, and the Wea), and many of the inhabitants had participated in the attacks on Fort Wayne and Fort Harrison.

On November 25 Harrison detailed Lieutenant-Colonel John B. Campbell, of the Nineteenth Infantry (one of the eight new federal regiments authorized in June), with Major Ball as second in command, to lead an expedition against the Miami villages. Campbell was to leave Franklinton (now Columbus) and to avoid contact with the friendly Delaware by traveling via Springfield, Xenia, and Dayton to Eaton for final provisioning and assemblage of guides before marching to the Mississinewa.[10] Certain friendly

Miami Indians were to be spared if possible, but the rest of the warriors were to be captured or killed.

The 600-man force consisted of Simrall's Kentucky mounted men, Ball's command of the Second Dragoons, an infantry company of the Nineteenth, a militia company of Pennsylvania riflemen, a company of spies or scouts, and the well-known Pittsburgh Blues (a regular company of one-year volunteers under Captain James Butler, allowed to use their name because of past service). Campbell quickly moved his command to Dayton, stayed there until he got sufficient pack horses for his infantry, and moved to Greenville. On December 14 the men left Greenville and arrived at the site of the first Miami village in the early morning of December 17. Campbell's men thought that they were at Silver Heels' Town, one of the chief Miami villages, but instead it was a minor village containing a few hostile Delaware and Miami.[11] Although they attacked quickly, some of the Indians escaped. But eight warriors were killed and another eight braves and thirty-four women and children captured. The infantry guarded the prisoners and constructed a fortified camp, and the mounted men set out for Silver Heels' Town, some two miles away. The village was vacant, and Campbell ordered it burned, as well as two other villages.

Just before dawn the next morning, while the officers were holding a council to decide on returning home, advancing to other villages, or searching for the Indians of the destroyed villages, the Indians launched an attack against the camp. In an hour's decisive fighting, the Americans beat off the attack. Campbell reported his losses as eight killed and forty-eight wounded (two died later), but believed, from later evidence, that at least thirty Indians had been killed.[12] Many of his horses had been killed, his men had severe cases of frostbite, the prisoners had to be guarded, and his most seriously wounded had to be carried in litters. Consequently, even though a small reinforcement met him halfway, Campbell did not reach Greenville until Christmas Day.

The expedition had been successful in removing one part of the threat to Winchester's supply route. Harrison received the news late on New Year's Day, and his first general orders of the new year declared that Campbell's exploit shed luster on the entire army. It was the most successful of the various expeditions that had been sent out that fall and, with the others, went a long way to ensure the security of the frontier the next spring.

While the expeditions were engaging in frontier actions, Harrison's main army had been hard at work. Three small forts had been built to guard the supply route from Piqua to old Fort Defiance: Fort Barbee at St. Mary's, Fort Amanda (south of modern Conant, on the Auglaize), and Fort Jennings (on the Ottawa River, south of Gomer). A larger post, Fort Winchester, had been constructed on the west bank of the Auglaize, below old Fort Defiance and over a mile from the Miami River, at a site selected by Harrison. This fort, built in the form of a parallelogram, enclosed three acres, had two-story blockhouses at the corners, a gate with projecting overhead sentry boxes in the middle of each face, and an underground passageway from the blockhouse on the northeast corner to the river.[13] The usual features of regular forts were included—storehouse, hospital, barracks, and powder magazine.

Winchester had retained his fortified camp across from the mouth of the Tiffin River while the fort was being constructed and, then, after detailing a garrison for the fort, had established a new camp along the point of land below it. He had few artillery pieces for either field or garrison use, but his most crucial shortage was in winter clothing for his command, and the adverse weather aggravated the fevers already sweeping through his regiments.

With the sick report increasing and deaths occurring daily, Winchester twice moved his camp in an attempt to find more healthful ground and a handier wood supply. His second regular camp (third, counting the one opposite the Tiffin) was established early in November on the north side of the Miami, more than three miles below the junction of the Auglaize. About two weeks later his camp was moved some five miles farther down the north side of the Miami. He was at least inching toward the Rapids, but with winter setting in, he ordered his camp picketed and huts built by the men. While some of the men worked on the fort, others began the construction of pirogues,[14] which Winchester hoped to use to ferry supplies for his movement to the Rapids.

The late fall had brought a series of hard frosts and thaws, which often left the road to Fort Winchester impassable for sleds or wheeled vehicles and so exhausting to pack horses that they had to be replaced frequently. Only a trickle of supplies came to Winchester's camp and, far from building up a surplus of provisions for the move to the Rapids, the General was frequently forced to put his men on reduced rations.

Winter clothing had been ordered for his regulars from Pittsburgh in September,[15] but it failed to arrive in quantity for distribution to Wells's regulars before the end of the year. The militia was in even worse shape. Harrison had confiscated stocks of heavy cloth originally intended for distribution to Indian tribes as part of the regular annuities. From this, the women in Dayton had made 1,800 heavy shirts,[16] but not enough of these were sent to Fort Winchester. Even shoes were lacking for many of the men, and only in December did they become available for the regulars and the most needy of the militia.

It is small wonder, then, that Winchester, faced by a minor Valley Forge, was unable to move toward the Rapids; and it was fortunate, for him, that the other columns were not ready to advance.

Harrison, usually headquartering at Franklinton but occasionally at Delaware, tried in vain to improve the provision situation for his entire command. But the major contractors were unable to furnish the required number of rations on regular schedule, and Harrison attributed this to the fact that they sought excessive profits and let subcontracts at such low figures that the holders were unable to fill them. The central column was trying to stockpile provisions at McArthur's Blockhouse and, protected by Tupper's men, advance them. However, they encountered the same difficulty that Winchester's men did and there, too, the flow of provisions nearly halted.

A bright spot in Harrison's situation was the fact that the right wing was beginning to show some semblance of order. Following Hull's defeat, Major-General Elijah Wadsworth had called out his entire Ohio militia division from the Western Reserve area. Too old for an active campaign, he had appointed Brigadier-General Simon Perkins to command the portion turned over to Harrison. From supply points at Wooster and Mansfield, Harrison began to order these men, together with the Virginia and Pennsylvania men when they arrived in November, to Upper and Lower Sandusky. The former post was about four miles east of the modern city and the latter was at modern Fremont, less than fifty miles north. A small post, Fort Stephenson, was built at Lower Sandusky, and two small stockades, Fort Seneca and Fort Ball (at modern Tiffin), were constructed between the two Sanduskys to protect the route. When ordered, the right wing would advance from Lower Sandusky to the Rapids, less than forty miles away.

Before Harrison had assumed command, Meigs had offered Perkins' division and other militia extra pay to construct a road from Upper to Lower Sandusky. At Harrison's later urging, Meigs also authorized extra money for Perkins' men to begin construction of a road toward the Rapids, including a fifteen-mile causeway across the Black Swamp.

The Pennsylvania troops had brought a few artillery pieces, but the major supply of artillery to be dispatched from Pittsburgh had not arrived. By December 12 Harrison complained, only 28 pieces had been delivered including 10 six-pounders, which had limited use and which he already had in sufficient numbers. His need was for big guns to oppose enemy garrison artillery.

Nevertheless, provisions continued to be Harrison's chief concern. Considering it safe to advance from the Rapids only when he had a million rations on deposit there, he concentrated on this objective. To shorten his current supply lines and help build up stocks at the respective points closest to the Rapids, he had even held back the advance of some of his men. Forage for his horses proved so difficult to transport to forward points that he curtailed the movement of his mounted men toward the Rapids, instead stationing them in the settled parts of Ohio. Some progress was made by driving livestock to Fort Winchester and other advance areas, where the meat was butchered, salted, and barreled. Until the weather improved there was little else he could do. Understandably, the men at Fort Winchester were never far from mutiny; the Pennsylvania men, Harrison complained, were so unjustly insubordinate that he would have dismissed them, if not afraid of "wounding the reputation of the State." [17] Harrison, like Hull before him, was having his fill of troubles with militiamen.

All in all, it is not surprising that Harrison's letters began to reflect some pessimism concerning his chances of regaining Detroit that winter. On December 12 he wrote that, unless political considerations definitely forbade the canceling of his offensive plans, his advance forces should remain where they were. This would avoid any further outlay of the tremendous extra funds necessary for a winter campaign and allow time for the establishment of naval superiority before advancing.[18] In any case, he continued, Fort Malden should be the point attacked because, if the British were there in force, anyone holding Detroit would require a garrison twice the size of the enemy's force, as well as an additional force, at least the size of the British, to guard the supply route. However, until receiving orders to the contrary, he planned to continue with his offensive plans.

Logan, the friendly chief, given the rank of captain, had succeeded in scouting the Rapids and reported no enemy concentrations there. However, his party had been surprised by a British scouting party and, although Logan killed Winnemeg (who had become an active supporter of the British), he was severely wounded and died soon after reaching Winchester's camp. Harrison acted on Logan's information and, about December 10, ordered Winchester to advance to the Rapids as soon as practicable.

With more favorable weather, Winchester ordered his advance for December 23, but countermanded the order when expected supplies of flour failed to arrive. Finally, on December 29, his advance began. Delayed by inability to sled most of his supplies, he arrived at the Rapids on January 8 and immediately began the construction of a fortified camp.

Following the capture of Detroit, the British had not been completely inactive in the Detroit region. The day of surrender, Brock had issued a proclamation pledging protection of property and religion, authorizing the continuance of the present laws until further notice, and entreating the subject population to surrender public property and arms of all kinds.[19] Shortly afterward he had departed for Fort George, leaving Procter in active command. Procter had asked Judge Woodward, the highest remaining official, for a detailed summary of the Territorial boundaries and of the duties of various governmental officers. Acting on this information on August 21, he proclaimed himself the Civil Governor, named Woodward the Secretary, retained the minor officials not prisoners of war, and authorized the appointment of others.

Militarily, as has been seen, Procter had attempted little beyond the occupation of River Raisin, Muir's expedition toward Fort Wayne, and the unsuccessful expedition to the Rapids. Prevost had left the question of the evacuation and destruction of Fort Detroit to Brock's discretion, and Brock had retained it because he feared that its abandonment might result in the massacre of the residents by the Indians or that it might be interpreted as a sign of British weakness and thus influence the Indians to change their allegiance to the American side.[20]

About October 5 two vessels were dispatched from Fort Malden on a routine trip to the Niagara frontier—the *Caledonia,* a private vessel with a cargo of furs, and the old *Adams,* captured and renamed the *Detroit,* carrying some of the captured guns and ordnance stores. Anchored near Fort Erie on October 8, the vessels were boarded that night by a daring group of Americans led by Lieutenant Jesse D. Elliott of the navy. Elliott's followers, some civilians, got the *Caledonia* safely to American territory but grounded the *Detroit* and abandoned her in the face of British gunfire. The British reboarded, threw the valuable guns overboard, and left; the Americans again went aboard and once again were forced to abandon the ship, but not before setting it afire. Both sides had suffered casualties, but the Americans had recaptured over twenty prisoners of the Fourth Regiment aboard the *Detroit.* Two developments caused this incident to be long remembered. First, Hull's papers were on the *Detroit* and were burned and, with their loss, Hull's best chance of subsequently clearing his name disappeared. Second, Brock's official report,[21] also destroyed, proved to be the last of his career.

The American forces along the Niagara River, commanded by General Stephen Van Rensselaer, a militia officer, numbered about four times the size of the British forces across the river. Even though the ranking officer of the regulars, Brigadier Alexander Smyth, refused to co-operate with him, Van Rensselaer decided to cross from his headquarters at Lewiston and attack Queenston. The attack began on October 10, but it was poorly conducted, boats were not available, and the undertaking was soon canceled.

Three days later another attack was launched. An American force landed on the enemy shore and stormed Queenston Heights. Brock, who had hurriedly ridden to the scene from Fort George to rally his men and to lead a counterattack, was killed. Lieutenant-Colonel Macdonell was severely wounded and died the following day. Had Van Rensselaer been able to send reinforcements, he might have carried the field. But many of his militia refused to cross the river and, when Major-General Roger Hale Sheaffe arrived with an infantry force from Fort George, the Americans were forced to surrender.

Van Rensselaer resigned his command, and Smyth, his successor, signed an armistice with Shaeffe. The armistice terminated on November 20, and a few days later Smyth ordered an invasion which failed miserably. Action along the Niagara ended for the year. When one considers their comparative chances of success, the Niagara campaign had been a far greater failure than Hull's. Obviously Harrison would be little aided by any diversion from Niagara that winter.

With the death of Brock, the British lost their only brilliant officer in the West. Sheaffe was appointed to Brock's command in Upper Canada, but no one could really replace the British hero.

By one means or another, the British had been more successful than the Americans in solving their provision problems: Procter's men had scoured the countryside for provisions; some of his Indians had been maintained for a time at the Rapids; and some supplies had come by water. Later in 1812, Procter was able to report that he had sufficient provisions until the opening of navigation in the spring. His regulars at Detroit and Malden at the end of

November had been reduced to an officer and 25 men of the Royal Artillery, a captain of the Royal Engineers, 9 officers and 270 men of the Forty-first, and an officer and 70 men of the Royal Newfoundland—a total, including himself, of 13 officers and 365 men.[22] Obviously, successful opposition to Harrison's large army still depended on the militia and Indians.

By January 13 Procter had learned of the presence of the Americans at the Rapids and quickly recalled the portion of the Essex Militia that had been released to their homes that fall. He had no plans to force the residents of Michigan to perform military service, but he did reinforce the few British at River Raisin, in the belief that he might find it necessary to oppose Winchester's men at the Rapids.

As Harrison approached the crucial phases of his campaign, changes occurred in Washington which were to effect him. Secretary Eustis yielded to political pressure and resigned his post about Christmastime in 1812. James Monroe, Secretary of State, assumed the temporary direction of the War Department, acting until January 13, 1813, when Eustis' resignation became official and John Armstrong took office as the new Secretary. While Monroe was in control he addressed a long letter to Harrison, dated December 26, 1812.[23]

In it, he expressed concern over Harrison's delay, especially in view of the fact that the term of service of his six-month militia would soon expire (the service of the Ohio troops ended in February and that of the Virginia and Pennsylvania troops in March). He questioned whether the campaign should be postponed until spring. While Harrison was still given discretion to decide, he was to notify Monroe immediately of his plans and, if the campaign were abandoned, was advised to attempt to destroy the portion of the British navy then in winter quarters at the Malden naval yard. Finally, Monroe wrote that President Madison contemplated an expedition of a thousand mounted men who would advance from Kentucky in February, move to Fort Wayne, and then destroy the numerous Indian villages along the southern end of Lake Michigan and the Illinois River.

161

By January 4 Harrison had received Monroe's letter and addressed a reply. He pointed out that his last letter, on December 12, had covered the situation, but again summarized his troubles. He said that, although he had been given complete discretion to advance that winter or wait until spring, he had received no reply to his question as to whether the expenditure of extra money for winter movement was to be considered a prime factor in his decision. Consequently, he had concluded that political considerations outweighed the financial aspect of the matter and planned to advance with a picked force from the Rapids about the end of January, feint toward Detroit, cross the ice in the Detroit River, and attack Fort Malden. He was not able to state the size of his attacking force at that time, pointing out that the failure on the Niagara frontier increased his potential opposition; and that, if the weather were such that he was unable to haul all his supplies with the main attacking force, he would need to use a sizable escort for the provision train, since it was unwise at any time to detach a force inferior to the total strength of the Indians.

In summary, Harrison explained to Monroe, he planned to move a minimum of 4,000 soldiers to the Rapids by January 20 and hoped that this would prove sufficient, cautioning, however, that his effectives usually ran only about two thirds of his total force. Should he be forced to abandon his campaign, he was still of the opinion that if naval control were secured the next summer, he could land below Malden, destroy the British, and quickly sweep to the Niagara.

Two days later, Harrison dispatched another letter to Monroe.[24] Again he stressed the importance of naval control, for the alternatives—crossing the ice to Malden (where a sudden thaw could cut off his only retreat) or moving to Detroit and constructing boats (which would require much time and many men to ensure provision supply)—left much to be desired. Furthermore, a naval force would be necessary in any case in order to regain Michilimackinac and end the possibility of a few British artillerists, with a large Indian force, suddenly landing at the southern end of Lake Michigan and attacking such vital points as Vincennes. If the winter campaign were abandoned, he would move against the British naval units at Malden. He admitted that he was vitally concerned about the approaching loss of his militia but hoped to induce many to remain as twelve-month volunteers for the regulars.

In regard to the President's plans for an expedition against the Indian villages, Harrison's previous letter advised against it at that time of the year: The warriors would be out in isolated hunting parties, and it had been his experience that the news spread so quickly when one village was attacked that the Americans would find the subsequent villages deserted. He himself had considered sending Campbell to the Mississinewa area again to finish the destruction of the villages there. However he had discovered that Simrall's Kentucky command was unable to march and had therefore abandoned the raid; he had ordered Simrall to discharge his five troops of cavalry, and had directed Major Ball to move his squadron to the settled parts of Ohio to recruit. One small battalion of Hopkins' men had been retained in service and placed under Colonel Russell's command at Vincennes, but the rest had been discharged.

It is apparent from Harrison's detailed reports that he was not wholeheartedly in favor of continuing his winter advance—that unless the weather and other conditions seemed extremely favorable, he would abandon it.

In another letter to Monroe from Upper Sandusky on January 15, Harrison reflected a note of confidence. The weather had been unusually favorable and, he reported, he had definitely decided to attempt an advance from the Rapids the first week in February.

But Winchester was to force the issue earlier than Harrison had anticipated. On January 13 Winchester had begun to receive messages from civilians in the River Raisin area. The first stated that the British knew of the American force at the Rapids and were rounding up the residents known to favor the Americans and taking them to Fort Malden. However, the message continued, there were not over 50 British and 100 Indians at River Raisin, and a rapidly moving American detachment could easily overcome them and gain possession of an estimated 3,000 barrels of flour and a quantity of corn and wheat before they could be transported to Fort Malden.[25] Several subsequent messages urged Winchester to prevent the expected destruction of the town and incarceration of the inhabitants.

Advised by Harrison to make no advance until ordered, Winchester at the urging of some of his militia officers, held an officers' council on the night of January 16. Most of his field officers voted for an immediate advance to the Raisin in spite of the strong dissent of his ranking regular, Colonel Samuel Wells.[26] Accordingly, Lieutenant-Colonel William Lewis left the camp early the next morning with about 550 men, followed later by Lieutenant-Colonel John Allen with over 100 more. The two groups joined later in the day and camped that night on the north side of what is now Maumee Bay. The next day they continued to advance on the frozen surface near the shore of Lake Erie and at about 3:00 P.M. approached the south side of the mouth of the Raisin River.

At River Raisin the British force was commanded by Major Ebenezer Reynolds of the First Essex and, except for a few regular artillerists with a three-pounder, probably consisted of about 50 militiamen and 200 or more Indians. They were aware of the Americans' presence and opened fire as the first men began to approach the south bank of the river. Lewis quickly ordered his men, marching in three columns, to form a battle line. The force crossed the river, forced the British to retreat, and pursued them for two miles. As the battle had lasted nearly three hours and it was then late in the day, the Americans abandoned the chase, allowing most of the British to escape with their fieldpieces. Lewis returned to River Raisin, checked his losses, and awaited reinforcements. Most of the people of River Raisin, then a village of thirty-three families living mainly on the north side of the river,[27] were overjoyed at the presence of the long-awaited Americans.

Lewis reported that, while only 12 dead Indians were discovered on the field and one Indian and two Canadian militiamen captured, many casualties were known to have been removed by the retreating British. He therefore believed that the total enemy force numbered 80 whites and 400 Indians.[28] While his figures

164

seem high for the British force, he could report more accurately his own casualties—12 killed and 55 wounded. Before he had encountered the enemy, Lewis had sent a message to Winchester informing him that a friendly Frenchman had told him that the British force then exceeded their original estimates. After the skirmish, he sent another message, informing Winchester of the successful outcome but requesting reinforcements to hold the position.

General Winchester ordered Wells's regulars to start for River Raisin the following day. Having left General Payne in command of the 300 men still at the camp, Winchester immediately set out in a cariole, passed Wells's men, and arrived at River Raisin that night. By the time Wells arrived on January 20, there were nearly a thousand men at the town. Even without artillery, they should have been sufficient to repel any British attack had they been properly deployed.

Lewis' command had encamped in rather haphazard fashion on the north side of the river behind an existing row of pickets, forming a rough semicircle. The river was at some distance to the rear, and the pickets did not extend all the way to it. Although the pickets had been strengthened and some sort of blockhouse constructed, the position was ill-chosen: They had no artillery and the pickets were emplaced in a large clearing at the end of the regular road from Detroit, allowing a clear field of unhindered advance for any British artillery. Lacking artillery, the Americans should have camped where the terrain would have restricted the British use of guns—on the south side of the river or in an area covered by woods.

Wells's regulars had been ordered to camp on the right of the pickets behind a rail fence, with no other protection. To make matters worse, some of the militia officers were quartered in houses at some distance from their men; Winchester had foolishly established his headquarters in the house of Francis Navarre, on the opposite side and over a mile up the river from his men.[29]

On the morning of January 21 Wells protested against the exposed position of his men and, although he and Winchester spent several hours checking more favorable locations, the General refused to allow the regulars to withdraw. Wells urged that scouts be sent to the Brownstown area to check reports that the British were rallying there for an attack, presumably on January 23, but Winchester calmly replied that the next day would be time enough.[30] However, he was not unaware of his danger—he wrote two messages to Harrison on that day stating that the enemy was reported to be preparing to attack and that his ground was unfavorable but that it was necessary to occupy it if the town were to be defended. Nevertheless, he refused to prepare an appropriate defense. His men did not have sizable amounts of ammunition (the regulars had only about 10 rounds a man), and the supply which had arrived from the Rapids was kept at Winchester's distant quarters.[31] Certainly one reason for this action was to prevent the weather from damaging the powder, but it could have been protected just as well in the rough blockhouse, readily available to the potential users. The general situation alarmed Colonel Wells. He secured Winchester's permission to leave the camp that evening —ostensibly to hasten the arrival of a small detachment of regulars bringing forward the heavy baggage—and rushed to the Rapids to consult with General Harrison.

Perhaps Winchester had come under the influence of a few Frenchmen who discounted the danger of a British attack. In any event, the fact remains that, through his virtually criminal negligence, his command was ill prepared to resist any British attack.

During the night of January 18 General Procter, at Fort Malden, had been awakened to be informed of the successful attack of Lewis' men and the retreat of Major Reynolds' command to Brownstown. He had immediately ordered the Kent Militia, from the Thames River, to augment the skeleton guards he planned to retain at Fort Detroit, Sandwich, and Fort Malden. After the Kent Militia had begun to arrive, he had led his force over the ice of the Detroit River to Brownstown. By the night of January 21, he had assembled his men at Brownstown, advanced to Stony Creek (some five miles from River Raisin), and waited to attack the Americans at dawn.

The British force at Stony Creek consisted of 25 officers and

166

512 enlisted men of the regulars and Essex Militia; 28 members of the Marine Department (from the ships laid up for the winter) ; 32 Indian Department men—a total of 597, of whom only a little over 200 were militiamen.[32] Tecumseh was absent in an attempt to induce other Indians to come to Fort Malden, and the ranking chief with Procter's force was Roundhead, the celebrated Wyandot. As usual, the British were reluctant to report the Indian strength, but apparently there were over 600; one British participant reported 800.[33] Thus, the total British force exceeded 1,200, perhaps 1,400, while the American strength was about 1,000. Furthermore, while the defense was usually thought to have an advantage over an equal number of attackers, this was more than outweighed by the poor disposition of Winchester's troops and the British possession of three three-pounders and three howitzers.

Just before dawn Procter moved his force into position, his artillery and regulars forming his center, Indians his right, and Indians and militia his left. Had the British advanced immediately, they would have completely surprised the Americans, who had no outpost guards; but when Procter paused to check his line and gun positions, the American sentries noticed his presence and sounded the general alarm. The Americans rushed to their positions behind the pickets or, in the case of the regulars, eagerly sought the meager protection of the crude rail fence breastwork.

They concentrated their fire on the British gunners or the more prominent of the enemy officers; the British artillery concentrated on the American right. When Winchester finally arrived, he saw that his regulars were being literally cut to pieces by the artillery and ordered them to withdraw to the north bank of the Raisin River. However, a few concealed Indians there slowed the regulars' movement so that the Indians on the left of the main British line flanked them. Lieutenant-Colonels Lewis and Allen each led a company of Kentucky men out of the picketed area, not yet the target of much British fire, in an attempt to aid the regulars. Many of the regulars did get to the river and tried to form. But they were forced to withdraw across the river, where they again failed to form, and the few who could do so kept retreating.

167

The American right was hopelessly defeated—Allen was killed, Lewis was taken prisoner; and Winchester was captured and escorted to Roundhead. The men still in the picketed area had scarcely lost a man; perhaps they could have won the day. However, the British worked on Winchester's fears. He had just seen what happened to his right; and the British convinced him that if the rest of his men did not surrender, the Indians could not be restrained from massacring his entire force. Not technically in command, as he was a prisoner, he sent a flag of truce to his men advising and ordering them to surrender. He had received Procter's promise to treat them as prisoners of war with the right to retain private property and the eventual return of side-arms.[34] The men, short of ammunition, accepted, and the battle ended before 11:00 A.M.

General Harrison, meanwhile, had been frantically trying to reinforce Winchester's premature advance from the Rapids. On January 16, when he first learned of Winchester's presence at the Rapids, Harrison ordered his artillery to advance from Upper Sandusky and departed for Lower Sandusky. The following day, in accordance with Winchester's request, he authorized the advance from Lower Sandusky of Major W. W. Cotgreave with a battalion of 200 Ohio militia of Perkins' command. Cotgreave's men marched the next day. On January 19, when Harrison learned of Lewis' advance to the Rapids, he ordered the rest of Perkins' men, about 300 under Colonel John Andrews, to march. He himself departed with General Perkins for the Rapids and spent that night at Cotgreave's camp, where he learned of Lewis' success. The next day he pushed ahead and arrived at the Rapids to learn that Winchester had departed for River Raisin.

Harrison promptly wrote Secretary Monroe that it was now necessary to hold River Raisin, but he feared that the British would attack before it could be reinforced. The morning of January 22, in view of Colonel Andrews' arrival with his force, he ordered General Payne to march the remaining Kentucky men to the Rapids. Cotgreave's men had spent the previous night near the mouth of the Miami and were advancing along the ice of

Lake Erie. When he was some fifteen miles from River Raisin, Cotgreave learned of the battle and circled to the road from the Rapids. Harrison himself got news of the battle about noon from a report sent back by Wells, who had left to rejoin his command. He ordered Andrews' Regiment to follow and set out with Perkins to overtake Payne's slowly marching men. Thus, that afternoon, there were about 900 Americans marching between the Rapids and River Raisin: Cotgreave's, Payne's, and Andrews' commands; and Harrison got them all united.

From the scattered reports of fleeing French and a few soldiers, together with the information that Wells could obtain in advance of Harrison's force, there could be no doubt that Winchester had been defeated and that there was nothing Harrison could do but attack. This he thought inadvisable: He had no artillery; he was then nearly thirty miles from River Raisin; and most of his men had already undergone a hard march that day. He ordered Wells to advance some distance with a large party of the strongest men to aid any who had escaped from the battle; he himself marched the rest of his men toward the Rapids.

Late that evening, Wells returned to Harrison's camp and attended an officers' council, as did Major McClanahan, the ranking survivor of the battle, who had escaped from the right wing. It was agreed that the Rapids could be defended against a British attack, but that the artillery advancing from Upper Sandusky was in danger of being cut off. On January 23 Harrison moved his force to the Portage River to ensure the safety of his artillery.

Harrison addressed two letters to Monroe, January 24 and 26, informing him of Winchester's defeat and summarizing his own views: While his officers might have pressured him into the action, Winchester's move to River Raisin had been contrary to Harrison's implied orders; once made, it was essential to hold the position to protect the settlers who had aided the Americans; he had done everything he could to reinforce the position; he had allowed Winchester too much authority in the past because of his high rank and experience.[35] Harrison was right—the disaster had not been of his making.

The historical importance of the Battle of River Raisin lies not merely in the battle itself but also in its tragic aftermath. Winchester was certain he had surrendered his force as legitimate prisoners of war, entitled to full British protection from the Indians. Testimony of other surviving Americans attests to their similar understanding. However, when the battle ended, Procter ordered those Americans who could to march with his force to the Stony Creek camp. The prisoners with him suffered indignities at the hands of the Indians and a few were murdered in the sight of British officers who failed to interfere. Procter was probably trying to protect the Americans, as well as to retain his force, by promising his Indians a big celebration that night—otherwise they might have seized the nearest prisoners and carried them off.

But that was not all Procter did. He left perhaps 80 American wounded at River Raisin with only four or five interpreters to save them from the wrath of more than 50 Indians who had remained to guard them. Captain William Elliott promised to rush to Malden to get sleighs to transport the wounded.[36] After he left, the Indians found some whisky. That night they murdered a few of the prisoners, and on the morning of January 23 a few others were killed. Some of those who were not murdered were taken to Fort Malden, but most of them were forced to travel to distant Indian villages.

Eventually, the people of Detroit (and of Canada, too) were able to ransom many of the prisoners the Indians had seized, and Procter regained others. The fact remains that Procter (who later discounted his responsibility by asserting the surrender had been without discretion) had proved either his unworthiness to command or his inhumanity, for he did little to remonstrate with the Indians or to prevent them from acting again in the same fashion.

The British had suffered 24 men killed, 12 officers and 149 men wounded.[37] Accurate figures of Indian casualties are unavailable. It is impossible to ascertain the American casualties; probably less than a hundred escaped to Harrison's camp. Certainly more than a hundred were killed in battle or died at the hands of the Indians. The name of Procter would long be reviled at many an American fireside. Neither Brock, now dead, nor Tecumseh, absent at a distant village, both gallant gentlemen, would have permitted such an ending to the battle.

Notes to Chapter VIII

1. Hopkins to Shelby, Ft. Harrison, Oct. 26, 1812, Dillon, *op. cit.*, p. 498.
2. Shelby to Harrison, Frankfort, Nov. 1, 1812, Esarey (ed.), *op. cit.*, Vol. II, p. 192.
3. Edwards to Eustis, Camp Russell, Madison County, Illinois Territory, Sept. 21, 1812, Carter (ed.), *op. cit.*, Vol. XVI, p. 265.
4. Russell to Eustis, Camp Russell, Oct. 31, 1812, *Ibid.*, p. 268.
5. Tupper to Harrison, Urbana, Oct. 12, 1812, Esarey (ed.), *op. cit.*, Vol. II, p. 169.
6. *Ibid.*, p. 170.
7. Tupper to Harrison, McArthur's Blockhouse, Nov. 10, 1812, *Ibid.*, p. 205.
8. Elliott to George Ironside, Foot of Rapids, Nov. 10, 1812, *MPHC*, *op. cit.*, Vol. XV, p. 179.
9. Tupper to Harrison, McArthur's Blockhouse, Nov. 16, 1812, Esarey (ed.), *op. cit.*, Vol. II, p. 217.
10. Harrison to Campbell, Franklinton, Nov. 25, 1812, *Ibid.*, pp. 228–29.
11. Campbell to Harrison, Mississinewa, Dec. 12, 1812, *Niles Register*, Vol. III, p. 316.
12. Campbell to Harrison, Ft. Greenville, Dec. 25, 1812, Esarey (ed.), *op. cit.*, Vol. II, p. 259.
13. Charles E. Slocum, "The Origin, Description and Service of Fort Winchester," *Ohio Archaeological and Historical Publications* (1901), Vol. IX, pp. 261–62.
14. Winchester's Gen. Orders of Oct. 16, 1812, *MPHC*, *op. cit.*, Vol. XXXI, p. 270.
15. Eustis to Gen. C. Irvine, War Dept., Sept. 22, 1812, **National Archives,** Letter Book 6.
16. *The Supporter*, Oct. 31, 1812.
17. Harrison to Eustis, Delaware, Dec. 13, 1812, Esarey (ed.), *op. cit.*, Vol. II, p. 245.
18. Harrison to Eustis, Delaware, Dec. 12, 1812, *Ibid.*, pp. 241–42.
19. Printed in Carter (ed.), *op. cit.*, Vol. X, pp. 402–03, and in other sources.
20. Brock to Prevost, York, Sept. 28, 1812, Wood (ed.), *Documents of the Canadian War*, *op. cit.*, Vol. I, p. 596.
21. Brock to Prevost, Ft. George, Oct. 11, 1812, *Ibid.*, pp. 601–03. There are two interesting eyewitness reports in the issue of *The Supporter*, Oct. 31, 1812.
22. Freer Papers, *MPHC*, *op. cit.*, Vol. XV, p. 208.
23. Esarey (ed.), *op. cit.*, Vol. II, pp. 265–69.
24. Harrison to Monroe, Franklinton, Jan. 6, 1813, *Ibid.*, pp. 299–307.
25. Isaac Day to Harrison, Otter Creek, Jan. 12, 1813, *Ibid.*, pp. 307–08. Day was captured and imprisoned at Fort Malden.
26. Wells to Thomas Cushing, Jefferson County, Kentucky, Feb. 9, 1813, *MPHC*, *op. cit.*, Vol. XL, p. 504.

27. Lossing, *op. cit.*, p. 352.
28. Lewis to Winchester, Frenchtown, Jan. 20, 1813, Esarey (ed.), *op. cit.*, Vol. II, p. 321.
29. Major McClanahan to Harrison, Portage (Carrying) River, Jan. 26, 1813, *Ibid.*, p. 339.
30. Wells to Cushing, Jefferson County, Kentucky, Feb. 9, 1813, *MPHC*, *op. cit.*, Vol. XL, p. 505.
31. McClanahan to Harrison, Portage (Carrying) River, Jan. 26, 1813, Esarey (ed.), *op. cit.*, Vol. II, p. 339.
32. Return of British force in action of Jan. 22, 1813, at Frenchtown, signed by Procter, Wood (ed.), *Documents of the Canadian War*, *op. cit.*, Vol. II, p. 10. The report lists the strength by rank and unit.
33. Casselman (ed.), *op. cit.*, p. 134.
34. Winchester to Sec. of War, Malden, Jan. 23, 1813, Esarey (ed.), *op. cit.*, Vol. II, p. 328.
35. *Ibid.*, pp. 331–33 and 335–38.
36. *Niles Register*, Mar. 6, 1813.
37. Report of Casualties, Wood (ed.), *Documents of the Canadian War*, *op. cit.*, Vol. II, p. 10. Lt.-Col. St. George was wounded at least four times, but recovered.

CHAPTER IX

SIEGE OF FORT MEIGS

AFTER MORE THAN SIX MONTHS OF WAR, the Americans knew too well that the conquest of Canada was no mere matter of marching. They had met with little but reverses, and were to suffer yet another defeat before their North Western Army would be organized effectively enough to strike back at the British.

On the last day of January, Harrison, still encamped at the Portage River, ordered Doctor Samuel McKeehan, surgeon's mate of the Second Ohio volunteers, to proceed under flag of truce to River Raisin to assist the wounded Americans wherever the British would permit. Late that night McKeehan and his escort (a French militiaman) camped near the Rapids and, in spite of a white flag attached to their cariole, were attacked by a party of Indians, who killed the militiaman and wounded the surgeon. McKeehan, taken to River Raisin and then to Fort Malden, was treated with contempt. Procter asserted the flag of truce and the letter of authorization from Harrison were merely pretexts to gain military information.

Harrison had requested McKeehan to secure from Winchester a letter with his report of the battle,[1] but such reports were within the routine military courtesy of the times—as in the case of Hull,

173

who had been allowed this privilege by Brock. Again, it was routine courtesy to pass medical men freely into enemy camps following engagements, although such rights were usually defined in capitulation terms. Neither side objected to the practice of some duplicity in sending dual-purpose flags (the British had clearly done so in another area that same month),[2] but medical men, whose profession was respected by all soldiers, were almost never involved in such transactions because they usually lacked the training necessary to take military advantage of the situation.

Perhaps McKeehan did not act wholly in good faith, but it seems a violation of military ethics to have refused him the right to perform his medical duties. Had Harrison intended him to act principally as a spy, he would have dispatched him sooner and provided him with more than the hundred dollars that he had to use for the physical aid and comfort of the wounded prisoners. Certainly Procter had little excuse for sending McKeehan to Montreal as a prisoner and for detaining him there for more than a month.

The once-confident Harrison began his return march to the Rapids on February 1. Never overly precipitant, he now, in view of the recent American reverses and in accord with a communication from Monroe, resolved to proceed slowly and to ensure the permanency of any gains rather than to strike boldly in surprise raids with the chance of being forced to retreat. He sought to enforce a recent directive from the Secretary of War which required his men to submit letters detailing troop strength or disposition to their immediate commanding officers for approval before transmission to newspapers. This was a measure long overdue; there were virtually no security regulations concerning such vital information, although both sides were avid readers of the other's press.

Arriving at the Rapids on February 2 with his advance force, Harrison issued orders for a general assembly of all units, retaining only small garrisons in the forts and blockhouses in his left and center. His major concern was that the majority of his militia had been assigned for a six-month period which would expire on February 15 for the first of his Kentucky men, and a month later for nearly all the other Kentucky and Ohio units. The respective states had offered bonuses to any militiamen who volunteered to stay for a longer period—but with little success. When these men left, the army, except for the regulars, would consist primarily of Virginia and Pennsylvania troops, nearly all of whose enlistments would expire before April 1.

However, Harrison had discovered that his men would serve beyond their enlistment periods if the army had actually begun a move toward Fort Malden before the expiration dates.[3] By February 6 the artillery was brought to the Rapids, and Harrison prepared to move against Fort Malden with more than 3,000 effectives. But February 15 passed, and still the force lingered in the camp. A long period of thawing weather rendered ice passage perilous and roads impassable. With no alternative, Harrison released the Kentucky men as their terms expired, and called off the winter offensive.

Harrison needed a more permanent position than that of Winchester's camp on the left bank of the Miami—one that would afford control of the river and could be easily defended from land attack. A site was selected on the southern bank just above the present town of Perrysburg, across the river and a bit below the old battleground of Fallen Timbers. The location was ideal—it was well elevated, yet less than 300 yards from the water, with a deep ravine at its rear and a small stream at its right. Here, Harrison had Captain Eleazer Wood, an engineer trained at West Point, lay out a major fortification. The area encompassed about eight acres and was to be strongly picketed with several batteries, seven large blockhouses, and two storehouses. Later named Fort Meigs in honor of the Ohio Governor, the fortification, when completed, would resemble a fortified camp more than a fort.

While most of the men were constructing the fort, the General learned that the British had recently laid the keel of a large vessel at Malden.[4] He then planned a surprise raid against all the British naval vessels laid up for the winter at the Amherstburg Naval Yard.

On February 26 a determined group of some 250 picked men, led by Captain Angus Langham, left the Rapids by sleigh for

Lower Sandusky. Having prepared various incendiaries, they advanced from Lower Sandusky on March 2, expecting to cross the ice of Lake Erie via the chain of islands there, camp on the furthermost island the next day, and on the night of March 3 advance under cover of darkness to burn the *Queen Charlotte* and any other vessels at Malden. When the guide in the lead sleigh discovered open water beyond Middle Bass Island, less than halfway across the lake, the detachment was forced to abandon the raid. Again unseasonable weather had prevented American offensive operations. The men dejectedly returned to the shore of Miami Bay and contacted Harrison, who was there commanding a reserve unit to cover their retreat.

Reasoning that the weather would prevent any serious British demonstration against Fort Meigs, Harrison, now promoted to the rank of a major-general, departed for Cincinnati on March 7 to arrange for reinforcements and to visit his family. Colonel Joel Leftwich, of Virginia, was left in command at the Rapids. Captain Wood had been ordered to Lower Sandusky to supervise defensive arrangements, and Leftwich allowed most of the work on the fort to cease. There was certainly some excuse for this: The supply of forage was nearly exhausted, and the horses were unable to work hauling timber or firewood. Firewood was to be found only at a great distance from camp because of extensive cuttings already made,[5] while the weather and the occasional presence of hostile Indians prevented the dispatch of small parties on wood details. Leftwich permitted some of the pickets to be used for firewood. Even with Wood's return on March 18 there was little work done until the weather improved. But the fort was nearly completed, and with favorable weather it could be finished speedily.

Until this time Harrison had been fairly free of restrictive orders. But as he proceeded toward Cincinnati he received two letters, the first of a series of orders, from Armstrong obviously aimed at lessening his authority and leading to the assumption of operational planning at Washington—though the failure of Hull must have demonstrated the weakness of such control.

True, there had been an appalling lack of co-ordination between the three frontiers of the war; yet to attempt to reorganize the direction of Harrison's supply and operational lines at that late date could well have been a crucial mistake. Armstrong, deeply involved in sectional prejudices and factional politics and admittedly having no high regard for Harrison and western militia, was determined upon such reorganization.

In his letters, Armstrong informed Harrison of a change in offensive plans: Harrison was to hold his positions if at all possible until May, when vessels then under construction at Presqu' Isle would be completed, and then to advance from Cleveland as his main base.[6] Meanwhile, he was authorized the use of only six regiments of regulars. These were the Seventeenth and Nineteenth (already with him but vastly understrength), the Twenty-fourth (then in southern Illinois), and three new regiments to be recruited in Ohio and Kentucky (the Twenty-sixth, Twenty-seventh, and Twenty-eighth). Only in case of dire need could he use the two Ohio militia regiments already requested by him, and no other militia could be ordered. Contrary to British views on the subject, McArthur and Cass were now considered by the American government as released from parole through exchange. They were to be promoted to the rank of brigadiers, for command of the two brigades to be organized from the new regular regiments.

Armstrong's first letter did relay some sensible regulations regarding the future use of militia; that requisitions for all militia should be by number of men desired rather than by units, and that when assembled they could be formed into the same size companies as the regulars used, namely, a hundred privates, eight noncommissioned officers, and five officers. This would correct the oversupply of officers resultant from calls by units and partly prevent the appearance of high-ranking militia officers to overawe regular officers of lower rank.

On March 17 Harrison drafted a reply to Armstrong's first letter, with additional comments made in another letter ten days later.[7] In regard to the immediate problem of man power he explained that he considered the retention of his position at the Rapids essential because it would be impossible to move his ordnance and supplies on a direct route to Cleveland through the swamp, while any circuitous route would produce either extremely slow progress or at least the stringing out of his command over a long line. In either case, it would be inviting an enemy attack. He could have designed a much smaller post at the Rapids and protected it by some 300 men. But such a small force would be unable to oppose the British in the field or even act as a threat against Detroit; and it would not serve to block the British in any westward movement against other posts, since they could circle the Rapids. Moreover, he had never believed he would be restricted in the use of militia, at least not until the regular regiments were formed and in position.

Inasmuch as nearly all Indians of the Northwest were open enemies or dubious neutrals, Harrison continued that he hoped for authority to maintain at least 2,000 effectives to protect his seven western forts (Loramie, St. Mary's, Amanda, Jennings, Brown [on the Auglaize near modern Oakwood], Wayne, and Winchester); Upper and Lower Sandusky; McArthur's and Findlay's blockhouses (provisions were currently stored in each); and Fort Meigs. Before receiving Armstrong's orders, he had already called for Kentucky militia, and early in February the Kentucky legislature had authorized the organization of 3,000 militia for a six-month term in federal service, with Governor Shelby agreeing to lead the force. Shelby had written Harrison on March 20 that Brigadier-General Green Clay had been ordered to assemble half of the force for the march to Cincinnati and the Rapids, as Harrison's letter of March 12 had requested.[8]

Harrison had already called out the two authorized Ohio regiments, but they had reported vastly understrength (one was only one sixth full strength). Since he had already written for the Kentucky men before receiving Armstrong's orders, he had not countermanded the request. Even if the new regular regiments could be raised in time to use that spring, there would be no opportunity to train them and they would be little different from militia. Without the Kentucky militia, many of his posts would be guarded by only fractions of a company, and after April 2 Fort Meigs would have virtually no garrison.

178

Harrison continued to insist that the Rapids, not Cleveland, was the better assemblage point. Movement of supplies to Cleveland was impossible, and any concentration at Cleveland would be worthless if the Americans failed to gain control of Lake Erie. (Furthermore, since Cleveland must have been 130 miles by land from the Rapids, a movement there would render the West incapable of repelling Indian raids before they reached the fringe of the settlements). If naval control were first secured, it would be a simple matter to move the supplies in small boats from the Rapids to Miami Bay, and thence to any destination. Also, he felt the maximum number of men for his area too small—six regiments of 1,000 men each—considering the need for maintaining garrisons and allowing for vacancies and sickness.

Armstrong had taken contrary views as an economy measure and because he was opposed to the use of militia. Perhaps he had been influenced by opinions of others such as Lewis Cass, who had written that militia were not dependable for offensive measures, commenting, "I am well convinced the drafted Militia will never cross the Detroit River." [9] Certainly Armstrong and Congress were justified in seeking to convert to a system of long-term regulars. And they were wise to reorganize the basis for the defenses of the country and authorize a total of 52 regular regiments— moves which should have been made long before. But Armstrong was just as wrong in trying to force Harrison into the predicament of the man trying to change horses in midstream who, upon abandoning his first horse, discovered that he had no other. Harrison just did not have the regulars—they existed on paper only.

In late March Harrison learned that the British were preparing for an attack on Fort Meigs, that navigation on the Lakes would open before the normal time, and that his Pennsylvania and Virginia men would not stay beyond the expiration of their terms. This news boded ill for the security of Fort Meigs, so he left Cincinnati on March 31. His plans were to proceed to the Rapids, stripping posts en route of all but a few men and hoping that Colonel John Miller of the Nineteenth, recently ordered to command Fort Meigs, had preceded him with similar reinforcements.

Colonel Joel Leftwich had left Fort Meigs on April 2 after turning over the command to Major Amos Stoddard of the regular artillery. With this change and an improvement in the weather, work on the fort was resumed, but the small work parties were continually threatened by roving Indians. One soldier was killed on April 4, and four days later another was killed and two were captured.[10] Reinforcements of militia and regulars began to appear at the fort, with the arrival of a militia company on April 8 and Major Ball's squadron of regular cavalry on the following day. On April 12 scouts reported the arrival of Colonel Miller with 140 regulars and 100 militiamen and, knowing that Harrison was accompanying them, Stoddard ordered a fifteen-gun salute.

Arrival of reinforcements permitted the withdrawal of the last of the eastern militia, some 200 Pennsylvanians who had volunteered to stay after their expiration date. However, there still were a few companies of Virginia and Pennsylvania 12-month volunteers. Harrison was pleased to observe that the seven blockhouses, five batteries, picketing, and the earthen parapet around the entire camp were nearly completed. The addition of an interior well and traverses would render it defensible. The fort was well gunned: More than twenty pieces were mounted. Big Battery, the main installation, located at the front of the fort, possessed four eighteen-pounders, the heaviest guns available.

Rumors of British preparations to attack continued to seep into camp, and Harrison employed several friendly Indians to gain other information. Upon learning that several British officers had examined the ground opposite the fort for artillery sites, he ordered the removal of many of the supplies at Lower Sandusky to the greater safety of the interior. In the closing days of April the Grand Traverse was begun—a bank of earth, ten feet high and twenty feet thick, parallel to the river and through the middle of the camp, with a smaller parallel traverse and several perpendicular ones. With probably nearly 2,000 men on hand and more on the way, Harrison wrote Armstrong on April 21 that he would welcome attack. He was soon to get his wish, for on April 28 enemy gunboats and columns were in sight.[11]

After River Raisin, Procter had made no attempt to follow up his victory. He made no move to occupy the Rapids when Harrison had withdrawn; he had too few regulars to establish a post there and already regretted the necessity of maintaining garrisons at Fort Malden, Sandwich, and Detroit and of sending frequent detachments to such places as River Raisin. He was forced to retain his Indians even though they presented constant rationing and supply problems out of all proportion to their usefulness. The French aid to the Americans at River Raisin had convinced him that, given the opportunity, the people of Detroit would do the same. To counteract this possibility, he ordered a number of prominent Detroit residents to leave the Territory, planning to send them to Fort George for disposition at Sheaffe's headquarters.

This action brought a quick reaction from the Detroit residents who were to be evacuated. Twenty-nine of the men, led by Elijah Brush, signed several resolutions dated February 1, stating their views to the effect that such a move was contrary to the Articles of Capitulation, that it was inhumane to separate them from their families, that they had been given their military parole.[12] Woodward, who had been shocked at the aftermath of River Raisin, delivered the document (he may have been the author) to Procter.[13]

Probably as a result of the resolutions, the execution of Procter's order was delayed, but martial law in Michigan was declared— and one must admit that military necessity justified such action. Unless many more men crossed to Canada to take the oath of allegiance, Procter would be little concerned over the eventual fate of the inhabitants of Michigan. Even slightly friendly relations between Woodward and Procter ended when the Judge left for the East, and the civilians were left without a former high official to plead their cause.

Reinforcements of nearly a hundred men of the Forty-first and a few artillerists reached Fort Malden early in February. Within a few days the disposition of Procter's 440 regulars was: 242 at Amherstburg, 117 at Sandwich, and 81 at Detroit. None of these figures included commissioned or noncommissioned officers and probably not even drummers.[14] Procter felt this number insufficient. Perhaps with his approval, 47 prominent Canadians ad-

181

dressed a memorial to Prevost. They stressed the importance of retaining Michigan, indicating a present danger and pleading for the enlargement of the regular force in the vicinity. They pointed out that the harvest had been reduced the past year in the forced absence of the militia and that a crucial food shortage would develop if similar conditions prevailed in 1813.[15] Certainly Procter was glad to have the citizens' petition; even if he got more regulars, he could still call out the militia at need.

Some minor relief was forthcoming for Procter. A naval vessel of size was under construction at Malden, while gunboats were started in the Thames River area. Procter had been promoted to brigadier-general for his success at River Raisin, and Lieutenant-Colonel Augustus Warburton had been detached from service with the Incorporated Militia and ordered to Amherstburg to replace the severely wounded St. George.

Even further relief might come from a plan being formulated to create a ranger unit to co-operate with the Indians, quite independent of regular forces. Procter had enthusiastically replied to Sheaffe's request for comment but indicated that he foresaw an organization of perhaps 500 men serving for the duration of the war—a force that could be used by him in lieu of militia, as well as for service with Indians.[16] Sheaffe and Prevost contemplated only a company or two, but all agreed the leader should be William Caldwell, a colonel in the militia and a veteran of ranger service in the Revolution. More urgent matters arose at the Rapids, and the plan was dropped.

Procter had determined to attack Fort Meigs before the garrison there could receive large reinforcements. His forces were gathered, but incessant rainfall delayed his departure. Tecumseh, who was to lead the Indians by land, was to join the British near the Miami River. On April 24 Procter boarded the *Lady Prevost*, and the expedition set forth. There were six vessels of some size, two gunboats, and several bateaux carrying 26 regular officers, 27 regular sergeants, 469 regulars of lesser rank, 34 militia officers, 22 militia sergeants and 406 militiamen—a total of 984,[17] not including various Indian Department officials traveling by land, a few volunteers, a few men at River Raisin, and the Marine Department under Commodore George Hall. It would be a major demonstration.

Procter stopped well above the mouth of the Miami, where he received reports of scouts sent to the Rapids. On April 27 he moved to Swan Creek to hold an Indian Council. The 1,200 Indians (making a probable total force of nearly 2,400), led by Tecumseh and Roundhead, agreed on the plan of attack, and the force moved to camp on the left bank of the Miami, advancing April 28 to a position below the ruins of old Fort Miami and beyond artillery range of Fort Meigs.[18] This was to be no surprise assault but a careful siege, so the British carefully positioned their artillery within range of the fort—on this could depend the success of the operation.

Captain Dixon of the Royal Engineers had already examined the ground and selected the site for the batteries. The rest of April 28 was spent in unloading and preparing equipment for the batteries, while the Indians crossed the river and captured some livestock before being driven away by artillery fire. Work began that night on the digging of the batteries and continued intermittently the next day; the Indians meantime discharged a covering fire and were also much in evidence on the American side. The American gunners fired a few eighteen-pounders at the forming batteries, but with a supply of only 360 could ill afford to use many until the enemy guns were in position.

The Americans, now aware of the location of the pits, trained a gun on the position for use that night, but the British succeeded in getting most of their artillery (some of it captured at Detroit) positioned by dawn on April 30.

The Americans, having finished their traverses, moved their tents from the river side of the fort to reveal to the British the extensive internal elevated works. The day brought fire from both sides and, even with earthen protection, the Americans had one man killed and six or seven wounded.[19] Furthermore, the Indians had captured the mail from Sandusky.

That night the British gunboats, *Eliza* and *Myers*, each mounting at least a nine-pounder, slipped upstream and shelled the fort, while the British got the last of the guns in place. A British officer

183

listed the four batteries as: two twenty-four-pounders and an 8-inch howitzer, two 5½-inch mortars, two twelve-pounders, and a single twelve-pounder, probably manned by sailors.[20] On May 1, when the real siege began, fire from most of the guns lasted throughout that day and the next.

In these two days the British fired 590 ball shot or shells (some of it red-hot shot, in hopes of blowing up a powder magazine), killing 6 men and wounding 11 others.[21] Indians on the American side of the river fired small arms at the fort. Actually, the damage was small for the total metal discharged by the British. The Americans had no twenty-four-pounders, the British no eighteen-pounders; but Harrison's men recovered spent British twelve-pound balls, thereby increasing their scanty supply.

On the morning of May 3, as the Americans crawled from their cold and muddy underground shelters, they lost some of the complacency they had had during the three days of siege. During the night the British had constructed a battery on the American side of the river only 300 yards below the fort. With this battery (a six-pounder, a 5½-inch howitzer, and a mortar of the same caliber), the British had established a cross fire. Harrison ordered another traverse, and the artillery duel continued that day and the next. He refused Procter's surrender demand of May 4: The fort was in no immediate danger of falling—his men were fairly safe and could cover up the crucial powder magazines faster than British artillery could plow the dirt off. The British were causing damage —the roofs of the blockhouses were about shot off—but Harrison knew that sizable reinforcements were on the way.

Just before midnight on May 4 Harrison received a message from Brigadier-General Green Clay stating that he and his force of 1,200 Kentucky men (not counting officers) were traveling down the Miami in eighteen boats and were within two hours of the fort. Harrison decided to use this force to capture the British batteries across the river, while his own men silenced the small battery below the fort. Clay had waited for daylight to attempt the somewhat dangerous passage through the Rapids and there received orders from Harrison's messenger, Captain John Hamilton. Clay was to detail 800 men, order them to land on the left bank at a spot selected by Hamilton well above the British batteries, capture the batteries, spike the cannon, and destroy the carriages. They were then to retreat *immediately* to the boats and cross to the fort before the main British camp could oppose them.[22] The rest of his force was to land on the right bank above the fort and, with a guide, cut their way through the Indians to safety.

Clay's brigade was already traveling in battle order, so it was a simple matter to direct the leading twelve boats to attack the batteries as ordered. This was the regiment of 796 officers and men commanded by Lieutenant-Colonel William Dudley.[23] Clay, in the thirteenth boat, would land on the right bank with the five boats to his rear, containing William Boswell's Regiment of 623 officers and men (apparently less one company on duty at McArthur's Blockhouse).

Having been assured by Hamilton that he had gun spikes, Dudley's command landed as directed and advanced undetected toward the batteries. Clay, in the lead of the other section, found no guide posted on the shore to designate his landing spot. He started across the river to join Dudley, but discovered that the current would sweep him past that spot. He therefore recrossed the river to land on the right bank below Hollister's Island, much closer to the fort than originally planned. His actions had been observed, and his landing was made under long-range British artillery fire and musket fire from scattered Indians. American artillery dispersed his Indian pursuers, possibly aided by the appearance of Ball's dragoons outside the fort, while Clay reached the fort safely with the fifty men in his boat.

Boswell had seen Clay's attempt to land on the left bank, crossed his five rear boats to Dudley's landing spot, was ordered by Captain Hamilton to land as previously directed, and recrossed the river to land above Hollister's Island. He was beyond range of British artillery, but the initial surprise was over and he was greeted by larger numbers of Indians. His men formed and advanced toward the fort, encountering only scattered Indian resistance. (Many of the Indians were apparently engaged in looting the abandoned supplies in the boats.) He was met by a sally consisting of the Pittsburgh Blues, a few other Pennsylvania and

Virginia 12-month volunteers, and a company of regulars. The combined force gave chase to the Indians but was recalled by Harrison when he noticed that they might be cut off, and all units returned to the fort with their casualties.

Meanwhile, Dudley had advanced in three columns toward the batteries: His left circled behind the batteries and took a position below them; his center acted as a reserve; and Dudley, in the right column, led a successful charge on the small guard at the gun positions. For some strange reason the guns were ineffectively spiked with musket ramrods instead of the normal softer and more expanding metal of regularly designed gun spikes. Dudley had been ordered to withdraw immediately after disabling the guns—this being the crux of the plan because their retreat lay across a level plain that had been cleared of undergrowth before the siege began, while Harrison already had several guns of the fort trained on the position to cut off any pursuit. Probably Dudley had not sufficiently explained the operation to his subordinates, but in any case, they failed to realize that numerous reserves were located in the British camp and that disaster would result if they failed to retreat according to plan.[24]

Perhaps the Kentuckians were just too eager to live up to their battle cry, "Remember the Raisin," and avenge that massacre. At any rate, the left column kept moving toward the British camp with an overzealous young captain, Leslie Combs, in command of the advance company. Harrison frantically signaled from the fort for Dudley to retreat but, whether the signals were observed or not, Dudley committed the majority of his force to aid his left. He should have abandoned these men if he could not recall them, but such objective hardheartedness—sacrificing a few for the safety of the many—is acquired only by long military discipline and, indeed, is not part of the American tradition. Dudley continued to rush after his left wing.

Upon discovering that his batteries had been seized, Procter hurriedly ordered a counterattack. Three companies of the Forty-first and several militia companies rushed from camp toward the scene, accompanied by some of the Indians. Procter recalled some of the Indians from across the river to help protect his main camp.

Perhaps the counterattacking force was outnumbered, but it was in no way confused as to its purpose and was led by probably the three steadiest and most able officers of Procter's command, Majors Adam Muir and Peter Chambers and Brigadier-General Tecumseh. Chambers' men charged and carried the batteries while most of Clay's force, confronted by Muir's group in the woods, lost all semblance of order. Overwhelmed by Indians on their flanks, they had little choice but to obey the British shouts to ground their arms and surrender. Some 150 of those left in the rear retreated in good order to the boats and reached the fort without the loss of a man—the rest of Dudley's force was killed or captured.

Dudley had been killed in the battle, as had several others; the rest were escorted by Indians and a token guard of soldiers toward the British camp near old Fort Miami, there to be loaded into the gunboats. As they neared the fort, the British escort was joined by large numbers of other Indians, and the Americans were forced to run the gauntlet. The survivors were forced inside the old fort, and a general massacre ensued, resulting in forty American deaths.[25] At least one British regular was shot trying to defend the prisoners, but Procter made no attempt to halt the massacre. It was not until Tecumseh arrived and quickly threatened to kill the next Indian that harmed a prisoner that the Indians stopped. Tecumseh is supposed to have inquired of Procter why he had taken no action and, when told the Indians could not be commanded, replied, "Begone! You are unfit to command; go and put on petticoats!"[26]

While the action had been going on both across the river and on the American left, a large sortie burst out to attack the British battery below the fort. Colonel John Miller commanded the force of 350 men: regulars, 12-month volunteers, and a small company of Kentucky militia. Holding their fire until within easy range, the attackers volleyed in unison, charged, and carried the position when most of the defenders retreated. While the guns were being spiked, Captain Uriel Sebree's Kentucky militia, in pursuit of Indians, were attacked by four times their number but held until reinforced—an unusual enough action by militia to warrant comment in Harrison's official dispatches.[27] The British and Indians were the more numerous force and when they formed a general counterattack, Miller sensibly withdrew. He reached the fort in safety with his wounded and 41 British prisoners, including Lieutenants Harris Hailes and Angus Macintyre.

The action of May 5 was over. The opposing sides could total their losses and re-evaluate their positions. Major Peter Chambers made the official report of British casualties: a drummer and 13 rank and file killed; a militia captain, a lieutenant, 4 sergeants, and 41 rank and file wounded (including 4 militia) ; 2 lieutenants, a sergeant, a drummer, and 37 rank and file prisoners (including a militiaman)—a total of 14 killed, 47 wounded, and 41 prisoners.[28] However his report was headed as the battle on May 5 and, although he did record the wounding of a militia captain on May 3 and his subsequent death (Laurent Bondy, who had been captured by Major Denny in the Turkey Creek action during Hull's campaign), he may not have reported any previous enlisted casualties. Certainly fire from American artillery during the previous five days must have caused some injury. Perhaps Procter had ordered him to minimize losses—Adjutant-General Baynes's issuance of Prevost's general orders of May 21 certainly reflects this view, for he failed to mention any British soldiers captured by the Americans in what must have been a further deliberate minimization, even though the men in question had by then been exchanged.

On the surface, the British losses seem rather light; but, as usual, no attempt was made to include Indian casualties—although they may have been large, estimates cannot now be made.

Harrison reported that 81 of his men had been killed and 189 wounded, but none captured.[29] A participant recorded that the British had fired 1,676 artillery shots or shells to that time, and that the Americans had had 12 killed and 20 wounded from this action.[30] This would indicate that roughly 70 were killed and 170 wounded in the sallies from the left and right of the fort on May 5.

Of the action near the British main batteries, Chambers reported capturing a total of 547 (including 21 regulars) but Procter, while enclosing the report in his letter of May 14 to Prevost, noted that the Indians had brought in more than 80 since that time, making a total of perhaps 630.[31] Whether the captured regulars had been sent from Fort Meigs to assist in spiking the guns or had come down the river with Clay is unknown; Harrison did report the capture of Captain Samuel Price, of the Light Artillery Regiment, but without comment. Clay's brigade major reported a total of 635 missing from Dudley's Regiment on May 7.[32] It was known that no Americans were killed in storming the batteries on that side of the river and since only 45 bodies were discovered on the scene after the British withdrew, Harrison believed no more than 50 Americans had been killed there in the later action.

There is some discrepancy in the figures, but available information would indicate that the Americans had experienced a total of 130 killed, 189 wounded (not counting wounded prisoners), and over 600 prisoners.

The real action of the fifth was over, indicated by the British that afternoon when they unplugged some of their guns and fired a salvo. This apparently caused further casualties among the unsuspecting Americans. Procter then dispatched Chambers to carry another surrender request to Harrison. Reiterating his ability and determination to fight, Harrison allowed Chambers to take the two captured British officers with him after a mutual pledge to arrange terms for the other prisoners. During the truce Harrison deployed most of his garrison outside the fort to protect it against any Indian violations and secured the boats abandoned on the right bank by Clay's men. The following day was as rainy as the previous ones had been and, with the passage of various flags back and forth across the river, no fighting occurred.

The terms, apparently arranged on May 7 but formally dated two days later, provided for the immediate and mutual exchange of all regulars held prisoners but with the pledge that they would not serve for the period of a month except on garrison duty.[33] The Kentucky men were to be taken to the vicinity of the Huron River near Sandusky and released under pledge of no further service unless later exchanged.

Procter, now free to renew the siege on a full scale, found he was quite unable to do so. Most of his Indians had left for their villages in the boats captured from the Americans. It was more interesting to them to display their plunder and the captives they held concealed from the British than to watch a fruitless long-range siege of the fort. Too, they realized that the British would not assist in a typical Indian-fashion assault.

Procter's militia displayed a similar impatience but for different reasons. The day before, Procter had received a notice signed by eight militia captains of the Kent and Essex regiments stating that much of the small wheat crop had been winterkilled; that a small crop of spring wheat had been planted; and that, if the militia-farmers were not able to get home soon, it would be too late to plant corn and the entire area would be faced with famine. Indeed, most of their men had already left.[34] It was a *fait accompli* —Procter could only arrange to recover his artillery and stores and raise the siege.

By the morning of May 9 Procter and his regulars, Tecumseh and the few remaining Indians, and a few militia had loaded their artillery on the gunboats and departed to board their larger vessels for Amherstburg. Apparently the Americans fired a few last salvos at the retreating foe and, in return, suffered a few more casualties from the fire of the gunboats.

The battle and the siege were over. Harrison was really in about as good condition as when the action began. The British could boast of winning the action, but they had been unsuccessful in the siege. Two questions remain to be answered: Why did Procter make no attempt to attack other areas, and why did Harrison not pursue Procter's inferior forces after the departure of the Indians?

The first question is the more difficult to answer. If, following the battle, Procter had asked the Indians to attack Fort Winchester or advance to Fort Findlay or other posts along Hull's trail, they would probably have done so. Had he immediately raised the siege and moved by water to attack the Sanduskys (as he did a few months later), he probably could have held both militia and Indians. Why he took no action is a mystery; he had had no great casualties and seems to have had ample ammunition and supplies. The answer must be that he was concerned only in holding Detroit and was uninterested in offensive action in strength, seeing River

Raisin and the Battle of the Miami as purely defensive measures. He missed his last chance to assume the offensive because he had left a powerful enemy buildup within striking distance of his center. The tide had turned; no longer would the British be able to stop American forward moves by a few scattered skirmishes. Pure weight of numbers was beginning to tell, and Procter refused to counteract it in the only way he could have done so—by taking advantage of the great mobility of his Indian force.

It is easy to determine why Harrison made no attempt to pursue Procter. Inasmuch as he would be forced to move by land and had been warned that any territorial gains must be of other than a temporary nature, his forces were far below the number he felt necessary for such a move. Too, he was no longer completely on his own in undertaking offensives. Armstrong's letter of April 3 forbade the use of a land route to Fort Malden, ordered Harrison to await water transportation, and authorized him to use only militia for the defense of the Miami posts.[35] Harrison could do nothing but wait for the effect of the new reorganization policy to provide sufficient regulars and for the naval forces to gain control of Lake Erie and provide transport.

On May 11 Harrison turned the command of Fort Meigs over to General Clay and left for Lower Sandusky to ensure the safety of that area and to arrange some protection for the Kentucky militia soon to be released by the British in the woods to the eastward. At Lower Sandusky he dispatched to Armstrong a proposal that Procter had made, to exchange all the friendly Indians in American territory for the Kentucky prisoners[36]—he was sure that the government would refuse such a nefarious exchange, but he had agreed to forward it. He discovered that men were heading for Fort Meigs from all directions; Cass, with the men he had gathered while on recruiting duty since the end of March, and Meigs, with militia, arrived at Lower Sandusky on May 13. Harrison ordered the recruits back to the interior and sent messengers to turn back militia. His orders precluded any possibility of retaining them on duty, but he was able to salvage some 200 of the Ohio men Meigs had brought, on the grounds that they made up for the deficiency in previous Ohio drafts. These he retained at Lower Sandusky, releasing a similar number already on duty there (from the Western Reserve) to reinforce Cleveland. McArthur was moving up Hull's road with recruits he had assembled, and Harrison ordered some of them to reinforce the scanty garrison at Fort Winchester. Cass and McArthur were ordered to return to their recruiting duties.

Perhaps, as he proceeded to Franklinton to oversee the gathering of his forces for the expected campaign against Fort Malden, Harrison gave thought to the effect of the new reorganization plan. Part of the plan was the creation of nine military districts within the United States, the Eighth comprising Kentucky and Ohio and the territories of Indiana, Illinois, Missouri, and Michigan. The officers assigned to this district had been announced in April. The major ones were Harrison, Major-General in command; Cass and McArthur, Brigadiers commanding the expected two brigades; and Brigadier-General Benjamin Howard, commanding at St. Louis.[37]

If Harrison gave any thought to the problem, he must have realized that he would be ringed with restraints in the forthcoming campaign. What he could not have realized was that the Americans had suffered their last decisive defeat in the West—for that was the significance of the Battle of Fort Meigs.

Notes to Chapter IX

1. Harrison to McKeehan, Hq., Jan. 31, 1813, Esarey (ed.), *op. cit.*, Vol. II, p. 346.
2. See Lt.-Col. R. H. Bruyeres to Prevost, Kingston, Jan. 19, 1813, Wood (ed.), *Documents of the Canadian War, op. cit.*, Vol. II, p. 67.
3. Harrison to Sec. of War, Miami Rapids, Feb. 11, 1813, Esarey (ed.), *op. cit.*, Vol. II, p. 357.
4. Harrison to Armstrong, Miami Rapids, Feb. 20, 1813, *Ibid.*, p. 365.
5. Harlow Lindley (ed.), *Captain Cushing in the War of 1812* (Columbus: Ohio Archaeological and Historical Society, 1944), p. 91. Daniel Cushing served in the Second Regular Artillery and commanded the major battery at Fort Meigs. He was drowned in 1815. His diary affords the best picture of life at Ft. Meigs.
6. Armstrong to Harrison, War Dept., Mar. 5 and Mar. 7, 1813, Esarey (ed.), *op. cit.*, Vol. II, pp. 378–81.

7. Harrison to Armstrong, Cincinnati, Mar. 17 and Mar. 27, 1813, *Ibid.*, pp. 387–91 and 400–03.
8. Shelby to Harrison, Frankfort, Mar. 20, 1813, *Ibid.*, p. 392.
9. Cass to [Eustis?], Zanesville, Nov. 6, 1812, *MPHC, op. cit.*, Vol. XL, p. 499.
10. Lindley (ed.), *op. cit.*, pp. 97–98.
11. Esarey (ed.), *op. cit.*, Vol. II, p. 430. The letter was carried out of camp by William Oliver, the hero of Fort Wayne.
12. *MPHC, op. cit.*, Vol. XXXVI, pp. 283–85.
13. Frank B. Woodford, *Mr. Jefferson's Disciple: A Life of Justice Woodward* (East Lansing: Michigan State College Press, 1953), p. 118.
14. Signed by Lt. Troughton (Actg. Dep. QMG), William Woodbridge Papers, Burton Historical Collection.
15. Sandwich, Feb. 26, 1813, *MPHC, op. cit.*, Vol. XV, p. 251.
16. Procter to Sheaffe, Sandwich, Mar. 20, 1813, Wood (ed.), *Documents of the Canadian War, op. cit.*, Vol. II, pp. 28–30.
17. Embarkation return signed by Maj. Peter Chambers, Apr. 23, 1813, *Ibid.*, p. 38.
18. Chambers to Noah Freer, Amherstburg, May 13, 1813, *MPHC, op. cit.*, Vol. XV, p. 289.
19. Lindley (ed.), *op. cit.*, p. 101.
20. Chambers to Freer, May 13, 1813, *MPHC, op. cit.*, Vol. XV, p. 290.
21. Lindley (ed.), *op. cit.*, p. 101. Maj. Stoddard was one of those wounded and died a few days later of lockjaw.
22. Clay to Harrison, Ft. Meigs, May 13, 1813, Casselman (ed.), *op. cit.*, p. 173.
23. Report signed by Brigade Maj. Thomas W. Pinoitt, Fort Meigs, May 7, 1813, Green Clay Papers, Burton Historical Collection.
24. Lossing, *op. cit.*, p. 486.
25. Casselman (ed.), *op. cit.*, p. 154.
26. Lossing, *op. cit.*, p. 489, note 7.
27. Harrison to Armstrong, Lower Sandusky, May 13, 1813, Esarey (ed.), *op. cit.*, Vol. II, p. 444.
28. Casselman (ed.), *op. cit.*, p. 166.
29. Harrison to Armstrong, Fort Meigs, May 13, 1813, *Ibid.*, p. 170.
30. Lindley (ed.), *op. cit.*, p. 128.
31. Wood (ed.), *Documents of the Canadian War, op. cit.*, Vol. II, p. 39.
32. Green Clay Papers, Burton Historical Collection.
33. Printed in Casselman (ed.), *op. cit.*, p. 152, note 1.
34. Statement of Militia Captains, *MPHC, op. cit.*, Vol. XV, p. 280.
35. Esarey (ed.), *op. cit.*, Vol. II, pp. 412–13.
36. May 13, 1813, *Ibid.*, p. 444.
37. C. K. Gardner, Ass't Adj. Gen., Washington, Apr. 27, 1813, *Niles Register*, Vol. IV, p. 148.

CHAPTER X

FRONTIER EXPEDITIONS; BATTLE OF LAKE ERIE

THE PRESENCE OF A FAIRLY LARGE main force in the north deterred large-scale Indian raids in the settled portions behind, or even west of, the American lines, as Hull and Harrison had believed. Small raiding parties did plague settlers in the interior, just as they had before the war, and led to a series of militia expeditions independent of the main forces. Such an expedition, it should be remembered, had been directed against Peoria in the fall of 1812. But Hopkins' detachment had retreated before reaching the village, and Edwards and Russell had circled it and attacked above. There had, however, been yet another element in the attack— Governor Edwards had ordered Captain Thomas E. Craig's company to Peoria by boat to arrest Indians in the settlements. Arriving there on November 5, Craig was able to occupy the small village inhabited by a few traders and their families. All but a few Indians were absent.

Craig was assured by the Indian Subagent, Thomas Forsyth (who returned with a group of his men to Peoria, his headquarters, on the following day), that Indians near Peoria had participated in raids but they were not then in the area and that the villagers had not aided them. Perhaps Craig might have returned southward without taking any action but that night, as his men were sleeping on the two boats, they were fired on. Craig discovered tracks leading to the village and was convinced that either the villagers had fired or that they were involved in the Indians' activities. He arrested all the men, including Forsyth, and confiscated all arms. By November 9, convinced that neither Edwards nor Hopkins was coming, he burned four houses and barns (more than half of the settlement), assembled the population of forty-two, and took them prisoners to the area of St. Louis, where he released them.[1]

Craig's expedition was unfortunate because Forsyth had some influence over the Indians and apparently had been sending to interior officials all the information he could gather about Indian activities in the Northwest. His removal left no American official between the northern posts on the Mississippi and the forts of Harrison's main force. The following spring Forsyth indicated he would be willing to return to Peoria, but the damage had been done—the Indians had gone over to the British. However, it should be pointed out that Craig had only carried out his orders and that the Indians undoubtedly would have joined the British even if Forsyth had been there. In fact, many of them had done so before Craig's expedition arrived.

Militarily, the Hopkins-Edwards-Craig expedition illustrated the hopelessness of rendezvous-point operations of joint forces by all but the most precisely conducted forces—surely not a job for the average militia unit.

The British were more experienced than the Americans in establishing and maintaining backwoods posts of influence. True, the Amherstburg Indian Department had stagnated under the headship of the nearly eighty-year-old Matthew Elliott. His personal influence could be exerted only when various Indians came to him, and maximum use of the western Indians had not been made. The situation was corrected with the appointment of Robert Dickson as agent for the Indians west of Lake Huron, effective January 1, 1813. Dickson was highly respected by the British—an indication of this was the fact that Prevost reimbursed him for his unofficial expense of the previous year and provided him with a salary of £200 (the same as Elliott's) plus a £300 travel allowance in addition to the customary perquisites of his position.[2]

Dickson's orders were concise: He was to gather as sizable a force of Indians as possible to fight the Americans. Dickson repeatedly produced warrior contingents of most of the western tribes, some to join Procter's forces, some to fight the enemy separately. His appointment was a wise move on the part of the British; on June 21, 1813, for example, Dickson reported at Michilimackinac with 623 warriors.[3]

Until the summer of 1813, Indiana, as well as the other western territories, did what it could to protect itself from Indians. Fort Knox had been moved to Vincennes, and the seat of the Indiana government had been transferred in May to a more sheltered location at Croyden. A new governor, Thomas Posey, a veteran of the Revolution and a former brigadier-general under Wayne, had been appointed in March to succeed Harrison. But the main threat to Indiana had come during Acting-Governor Gibson's period of office.

In February, learning of Winchester's defeat, Gibson had ordered a number of militia companies to construct and garrison a chain of small blockhouses to the north of the settled parts of Indiana. In a way, the policy was successful, but the posts were usually understrength, and the militia and available rangers could scarcely prevent a few Indians from slipping into the interior. Between February and June several people were killed in unrelated instances near Vincennes, Fort Harrison (where a provision boat was attacked in March), and in the area of the Forks. The attacks on the latter area resulted in a series of militia actions.

The Forks, a settlement of more than a hundred families, was located at a fork of the Muscatatuck River and a stream known as Hite Creek. The settlers had erected several crude blockhouses, the largest being Fort Vallonia (near the modern town in Jackson County). Whenever available, United States rangers operated from these posts, but the usual defense depended on volunteers.

On March 18 one man was killed and three were wounded near Fort Vallonia. The next day Major John Tipton assembled twenty-nine militiamen and pursued the Indians upstream. His force sighted the Indians on an island later known as Tipton's Island (north of modern Seymour), killed one Indian, and reported that they believed the others must have drowned.[4]

On April 16 the Indians killed two more settlers and wounded another, and again Tipton's men rode in pursuit. One Indian was killed on the third day of the chase, and Tipton believed that the others would have been captured had not his men disobeyed his orders by firing prematurely.[5] It was generally believed that the raiders were based at the old Delaware towns along the west fork of the White River. On June 11 Lieutenant-Colonel Joseph Bartholomew, in an effort to prevent future raids, left Vallonia with a force of 137 mounted rangers and a few militia infantry. They marched the hundred miles to the Delaware towns, discovered most of them recently burned, found fresh signs around one empty village, and killed one Indian.[6] They destroyed 1,000 bushels of corn and were back in Vallonia by June 21, having failed to remove those responsible for the raids.

A larger expedition set out from Vallonia on July 1, a force of 573 effectives—parts of six ranger companies and Indiana and Kentucky volunteers, commanded by Colonel William Russell.[7] The men proceeded to the Delaware towns, to the Mississinewa area, down the Wabash to Prophet's Town, to Fort Harrison, and Vincennes. Although they destroyed several vacant villages on their 500-mile, four-week circuit, they saw no Indians. Russell believed the Indians had left Indiana for the summer—and, indeed, there were no more raids in Indiana that season.

The defense of Illinois presented somewhat different problems. Apart from the easternmost area, Illinois had more in common with Missouri Territory than with Indiana because Indians could easily reach either Territory by using the Mississippi or Illinois rivers. It was known that Tecumseh had requested that, since the majority of the warriors were in Canada, all the Indian villages be moved west of the Mississippi to facilitate defense. Illinois officials

197

believed that by late spring Indian squaws would be planting their crops in the western location. Furthermore, if the British were driven out of the Detroit area, they expected the Indians to continue the war from western bases. They were aware of Dixon's influence over the western Indians, especially the Sioux, and of the possibility of supplying munitions to these Indians by northern routes, even if the Americans were successful in gaining control of the Upper Great Lakes. Thus, the defense of Illinois called for both temporary and permanent measures.

Governor Edwards reflected the thinking of most people in believing that short-range protection could be best supplied by mounted rangers patrolling in advance of the settlements and by encouraging outlying settlers to congregate in defensible stockades. More permanent measures proposed the construction of small gunboats to patrol the major rivers, the emplacement of a string of forts, probably at Peoria, Prairie du Chien, and the mouth of the Rock River, and reinforcement of Fort Madison (in modern Iowa) and Fort Mason (near modern Hannibal, Missouri). This plan, officials believed, would furnish protection even if the British supplied the Indians with light field guns, and would also lead to permanent American influence over the Indians.

In the spring there had been murders in Illinois, too, especially in the area across the river from Vincennes. Governor Edwards had placed more than 300 militia volunteers in the field and supervised the construction of 17 small posts between the Mississippi and Kaskaskia rivers.[8] He requested authority from the Secretary of War to raise additional companies of United States rangers, in accordance with an act of Congress passed in February, authorizing ten additional companies for the frontier areas.

By April Edwards had learned that the Indians normally living near Peoria and other Indians of the territory, had constructed a fortified headquarters along the Bureau River (now part of the Mississippi and Illinois canal), some 60 miles up the Illinois River from Peoria. Five 20-foot blockhouses completely surrounded by a breastwork, protected by the river at the rear and an impassable swamp at the front, had been constructed.[9] The Indians were known to have been supplied with powder by the British. Therefore, this spot could become a vital threat to the security of Illinois. Late in April there were new raids east of Kaskaskia, and Edwards ordered all his mounted men to attempt to cut off the Indians' retreat. Columns advanced from four starting points and all sighted Indians but there was no real action. Again the Indians had demonstrated their ability to penetrate scattered settlements virtually at will. But a change in American policy would soon be in effect.

In a recess appointment on March 12, Governor Benjamin Howard of Missouri Territory was appointed to the rank of brigadier-general and ordered to command all forces of the entire Eighth Military District not directly assigned to General Harrison. By June 16 Howard had taken command of all military aspects of Illinois Territory, and Governor Edward's active field service ended. Howard was directly under Armstrong's orders so that the direction of the frontier defenses passed to Washington, thus representing a basic change in policy for the internal defense of the Territory.

With the series of Indian raids in check, any plans for the future security of the western territories would depend on the forthcoming campaign of the main army. General Harrison must have doubted that the Americans would have a fleet ready to contest British naval superiority on Lake Erie by June, as Armstrong had indicated. But he was committed to wait for such action before undertaking any general assault on Upper Canada. He could make good use of the extra time, for he had to divert part of his force to Cleveland. Besides, his newly assigned regiments were by no means fully recruited, to say nothing of being trained. While he planned to act only on the defensive until the expected naval battle, there was nothing in his orders to prevent him from undertaking reconnaissance operations or expeditions against the Indians. Such duty could be performed by Colonel R. M. Johnson's recently activated mounted regiment.

Secretary Armstrong had authorized Congressman Johnson to organize a regiment of mounted six-month volunteers in February, specifying that Governor Shelby would commission subordinate officers. Harrison had requested that this regiment be ordered on duty during the acute shortage of soldiers in April; but Shelby had received no direct authority to commission the officers and, since Kentucky law prohibited the awarding of a state office to a member of Congress, he took no action.[10] After the attack on Fort Meigs legal difficulties were quickly overcome, and Johnson's men were ordered to rendezvous on May 20. Harrison rescinded his request for the regiment as soon as the siege had been lifted, but Johnson continued to organize his unit. Meeting Harrison in Cincinnati on May 22, Johnson explained that his officers believed that the men would never serve if rejected for service at that time and, since Armstrong had been the grantor of the initial authority, Harrison accepted the regiment for federal service.

Harrison decided to order Johnson to Fort Winchester and then either employ the regiment against Indian villages or carry out his old plan of advancing by back trails to capture River Raisin and Brownstown. By June 7 Johnson's Regiment of 700 men had proceeded as far as Fort Wayne. Learning of an Indian raid in that area, they pursued the enemy to Five Medal's Village (near modern Elkhart), which had been destroyed in 1812. There Johnson lost the Indians' trail but continued to the St. Joseph River and White Pigeon's Town (in Michigan).[11] On June 14 they were back at Fort Wayne to report that their 200-mile scout had revealed no Indians in any great numbers.

By then, Harrison had learned of the American raid on York, the successful defense of Sackett's Harbor, and the capture of the British Forts George and Erie, on the Niagara frontier. He was also informed that it was believed Procter had moved eastward to bolster the attacked area.[12] Wanting to take advantage of this, Harrison dispatched a letter to Fort Winchester ordering Johnson to advance toward Brownstown with discretion to act as circumstances warranted. [13] At Fort Winchester, Johnson was forced to rest his horses and equip his men before attempting the march, and while waiting was ordered to Fort Meigs by General Clay, who had learned that the British were preparing a new attack on that post. And, indeed, Procter was preparing to move there, instead of to the Niagara area as reported to Harrison.

To assist Procter in guarding Detroit from a land invasion, Tecumseh's followers had settled along the lower reaches of the Huron River, with the Potawatomi further upstream and the Ottawa along the Rouge River. In order to remain secure, Procter needed reinforcements, provisions, and continued control of Lake Erie. Prevost had ordered the rest of the Forty-first to Amherstburg from the Lake Ontario area, but the move had been delayed by the refusal of the center division to release them from service in view of the recent enemy attack in that area. The normal supply lines to Amherstburg had been disrupted by American raids to the eastward, especially on Lake Ontario. Procter, with a growing number of Indians to maintain, was faced with dangerous provision shortages. This justified a further delay on the part of Sheaffe and Brigadier-General John Vincent in advancing the rest of the Forty-first, Newfoundland, and Glengary regiments to Malden.[14]

For the first time in the war the American left was benefiting from action in their center theater. Logically the British right, with what aid could be obtained from the center, should have concentrated on destroying the American fleet building at Presqu' Isle (then beginning to be known as Erie, Pennsylvania), for their security absolutely depended upon it. Just at the crucial time for such action, June, the British changed assignments of several of the highest ranking officers. Sheaffe was relieved from command of Upper Canada and ordered to command the Montreal garrison (a mild punishment for the recent reverses) ; Major-General Francis de Rottenburg was relieved at Montreal and ordered to command Upper Canada, effective June 16. Vincent had been promoted to the rank of major-general earlier that month and remained on assignment in the center zone. Captain Robert H. Barclay of the Royal Navy, an experienced officer who had lost an arm at Trafalgar, arrived at Amherstburg to command all naval units on the Upper Lakes and Lake Erie.

Procter was still high in favor with Prevost, and De Rottenburg was ordered to forward the previously requested reinforcements to him. Procter could not see why they had not been sent before.

201

He felt that, if he had more men, he could not only capture the needed provisions from the Americans, but also successfully lead a sea-land attack against Presqu' Isle [15]—an opinion in which Barclay concurred after having reconnoitered the Presqu' Isle defenses.

By mid-July Procter must have despaired of obtaining substantial reinforcements from De Rottenburg. He had received a letter from him to the effect that a naval struggle on Lake Ontario could be anticipated and that he would be unable to act in conjunction with Procter at present. He added that if the British lost control of Lake Ontario, he would be forced to retreat to Kingston. In such case, he advised Procter to retreat immediately to Lake Superior, avail himself of the transport canoes of the North West Fur Company, and proceed to Montreal by the Ottawa or Grand rivers.[16] Quite rightly Procter was concerned. He rushed a letter to Prevost, telling of De Rottenburg's communique but pointing out that the capture of the American vessels would aid the British center as well as the right, that there would be small chance of regaining naval superiority once it was lost.[17] Further, he continued, if he retreated, they would lose the support of the Indians; he could not attack Presqu' Isle without reinforcements, although he did plan to capture Sandusky.

On July 13 Procter wrote Prevost that his Indians had to be used immediately if he were to hold them, but that they had unanimously balked at attacking Sandusky, favoring another attempt on Fort Meigs. Procter felt such an attack hopeless without siege guns and naval support (the main naval units were en route to Long Point to attempt to get stores and men for operations on Lake Erie). However, since his major defense depended on the Indians, he was forced to accede to their demands.

Shortly after the middle of July, Procter set out from the Detroit area with a small detachment of regulars and militia and at least 1,000 Indians[18] and soon reached the area of Fort Meigs. His transport consisted of two gunboats and numerous canoes and small boats, but his largest artillery were six-pounders.

Harrison's total strength was greater than it had been in May, but his men were still scattered. He had no provision worries at any posts; in fact, he had sufficient rations to maintain his men until December 1.[19] To make sure that Procter would not capture provisions, he ordered men from the interior to bolster his advance posts.

As soon as Harrison received Clay's letter about the planned British attack on Fort Meigs, he ordered Colonel William P. Anderson with 300 picked men to Upper Sandusky. He also sent Colonel Samuel Wells to command at Lower Sandusky, with orders to destroy the stores and retreat if the British appeared. His other new regular regiments were still on only a skeleton basis. He wrote on June 23 that 140 of the Twenty-sixth were at Franklinton and that 300 new recruits were further south but many were paroled prisoners of war that had not yet been exchanged. He added that 60 of the Seventeenth were at Franklinton and another 50 were en route from Cincinnati, but his other partial regiments were unavailable at present.[20]

Harrison proceeded toward Upper Sandusky and arrived at Fort Meigs on June 28. He learned that Indians had been sighted near Lower Sandusky and he departed with Johnson's Regiment for that post on July 1. After learning that a few Indians had been in the area and had killed six civilians, Harrison, feeling there was no present danger to the post, pushed on for Cleveland.

Cleveland, then a town of some 50 residents, was the location of Fort Huntington, a small post established in 1812, presently commanded by Major Thomas Jessup with a 200-man garrison. Major Jessup reported no apparent danger. Harrison had checked his most advanced posts (Presqu' Isle was not under his command) and settled back to await Procter's move.

While at Cleveland, he received a letter from Armstrong ordering him to send Johnson's Regiment to Kaskaskia, Illinois, in answer to Governor Edwards' and General Howard's plea for more men. He immediately ordered Johnson to prepare to march, but the Colonel objected that he could not start such a long march without at least ten days' preparation. He had marched 730 miles in the past fifty days, and his mounts were in poor condition. Moreover, he could take only 400 men, and by the time he arrived there his term of service would be nearly over. On the other hand, if he were allowed to remain with Harrison, he could take a force of nearly 800 rested men on the campaign against Detroit. Therefore, he asked Harrison for permission to stay, accepting full responsibility for such action. In compliance with his orders, the General insisted that Johnson begin his march with as many men as were able, but wrote Armstrong that he believed Johnson would find it difficult to comply.[21]

The British and Indians first revealed their presence near Fort Meigs by killing or capturing a fatigue detail of six soldiers that had left the fort on the morning of July 21. The American artillery opened fire as soon as targets were sighted, but General Clay knew that the fort was in less danger than in May. The garrison was larger and better disciplined; the fort was at least as well gunned, provisions were greater; and the men were more rested and in better health. Clay could not then know that the British were weaker in every respect (except possibly numbers of Indians present) than in May.

When Harrison, at Lower Sandusky, learned the next night of the attack on Fort Meigs, he dispatched orders to McArthur to forward his men and to ask Governor Meigs to call out the militia as a precautionary measure. The rest of Harrison's new regular units were also ordered to march to the northern posts. He felt little apprehension over the situation at Fort Meigs and believed Procter would not attack Fort Winchester because of the danger of finding his retreat cut off. He was still convinced the real threat would be in the Sandusky area and moved his headquarters to Seneca Towns, ten miles south of Lower Sandusky, to await Procter's move.

On July 23 William Oliver, a genius at slipping through enemy lines, reported to Harrison concerning the occurrences of the past two days at the besieged fort. Procter, of course, lacked equipment for a proper siege and had no intention of storming the fort. Little action occurred through July 24, and the Americans had easily recovered the bodies of the men slain on the first day. The whole pretended siege was made to allow Tecumseh's Indians to try a simple ruse. The afternoon of July 26 the garrison heard the unmistakable sound of small arms fire interspersed with Indian yells:

204

Tecumseh's men were indulging in a purely sham battle among themselves, hoping a sally would rush out to the aid of the supposedly attacked Americans. The ruse would probably have worked, but a messenger from Harrison had reached the fort that morning, a Captain McCune of the Ohio militia,[22] who knew no Americans were en route.

The Indians, hoping that Harrison would divert his strength from the Sandusky area to Fort Meigs, staged their sham battle too late. The attack on the fort was clearly over. Procter raised the siege, if it can properly be called that, on July 28 and departed. No casualties seem to have occurred on either side except those on the first day and the subsequent wounding of two American express riders. Procter's judgment in thinking a second siege of Fort Meigs inadvisable had been vindicated, and he was now free to test his opinion that Lower Sandusky was vulnerable to attack.

Harrison, convinced that the Indians of the Sandusky area had been furnishing information to the British, had persuaded them in a council to abandon their nominal neutrality and declare openly for the American side. He could request only that they stand by, since he was not authorized to employ them as a full fighting force and did not yet trust them sufficiently to warrant their use on reconnaissance missions. The arrangement made travel safer through the region and, when Lieutenant-Colonel James Ball reported with 150 regular dragoons, Harrison ordered them to range toward Lower Sandusky. On July 31 Ball's command encountered a party of twelve British Indians and killed all but one.

Harrison had lookouts posted along Lake Erie to inform him of any British movement by water toward Cleveland. Should such a movement develop, he would march there with Ball's men and 200 mounted militia. Having received no word of the presence of any British force in the area, on August 1, as he was preparing to cancel the alert, he learned that Procter's men had appeared near Fort Stephenson.

Fort Stephenson was a stockaded post located at Lower Sandusky. Built in 1812, it had been strengthened since then. Harrison considered the post untenable and, since only some 200 barrels of flour were currently stored there, unimportant to retain. On July 29, believing Procter en route, he ordered Major George Croghan, then of the Seventeenth Infantry, to abandon and burn the post that night. Croghan did not receive the orders until the next day; he then wrote Harrison that he and his men were determined to hold the post.

Harrison sent Colonel Wells to take command of the fort and ordered Croghan to report to him immediately to explain his action. At the same time Harrison countermanded his orders to destroy the fort because he now believed that the British had returned to Malden. Croghan explained that he had received his orders too late to be carried out, that he felt it less dangerous to remain than to be exposed to an Indian attack in the woods, and that he had not meant his curt letter to reach Harrison but rather to be captured by the British. Croghan, a volunteer at Tippecanoe, was well liked by Harrison, and the explanation sufficed. On July 31 Wells was recalled, and Croghan was restored to command with new orders to retreat at the approach of a British force, if time permitted.[23]

On August 1 Procter appeared near Fort Stephenson and dispatched Colonel Elliott and Major Chambers to demand its surrender. Croghan sent a stanch Kentuckian, Lieutenant Edmund Shipp, of the Seventeenth, to parley. Shipp conveyed Croghan's refusal to surrender even in the face of the usual warning of an Indian massacre. Procter then began an intermittent cannonade of the fort from his gunboats and from a howitzer on shore. That night the British emplaced three mobile six-pounders within easy range of the fort and attempted to breach the stockade by artillery fire, concentrating on the northwest angle. The light guns proved ineffective and, on the afternoon of August 2, Procter ordered an assault. He later wrote that he did so only after pressure from his own officers and the Indians.

By 5:00 P.M. the British regulars had advanced in three orderly columns nearly to the edge of the protecting ditch surrounding the stockade. Until then they had been protected by dense smoke and by Croghan's orders to his men to hold their fire. Suddenly Croghan opened up with rifles, muskets, and his one artillery piece,

206

a six-pounder known as "Old Bess" or "Good Bess," loaded with grape and temporarily situated to bear directly on the defensive ditch at point-blank range. The Indians, expected to co-operate in the assault, quickly dispersed. The stockade was undamaged. It would obviously take a long time to create a breach by the use of axes and sabers—too long, considering the casualties among the attackers. Procter recalled his survivors to a position behind a ridge at some distance from the fort, where they remained until full darkness.

The Battle of Fort Stephenson was over. About 9:00 P.M. the British retreated to their boats and began their return to Fort Malden, the Indians following by land. Only one American had been killed and seven wounded.[24] Prevost ascribed the British defeat, in his orders of September 3, to the lack of heavy siege guns and to the unfamiliarity of the Indians with formal assaults. He reported the British losses as: 3 officers (including the assault commander, Brevet Lieutenant-Colonel William Short) and 23 men killed; 1 sergeant and 28 men prisoners; and 3 officers (including Captains Dixon and Muir) and 38 men wounded—a total of 96 British casualties.[25]

Procter could not have been surprised when he received a mild rebuke from Prevost for allowing "the clamour of the Indian warriors to induce you to commit a part of your valuable force in an unequal & hopeless combat." [26]

From his partly fortified camp at Seneca Towns, Harrison had heard the initial cannonade and had sent reconnaissance scouts who assured him the Indians had circled Fort Stephenson for some distance. He hesitated to march against the British until expected reinforcements reached him, but when McArthur and Cass arrived with their men, he sent them (with added Ohio militiamen) to the besieged fort. However, they arrived after the British had retreated and were unable to overtake the Indians.

Harrison lauded the valiant defenders of the fort in his orders of August 8. Croghan was later brevetted a lieutenant-colonel, and his little more than 200 men who had defended the fort received the deserved plaudits of their country. No longer would the Americans be at a psychological disadvantage from undue fear of the

British and Indians; no more would their present posts be attacked by Procter's men.

The British high command had made a fundamental error in strategy by not attacking the American installation at Presqu' Isle; they would soon pay the full penalty for their shortsightedness.

The construction of an American fleet and the subsequent Battle of Lake Erie are outside the scope of this account of the land war in the Northwest, but a summation is germane since, as Hull had predicted, the West was won through these events.

In July of 1812 Daniel Dobbins, master of the *Selina*, had been captured by the British at Fort Michilimackinac. After his release he had reached Detroit in time to be included in that surrender, and had then proceeded to Washington. Before a cabinet meeting, he had recommended that the landlocked harbor of Presqu' Isle (or Erie, Pennsylvania) was the best position for the construction of a fleet for Lake Erie. Dobbins had been appointed a Sailing Master and ordered to Erie to construct gunboats.[27] The Administration had finally decided to act on the suggestion of Hull and others that naval control of the Upper Lakes would greatly aid even large land forces.

Construction had begun by late October. By December Dobbins had reported that a shipwright and ordinary house carpenters had succeeded in laying on the stocks two gunboats with 50-foot keels.[28] When Commodore Isaac Chauncey, Commander of the American Navy on the Great Lakes, had visited Erie shortly afterward, he had approved the existing work, and had ordered Dobbins to cut timbers for two larger vessels. By the middle of March, Noah Brown, a noted shipbuilder, had arrived with experienced assistants and had begun the construction of two brigs above the village. Shortly thereafter, Lieutenant Oliver H. Perry had arrived to command the entire installation and the future navy on Lake Erie.

As the ships began to take form, the danger of British attack increased, and Pennsylvania militia were detailed to guard the site. Presqu' Isle, once the site of a French fort, was now restored with outlying blockhouses constructed at strategic points. Other keels were laid at Erie; and boats large enough to carry fifty equipped soldiers were ordered constructed at Cleveland under the supervision of Major Jessup. Timber was no problem, but Perry was hard pressed to secure ordnance and crewmen because Chauncey, his immediate superior, was seeking to build up his strength on Lake Ontario and released only driblets for service on Lake Erie. The American victories along the Niagara permitted Perry to conduct five vessels from Buffalo to Erie to join his potential fleet. By July 10 his ships were ready, but he lacked men to man them and had yet to force his brigs over the shallow bar at the entrance to the harbor. That occasion, Perry believed, would be the logical time for the British to attack.

The British, with a navy to begin with, had embarked on a less extensive building plan of their own—two gunboats in the Thames area and a sizable ship at Amherstburg. Nominally Barclay commanded the naval units on Lake Erie but he had orders to cooperate with Procter. Moreover, British regulations for combined naval and land operations (and the present situation could be considered such) provided that the senior officer of either service be in command. Brigadier-generals were the equivalent of commodores, so Barclay, rated a captain, was junior to Procter. After Procter's promotion to the rank of major-general in August, the gap was even wider. Thus, Procter could and did influence naval policies on Lake Erie, although the regulations denied him direct command over Barclay's men.

Barclay encountered as much difficulty in getting men from his superior, Commodore James Yeo, as Procter had experienced with De Rottenburg—neither got more than a fraction of his requests. The *Detroit*, the new vessel constructed in the Malden Naval Yards, was launched in July, but there was no available crew and there were few local Canadians who had had experience sailing anything larger than small boats. Barclay believed his force, without the *Detroit*, weaker than Perry's and felt it impossible to attack Perry's ships even while they were still unfinished. Both Procter and Barclay were convinced that the British would be literally starved out of the Detroit area unless provisions were transported rapidly from the East. Thus, the mere existence of Perry's fleet, threatening the security of provision transport by small boats, kept the British vessels impotently standing by, awaiting hoped-for convoy duties for provision boats, just when they should have been concentrating on blockading or destroying the American vessels. Even this worked against the British. The hoped-for provisions failed to arrive, and Yeo had no intention of releasing enough experienced men to man Barclay's vessels.

There was a rather curious parallel in the fact that both the American and British commodores were concentrating on their own fleets on Lake Ontario and denying proper support to their subordinates on Lake Erie. But time worked against Barclay; Perry was constantly getting stronger. Either because he expected eventually to fight with a fully manned fleet, or because he simply overestimated the time required for the operation, Barclay left his anchorage at Long Point too late to attack Perry while he was in the vulnerable position of transporting his brigs over the bar at the mouth of Erie harbor. Thus, on August 5, Barclay set sail for Amherstburg, and Perry's fleet was loose on Lake Erie—two brigs, the *Lawrence* and *Niagara,* each mounting eighteen thirty-two-pound carronades and two long twelves; the *Caledonia* of 3 guns; the *Ariel* of 4; the *Scorpion,* 2 guns and 2 swivels; and the *Trippe, Tigress, Porcupine,* and *Ohio,* each mounting at least one gun.

Perry slowly cruised on Lake Erie looking for enemy provision boats and accustoming his crew to their new vessels. He soon received an additional complement of sailors from the East and invited Harrison to his flagship to discuss future plans. Harrison, who had already dispatched more than a hundred experienced sailors serving in his army, agreed with Perry that the British fleet should be engaged before any invasion of Canada was attempted. Perry was willing to attack Barclay in the Detroit River, if necessary, but he knew the British shortage of provisions would force Barclay to accept combat in the wider waters of Lake Erie. The British had to hurry if they were to provision Amherstburg before the close of navigation; it was already late for slower methods by land. Even if Barclay won the naval battle, Harrison

210

had the largest army ever assembled in that area ready to advance by land. Only an overwhelming and sudden British naval victory could save Procter and even this, granting Harrison were allowed to retain his forces for a winter campaign, could only postpone the inevitable.

Accordingly, Captain Perry (captain by virtue of commanding a vessel, not by permanent rating) stationed his fleet near Put in Bay, establishing a land lookout and dispatching scouting vessels to await Barclay's challenge.

Barclay had meanwhile distributed his crews to man all his vessels, moving his flag to the *Detroit*. He was so careful of his resources that he employed only canoes to reconnoiter Perry's fleet, while hoping for the arrival of a party of seamen known to be en route via land. By September 6 the disappointingly few sailors had arrived and he had no notice of others on the way. He had long since made use of soldiers from Procter's command for the ordinary unskilled labor necessary. On the afternoon of September 9, Barclay set sail to emerge from the Detroit River and attack Perry. The British fleet consisted of: the *Detroit*, 19 guns; the *Queen Charlotte*, 17 guns; the *Lady Prevost*, 13 guns; the *Hunter*, 8 guns; the *Little Belt*, 2 guns; and the *Chippeway*, 1 gun.[29]

Barclay had a slight advantage in the number of guns and had more long-range guns, but Perry's fleet had larger caliber guns and could discharge twice the weight of shot in a general broadside. Barclay brought but six craft to the fight, and Perry eight (the *Ohio* was at Erie at the time). While the combined tonnage of the largest three vessels on both sides must have been about the same, the total tonnage of the British was considerably less than the American. Barclay would seek to fight at a distance to utilize his longer range weapons; Perry would try to close in to take advantage of his thirty-two-pound carronades. The Americans would have the theoretical advantage, but battles had been won by the British against greater odds.

By daybreak of September 10, Barclay's fleet had been sighted from Put in Bay. Perry sailed out and both commanders adopted battle lines, covering their largest vessels. By 11:00 A.M. they were drawing near, a light wind from the southwest at Barclay's back.

Perry continued to advance, but the wind suddenly shifted to the southeast, now favoring Perry. The British lead vessel opened fire shortly before noon; more than three hours later the Battle of Lake Erie was over. The entire British fleet was in American hands. Perry dispatched a hasty note to Harrison, "We have met the enemy and they are ours. . . ."

Factors contributing to the American victory included the wind advantage, the loss of all senior British officers from death or wounds (only partly accounting for the superior maneuvering of the American fleet), and a fluke accident that caused the *Queen Charlotte* to foul the *Detroit* and virtually incapacitate them both. The British had suffered nearly 40 killed, the Americans less than 30; each had about 100 wounded.

In spite of the fact that Prevost had ordered a message sent to Procter stating that, if necessary, Barclay's fleet was to be "sacrificed to the last atom," [30] Barclay was personally blamed by many higher commanders for engaging Perry's fleet. He was eventually exonerated by a court-martial held in England in 1814. But the fact remained that the Battle of Lake Erie left the Americans in absolute control of Lake Erie. Procter would have to depend on his existing resources to defend his sector.

Notes to Chapter X

1. The most informative documents for Craig's expedition are: Craig to Edwards, Shawneetown, Dec. 10, 1812, E. B. Washburne (ed.), *The Edwards Papers*, Vol. III, Chicago Historical Society's Collection (Chicago: 1884), pp. 86–88; and Forsyth to Sec. of War, St. Louis, Apr. 10, 1813, Carter (ed.), *op. cit.*, Vol. XVI, pp. 310–12.
2. By Command of Prevost, Quebec, Jan. 14, 1813, *MPHC, op. cit.*, Vol. XV, pp. 219–21.
3. Dickson to [?], Michilimackinac, June 21, 1813, *Ibid.*, p. 323.
4. Tipton to Gibson, Vallonia, April 24, 1813, Dillon, *op. cit.*, p. 521.
5. *Ibid.*, p. 522.
6. Bartholomew to Gov. Posey, Vallonia, June, 1813, *Ibid.*, pp. 524–25.
7. Russell to Posey, Vincennes, July 25, 1813, Esarey (ed.), *op. cit.*, Vol. II, pp. 497–99.
8. Edwards to Armstrong, Northern Frontier of Illinois Territory, Mar. 13, 1813, Carter (ed.), *op. cit.*, Vol. XVI, p. 304.
9. See Auguste La Roche and Louis Chevalier to Howard, St. Louis, Apr. 4,

1813, and Edwards to Armstrong, Elvirade, Apr. 18, 1813, *Ibid.*, Vol. XIV, pp. 312–14.

10. Shelby to Harrison, Apr. 18, 1813, Esarey (ed.), *op. cit.*, Vol. II, p. 420.
11. McAfee, *op. cit.*, pp. 318–20. McAfee was a captain in Johnson's First Battalion and went on the expedition.
12. Harrison to Armstrong, Franklinton, June 11, 1813, Esarey (ed.), *op. cit.*, Vol. II, p. 471.
13. Harrison to Johnson, Franklinton, June 11, 1813, *Ibid.*, pp. 468–70.
14. Vincent to Baynes, Bazyley's, June 4, 1813, Wood (ed.), *Documents of the Canadian War*, *op. cit.*, Vol. II, pp. 137–38.
15. Procter to McDouall, Sandwich, June 16, 1813, and Procter to Prevost, Sandwich, July 4, 1813, *Ibid.*, pp. 243–44 and 42–43.
16. Twelve Mile Creek, July 1, 1813, *MPHC*, *op. cit.*, Vol. XV, *pp.* 328–29.
17. Sandwich, July 11, 1813, Wood (ed.), *Documents of the Canadian War*, *op. cit.*, Vol. II, pp. 253–54.
18. Casselman (ed.), *op. cit.*, p. 177. Prevost reported to Bathurst that there were 3,000 to 4,000 Indians, but the number seems excessive.
19. Harrison to B. G. Orr, Franklinton, June 22, 1813, Esarey (ed.) *op. cit.*, p. 476.
20. Harrison to Armstrong, Franklinton, June 23, 1813, *Ibid.*, p. 477.
21. Cleveland, July 12, 1813, *Ibid.*, p. 490. Esarey also prints the other pertinent letters of Armstrong, Harrison, and Johnson.
22. Harrison to Armstrong, Seneca Towns, July 28, 1813, *Ibid.*, p. 501.
23. Croghan to Editor of *Liberty Hall*, Lower Sandusky, Aug. 27, 1813, *Ibid.*, pp. 527–29.
24. Croghan to Harrison, Lower Sandusky, Aug. 5, 1813, Casselman (ed.), *op. cit.*, p. 184.
25. Wood (ed.), *Documents of the Canadian War*, *op. cit.*, Vol. II, pp. 50–51.
26. Hq., St. Davids, Aug. 22, 1813, *Ibid.*, p. 48.
27. W. W. Dobbins, *History of the Battle of Lake Erie*, Second Edition (Erie: Ashby Printing Co., 1913), originally published in 1876, it contains an interesting account of the construction of the fleet by the son of the Sailing Master.
28. Lossing, *op. cit.*, p. 509, note 2.
29. Testimony of Lt. Francis Purvis at Barclay's court-martial, Wood (ed.), *Documents of the Canadian War*, *op. cit.*, Vol. II, p. 315.
30. Baynes to Procter, Kingston, Sept. 18, 1813, enclosed in Harrison to Armstrong, Detroit, Oct. 17, 1813, Esarey (ed.), *op. cit.*, Vol. II, p. 583.

CHAPTER XI

BATTLE OF THE THAMES

FOLLOWING THE DISASTER on Lake Erie, General Procter was in an increasingly difficult position. His provisions were low, with little prospect of improvement. He knew Harrison's forces were assembling, while he had growing doubts about the dependability of his Indians, the local Canadians, and probably his immediate higher command.

Certain minor details were in his favor. He had perhaps the largest contingent of Indian warriors yet assembled, and they had been somewhat placated by official notification that those chiefs who had assisted in the capture of Detroit would share in the prize money as subalterns, while the warriors would share as privates. Too, official scales of pensions and death benefits had been announced earlier in the summer to provide for Indian casualties. However, Procter feared the Indians would rebel if he took advantage of his temporary opportunity to retreat eastward with his force.

He still commanded a sizable force of regulars. He had lost 4 officers and 246 men serving under Barclay, but retained command of 48 officers and 831 men.[1] De Rottenburg had finally released most of the Forty-first, which he had been retaining contrary to orders. Some 400 officers and men, mainly of the Forty-first, had arrived at Amherstburg during the previous two months.[2]

His over-all forces were never larger than in September, his provisions never lower. It was not the present that Procter feared, but the future. He had been operating for more than a year at the end of an extremely extended line, constantly faced by greater potential enemy forces and the reluctance of his superiors to maintain his area. He had been proceeding by the book, but the book had never been written to cover his special problems. An outstanding officer might have surmounted his obstacles, but Procter gradually succumbed to continued stresses and soon began to crack under the strain.

On September 12 Procter addressed a letter to De Rottenburg informing him of the probable loss of the navy and that his best course would be to retreat to the Thames River before undertaking any other action. A movement up the Thames past a point of possible navigation would neutralize the American navy, shorten overland supply routes from the East, and permit an easy junction with De Rottenburg, if necessary. Procter knew he could count on obtaining limited provisions along the Thames; De Rottenburg, believing Barclay's ships could carry supplies to Malden with greater safety than via Lake Erie, had ordered them sent there before the Battle of Lake Erie. The chief deterrent to such action would be the effect on the Indians. Instead of consulting the Indians, Procter procrastinated, hoping De Rottenburg or Prevost would approve the plan and thus assume responsibility. True, Prevost then was at Kingston and could be expected to decide immediately, but valuable days were wasted which Procter should have spent in preparing for either the complete evacuation or full defense of his area.

Procter did proclaim a limited martial law on September 13 for western Upper Canada to enable the army to impress supplies and remove disaffected persons from danger points. Slowly, too, he began transferring equipment toward Sandwich but delayed any action that would commit him to evacuation.

As a result of British reverses on Lake Ontario and the possibility that De Rottenburg himself would retreat eastward, a series of letters had been exchanged in July and August concerning Procter's position. De Rottenburg had proposed that if Procter were unable to join him in time for an eastward movement, Procter's isolation would necessitate the abandonment of Amherstburg. In that event, Procter should move to Michilimackinac and use fur company transport canoes to move his force to Lower Canada. Procter had replied indignantly that he had no intention of retreating and that such a move would completely alienate his Indian allies. He had addressed the letter to Prevost over De Rottenburg's head, and the latter protested this action. Of course, De Rottenburg had not retreated (he might have if Prevost had not come to eastern Upper Canada to assume temporary command), and the incident blew over. But Procter's letter of September 12 proposing his own retreat naturally met a cool reception from De Rottenburg.

On September 17 De Rottenburg instructed his adjutant, to reply: Procter was not in a sufficiently dangerous position to warrant a retreat at that time, that he should concentrate on his defenses and consider fortifying the narrows of the St. Clair River to prevent American passage to Lake Huron. Prevost wrote Procter on September 23 loosely authorizing Procter's retreat, but notifying Procter that he was returning to Lower Canada and leaving De Rottenburg in full command. Procter informed Prevost of his plans more fully on September 21, but before receiving any reply to his previous letter he committed himself to retreat. Before the end of September De Rottenburg wrote that he now believed it was time for Procter to join him. Thus, there was a general, if belated, approval of Procter's move.

On September 18 Procter convened an Indian council at Amherstburg.[3] First, he proposed that the Indians retreat with the army to the Niagara frontier. Tecumseh, clad in his customary light-colored leather breeches and jacket and with an ostrich plume in his hair, majestically rose to speak. He pointed out that the British, having forsaken the Indians during the American Revolution, had promised that they would not willfully abandon British soil in this war. Nevertheless, they now proposed to retreat even though they had not seen a single American soldier and had not

216

suffered a single defeat on their own soil. Tecumseh asserted climactically that if Procter would release all the existing Indian supplies, the warriors would defend the area like men, without British help.

Unlike the Indians, Procter could not postpone his retreat until American forces appeared at Amherstburg. He therefore proposed that the Indians accompany the army to a defensible point up the Thames, probably below Chatham, and then make a stand against the Americans. Perhaps Procter sought agreement on this proposal all along and had offered the Niagara plan only for its bargaining effect; he had lost all confidence in the Indians, as they had in him. Though the Indians accepted this proposal, Procter's inability to perform his command function is apparent from this time on.

In preparation for the retreat, orders were given to remove the supplies and men to Sandwich. Lieutenant-Colonel Augustus Warburton, in command of a detachment at Fort Malden, was to await Procter's orders to burn the fort and naval installations; eight days elapsed before these orders were given. Public buildings at Detroit and Sandwich and all excess supplies were similarly dealt with. Procter appeared to be in no haste; had he been, he would have had a protecting start. It was not until he learned that enemy sails had been sighted at the entrance to the Detroit River on September 26 that Procter ordered the move from Sandwich, and the march did not begin until late the following day. Instead of marching with a bare minimum of supplies, the British were encumbered with considerable baggage. Contrary to Procter's orders, they marched by easy stages. Proper rear guard action was also wanting in that they failed to destroy all bridges. The entire command seemed to be deteriorating. If Procter could not (or at any rate did not) do anything about it, Harrison could.

In late July, in the belief that he could field no more than 3,000 regulars, Harrison set about securing militia to bring his force nearer his authorized maximum of 7,000. Most of his Ohio militia and many of his Kentucky men were scheduled for discharge by the end of August. The bulk of his extra force was to come from Kentucky. He had written Governor Shelby on July 20 for 2,000

217

men, inviting him to lead the troops. He wrote, "I have such confidence in your wisdom that you in fact should be the guiding head and I the hand."[4] Shelby had responded with enthusiasm and ordered a rendezvous for all volunteers, preferably mounted, at Newport on August 31.

After the Battle of Lake Erie, Harrison had ordered Colonel Johnson's Regiment to Fort Meigs to await further orders. At the end of August he had requested the gradual assemblage of stores and men, principally from Fort Winchester, Fort Meigs, and Upper Sandusky. On August 29 Harrison had written that his force would be ready to advance by September 10. It was decided that Perry should first engage the British fleet, and Harrison would maintain his headquarters at Seneca Towns to await the naval battle. A secret Indian mission had visited the Wyandot chief, Walk-in-the-Water, and had reported to Harrison that he would try to sway the Indians from the British and, at Harrison's advance, seize and hold the old Huron Church at Sandwich.[5]

After Perry's victory Harrison pushed his preparations; by September 13 headquarters were established north of the mouth of the Portage River. Within two days Governor Shelby and General Cass arrived with the bulk of the invasion force; Johnson's mounted men were to advance overland. McArthur, then commanding at Fort Meigs and initially ordered to report with only his regulars, had requested permission to bring the Kentucky militia as well. Harrison replied that he had been led by General Clay and others to believe that the Kentucky men at Fort Meigs would not serve outside the country. However, he authorized McArthur to advance all but a guard of 80 men and proceed by small boats to join the main body.[6] These troops would complete Harrison's available force, which already included 250 Indians.

The Kentucky Militia were ordered to build a brush fence across the narrowest part of the peninsula south of the mouth of the Portage River and establish their camp in front of it. This simple device secured a safe pasture for the horses during the invasion. Most of the remaining Ohio men were stationed at Upper Sandusky or discharged. Some of the Pennsylvania militia refused to leave the country, but at least 100 elected to accompany Harrison.

218

Harrison, McArthur, and Cass moved all the regulars to Put in Bay on South Bass Island on September 20, the militia joining two days later. Colonel Christopher Rife had been left in command of the Kentucky men detailed as horse and supply guards at the Portage River camp. With a better chance on South Bass Island to ascertain his transport facilities, Harrison felt it necessary to discharge most of the remaining Pennsylvania men and some of the Kentucky militia previously at Fort Meigs. (Others were later discharged at Sandwich.) Delayed by bad weather, the army advanced to Middle Sister Island on September 25. Maximum use was made of Perry's ships and open boats in ferrying the men. A participant's estimate of 4,500 men as the strength at Middle Sister Island could not be far wrong.[7] Johnson's mounted men, ordered to advance to Detroit via River Raisin, would bring the total to 5,000.

Harrison joined Perry on the *Ariel* on September 26 to reconnoiter the approaches to the Detroit River. He discovered that a small blockhouse on Bar Point had been destroyed and that there were no soldiers in the area. (It was the sighting of this scouting vessel that gave Procter his first notice of Harrison's approach.) Back at Middle Sister Island, Harrison issued his invasion orders for the next day.

Detailed orders provided for the division of the landing force into two wings. The right, under Shelby, was to consist of the three militia brigades; they were expected to oppose the Indians who were presumed to be ranging the woods. The left wing would consist of the regulars, Lieutenant-Colonel Ball's dismounted dragoons in advance, followed by the major assaulting force of Cass's brigade, but commanded by Harrison. McArthur's brigade would form a reserve. The guns of the fleet would cover the initial landing, but three light fieldpieces would accompany the advance and other artillery could be landed where needed. Should the landing be unopposed, the front was ordered to wheel to the left and advance toward Amherstburg in two separate columns, being especially alert for an attack on the march.

About 3:00 P.M. on September 27 Perry's fleet hove to three miles below Amherstburg and landed the assault force. As soon

219

as they learned that the British had abandoned the town, the Americans quickly moved to Amherstburg and camped for the night.

Harrison led his force out of Amherstburg early the following morning, but not until the next day did the army reach Sandwich. The delay was caused by the necessity of rebuilding all bridges, maintaining an alert against Indian attacks, and proceeding without horses.

Harrison knew of Procter's plans to retreat along the Thames, but believed he could not pursue until Johnson's command arrived with mounts. British deserters and American citizens indicated that Procter's force consisted of 580 regulars and nearly 1,000 Indians.[8] Actually the estimate of regulars was low, but Harrison knew that Procter could assemble militia along the Thames and pick the battleground. He also knew that many Indians were still on the American side of the river and could either attack Detroit or join Procter. The threat to Detroit must have been the reason for detailing McArthur and his 700 men to Detroit, for McArthur, an officer in whom Harrison had great confidence, had led an expedition up the Thames the year before and should have been the logical choice to accompany the army against Procter.

Actually, the danger to Detroit was overestimated. While still at Sandwich, Harrison wrote that the Wyandot, Miami, and the few hostile Delaware had left the British and sought peace. Harrison had deferred the question for the time but indicated that he felt he should make an example of at least the Potawatomi (who had not yet sought peace), as they were guiltiest and were in the best position to do future harm.[9] He must have realized that the Indians' peace pretensions would be meaningless if Procter defeated him along the Thames. Nevertheless, he gave McArthur general authority to deal with the Indians at Detroit.

On October 1, after learning of the arrival of Colonel Johnson's mounted men at Detroit, Harrison secured the approval of Shelby and of the general officers' council to advance against Procter by land. Johnson arrived with his men later in the day. Cass's and Ball's men, who had left their knapsacks and blankets on Middle Sister Island, were ordered to remain at Sandwich until their equipment arrived, and then to follow Harrison. Cass himself was to accompany Harrison. Provisions, baggage, and ammunition wagons were to be transported by water under Perry's command. With nearly 1,500 men left at Detroit and Sandwich, the pursuit force totaled something over 3,000 men.

On October 2 the pursuit commenced. At noon the army paused along the shores of Lake St. Clair for their meal and heard the usual prebattle address by Harrison. The British failure to destroy the bridges much beyond Sandwich enabled Harrison's advance detachment to reach the mouth of the Thames late on the same day. Harrison was in earnest, if Procter was not.

Harrison's previous information had been that Procter planned to make a stand at Dolsen's, along the northern bank and probably fifteen miles upstream from the mouth of the Thames. Harrison expected to advance the majority of his force up the south bank. Thus, on October 3, his men crossed a small tributary of the Thames and learned that the advance, a detachment of Johnson's Regiment, had surprised a British lieutenant and eleven men engaged in destroying the next bridge, over Jeanette's Creek. The prisoners informed them that the next bridge had already been destroyed. Moreover, until now (since one British soldier had eluded Johnson's men), Procter had had no certain knowledge of Harrison's pursuit. The bridges were quickly repaired, and Harrison's men camped that night at Drake's farm, four miles below Dolsen's.

Until this point Harrison's men had been accompanied by three of Perry's gunboats. But now, though the river beyond was of sufficient depth, the bed was narrow and the banks were high and wooded, providing ideal cover for enemy sharpshooters to sweep the exposed decks. Consequently, the boats were left near Drake's farm with an infantry company for protection, thus reducing the effective force to well under 3,000. Perry joined Cass as a volunteer aide. Probably of more immediate help to Harrison was Matthew Dolsen, a former resident of the area and a relative of the owner of Dolsen's farm. He had joined the Americans as a guide, after deserting from the Canadian militia the previous year.[10]

Confidently the Americans pushed ahead on the morning of October 4. They encountered scattered Indian fire at Dolsen's, but

221

just before reaching Chatham they met their first formal opposition. Indians had torn up the bridge over McGregor's Creek and awaited American efforts to advance. Harrison, believing he was facing the main enemy force, formed full battle order. However, the two six-pounders quickly dispersed the Indians, the bridge was repaired, and the pursuit was continued for another mile. At this point a second creek was won by the mounted men, and its bridge was repaired. Later reports asserted that more than ten Indians were killed in the skirmishes at the two bridges, while the Americans had only two dead.

McGregor's Mills had been fired by the retreating British to destroy a quantity of stored wheat and was still smoking when Johnson's men arrived. Nor was this the only evidence of the nearness of the main British force, for just above Chatham a vessel (probably the gunboat *General Myers*) loaded with ammunition was likewise still burning. The Americans camped that night at Bowles's farm, on the south bank five miles above Chatham. Here the British had left two other burning vessels, possibly the gunboat *Eliza* and the small schooner *Ellen*. [11] Also a distillery containing 5,000 stand of small arms, previously taken from the Americans at various times, had been left in flames. Harrison's men were able to recover two twenty-four-pounders and various assortments of ammunition. Even if the Americans had not yet caught up with Procter, they were forcing him to destroy valuable equipment.

On the morning of October 5 Harrison's men captured two gunboats loaded with ammunition, as well as several bateaux and their crews. The character of the British retreat is obvious from the fact that the only remaining ammunition supply was kept far to the rear of their main body when it was known that Harrison was not far behind. By midmorning Harrison reached Arnold's Mills (modern Kent Bridge), the location of a deep ford, but the last one below Moravian Town. By noon his men had crossed by using the recently captured boats and by having each mounted man carry an infantryman behind him. Two hours and eight miles farther they reached Procter's camp site of the previous night. Three miles before reaching Moravian Town, Johnson's men captured an enemy wagoner, who informed them that the main British force was formed across the road a short distance ahead; American scouts confirmed the fact. Harrison had caught up with Procter, but the latter had chosen the battleground.

Actually Procter had had little to do with the direct command of the British retreat. He had usually been far in advance of his men and had not left sufficiently detailed orders for his second in command, Lieutenant-Colonel Warburton. Also, his later letters contained contradictory statements. For example, in one letter he indicated that he first expected to make a stand near the mouth of the Thames; in another, at Chatham. In reality, he probably still wanted to join De Rottenburg, but Harrison's rapid advance did not permit it. Absent on October 2 to scout the ground far in advance, Procter returned to the main force to find them camped at Dover instead of at Chatham, a few miles upstream. Probably he had left no orders to the contrary and, when he discovered that bake ovens had been constructed, he decided to allow them to remain. However, he left again the next morning for Moravian Town, seeing his family safely on the way to Delaware (west of London), but leaving no certain orders to defend Dover and taking the only experienced field engineer, Major Dixon, with him.

The British at Dover, having learned of Harrison's approach, moved to Chatham. There was a move to depose Procter from command for general neglect of duty, but Warburton refused to accept the command.[12] The British continued to retreat on October 4, but the Indians, although they had consented to the British withdrawal, remained at Chatham. Procter rejoined his troops on October 4 and ordered the further destruction of abandoned materials. Thus, the British fled up the north bank; the Indians, after the brief engagement at Chatham, up the south. Future British operations were seriously affected by allowing their ammunition supply on the gunboats to fall behind and be captured. They would have to fight the coming battle with only such ammunition as had been issued.

Fairfield, usually called Moravian Town from the Indian mission located there, was defensible. The artillery, except a six-pounder,

223

had already been emplaced on the heights. With the river on the left and a ravine in front, it might have been the logical place to engage the enemy. However, Procter, hoping to minimize the effectiveness of the American mounted men and use his own Indians to the best advantage, chose to defend a point two miles down river. If he met reverses there, he could fall back on the town.

Accordingly, the British were halted; the Indians advanced up the south bank and crossed the river at the ford above the town and joined them. Rather haphazardly one section of the British regulars formed two lines in open order across the road—their left on the river, their right on a narrow swamp, a six-pounder their only defense. The other section of regulars was formed in two lines with the narrow strip of swamp on their left. To their right was a large swamp with the Indians positioned just inside the border at an obtuse angle in advance of the British. Tecumseh commanded the Indians' left, Oshawahnah, the Chippewa chief, the right, both ordered to flank the American left.

With two major exceptions it was not a bad arrangement; ammunition for the six-pounder had been left behind; and the men, with less than a normal supply of ammunition, had no hope of securing more. The British had a defeatist attitude and had no confidence in Procter. Moreover, they expected Harrison to follow the customary procedure in employing his mounted men against the Indians, and Procter had thus ordered the British to form in the unusual open order. While on the field awaiting Harrison, he sent an urgent appeal to De Rottenburg for ammunition and provisions. Obviously, future supplies could not affect the battle, but Procter was more interested in his future retreat; and he would of course need supplies if he defeated the enemy attack.

Harrison first planned to use his infantry to make the initial charge against the British regulars, but changed his mind when he learned the Indians' position and that the British were in open order. His cavalrymen would be at a disadvantage fighting the Indians in a swamp.[13] So he decided to advance his cavalry against the British and order his infantry to hold the left flank against the Indians. This last-minute change of orders was probably responsible for the speedy American victory. Because part of Procter's force had already been captured, the Americans outnumbered the British and Indians by at least two to one.

Harrison's infantry regulars, about 120 men, were posted along the river and instructed to capture the enemy artillery. Three Kentucky brigades under Major-General Henry were formed in three parallel lines with their right on the road. The rest of the Kentucky infantry, under General Joseph Desha, were formed at an obtuse angle to Henry's men, their left to the rear, their right guiding on Henry's left. Shelby took station at the vital junction of Henry's and Desha's command; Harrison, Cass, and Perry at the right of Henry's first line. Johnson moved his mounted men in place and, because of the small stretch of swampy land in the middle of the British position, divided his command into two columns. Colonel Johnson led the column to the left of the narrow marsh, and his brother, Lieutenant-Colonel James Johnson, to the right.

The charge was sounded. A few minutes later resistance from the British regulars collapsed after they had fired less than three complete volleys. Colonel Johnson led his column against the Indians' left and met stout resistance from Tecumseh's men. However, Tecumseh was killed, probably by Johnson himself, and when Shelby sent reinforcements, the Indians, too, were forced to retreat. This time the Indians could not be blamed for the British loss; they were fighting more than a half hour after the British.

An American mounted force rode to Moravian Town and took it without opposition. A special detail sped after General Procter, who had fled the field at the first sign of the British collapse. But Procter proved that he could at least conduct his retreat and escaped, although only after abandoning his personal carriage.

One tradition has it that Tecumseh wounded Colonel Johnson before being killed in turn, but this seems open to question. Tecumseh's body may have been mutilated by American souvenir hunters, but there are some grounds for believing that this was a case of mistaken identity and that the Indians succeeded in carrying off Tecumseh's body that night. One thing is not open

225

to question; the Americans had won the Battle of the Thames.

Prevost later reported that 18 officers and 228 men of Procter's force reached Ancaster (south of modern Hamilton) by October 17, but that 28 officers and 606 men were killed or captured during the previous retreat and the battle of October 5.[14] Harrison's summary of the actual battle casualties is probably more accurate. He reported that the British had 12 killed and 22 wounded, while the Americans had 7 killed and 22 wounded, 5 of whom soon died.[15] He also reported 33 Indians dead on the field, but it was known that some Indian bodies were carried off and that some were probably lost in the swamp. Possibly 400 Indians eventually joined British commands to the eastward, but most of them had had enough and joined the Indians at Detroit in suing for peace.

The Americans had captured at least eight intact fieldpieces, two of them twenty-four-pounders, and had recovered another two or three from the river. Wagons and equipment of all sorts were also captured, the total in excess of a million dollars' valuation. Not the least valuable was the recapture of all the standards captured from Hull, Winchester, and Dudley, except that of the Fourth Regiment, which was not in Procter's possession.

Procter had issued orders for his survivors to rally along the Grand River in the area of Ancaster. A few of the sick had been started on their way before the battle; but Procter, knowing that his actions would be held in suspicion, outdistanced most of the others and, having reached Ancaster among the first, spread his version of the defeat. Procter waited until all his men had assembled and then marched them to Burlington Heights, at the head of Lake Erie, to join General Vincent. However, Staff-Adjutant John Reiffenstein, who had not been in the battle but had fled from Moravian Town at the first sign of reverses, had ignored Procter's orders and went straight to Kingston, spreading excited reports of complete disaster and of the imminency of American invasion farther into Canada.

Procter could complain about Reiffenstein's disobedience, but he had no choice except to request an official review of his own actions.

226

A year later in a court-martial at Montreal in December, 1814, Procter was found guilty of parts of all but the first five charges. It was recommended that he be publicly reprimanded and suspended from rank and pay for six months.[16] The specifications of which he was found guilty included: allowing his ammunition to be captured, not choosing the Moravian Heights as the battleground, not making the best disposition of his men for the battle, and not attempting to rally his men personally. Review by the British Commander-in-Chief confirmed the sentence.

Harrison's mounted men spent the night of October 5 in town; the others remained on the battleground, alert against possible Indian attacks. Provisions were scarce on both sides, and the town was stripped of food. The next day was spent in organizing the prisoners into better order and preparing for the return march to Detroit; pursuit of the few enemy survivors was unwise without additional provisions. Late that day, Moravian Town was burned to prevent its reoccupation by the British during the winter. The return to Detroit began on October 7; Harrison accompanied the mounted men and reached Detroit early on October 9. Shelby, with all the infantry and prisoners, arrived at Sandwich late the following day but was unable to cross the river because of a severe storm. By October 13 all the Kentucky militia, except Johnson's mounted men, had left for home. The prisoners were eventually taken to Camp Bull at Chillicothe, where the prisoners of the Battle of Lake Erie had been taken.

When Harrison had first occupied Detroit, he ordered a proclamation, dated September 29, re-establishing civil government in Michigan Territory. Hull was completely out of favor with the national administration, and Attwater, the legal Secretary of the Territory, refused to return from the East. So Harrison retained executive control of the Territory until Washington decided on a new Michigan governor. While Harrison was engaged in defeating Procter, McArthur, acting on his general instructions, had accepted the Indians' assurances of peaceful intentions, but as a precaution had required their women and children to remain near Detroit as hostages.

Harrison, when he returned from the Thames, indicated that he approved the pardoning of all the Indians except the Potawatomi and Miami; but he decided to pardon even these, partly because of McArthur's pledge and partly because he feared that at the first hostile sign on the part of the Americans, all the Indians would join the British.[17] He therefore determined to grant an armistice to all Indians that applied. Walk-in-the-Water had been fearful for the safety of his Wyandots if they came in contact with Johnson's men. Instead of occupying Sandwich, as he had promised, he had prudently withdrawn to the Thames River. From there he had notified Harrison of his location and, in compliance with Harrison's instructions, moved well up a small creek to be out of the way during the campaign along the Thames. The Wyandots had followed Shelby's men back to Detroit and would be included in any armistice.

The provisional Indian armistice was signed on October 14. It granted the Potawatomi, Wyandot, Miami, Ottawa, and Chippewa the right to occupy their normal hunting grounds until the holding of a formal peace council, providing they surrendered all prisoners, remained at peace, and furnished hostages.[18] A contemporary report stated that 3,419 Indians were provisioned at Detroit during the negotiations.[19] The armistice seemed a wise move because the Indians were anxious to return to their normal dwelling places and could be easily watched at these known locations. But it was inevitable that frontier settlers would again be uneasy.

With the Indian situation under temporary control, only the British occupation of Fort Michilimackinac kept the Americans from taking over all their former area. Harrison had planned to send McArthur's men to attack this post, but the storm of October 10 to 12 had blown two provision boats far to the east on Lake Erie, leading Harrison to believe them lost. The lack of provisions made it impossible for an expedition to leave for Michilimackinac before October 19, but a council of senior naval and army officers agreed with Harrison that it would be too late in the season to risk starting an expedition then. Actually, the post was isolated in winter and could easily be attacked in the spring. Moreover,

Harrison believed that the fort might already have been destroyed by the British and the garrison withdrawn to join General Vincent. Cancellation of the expedition northward left a disposable force at Detroit. When Armstrong had learned of the victory on Lake Erie, he had dispatched orders to Harrison to move his men eastward after defeating Procter. However, these orders had never been received because the bearer had been washed overboard during a storm on Lake Erie. Harrison was in doubt as to what to do; on October 19 he turned the command over to Cass and boarded Perry's ships with McArthur's men and the regular Rifle Regiment under Colonel Thomas Smith. A few of the 1,300 men were left at the Bass Islands, but Harrison arrived at Buffalo with most of them on October 24. After enjoying a series of celebrations, Harrison was ready to pursue the next phase of the war. Victory had been achieved in the West. Perhaps this could be the spark leading to victory along the Niagara front.

Harrison had issued a proclamation dated at Sandwich on October 17, permitting the civil officials in that part of Upper Canada held by the Americans to continue in office provided they took an oath to remain faithful to the United States during the occupation. The proclamation also offered parole to all Canadian militiamen, and, in accordance with Eustis' instructions of the previous year, pledged the protection of persons and property. The next day Harrison's general orders had assigned full executive powers under British laws to General Cass for that part of Upper Canada.[20] Cass later reported that this area extended for 130 miles and included an estimated 8,000 inhabitants.

To garrison Michigan and American-held Upper Canada, Cass commanded only 400 effective regulars and 1,300 Ohio militia, but, he reported to Armstrong, 370 more Ohio militia were on the way from Sandusky. Obviously, Cass could garrison only Detroit, Sandwich, and Malden but he relied on several secret agents to report any ontoward event in the rest of his part of Upper Canada.[21]

Cass's greatest initial problem in Michigan was in finding ways to assist the people in Detroit and especially in the River Raisin area to secure food for the winter. On the grounds that the enemy had been responsible for this condition, Cass doled out army provisions whenever he could possibly justify it and constantly appealed to Washington for more substantial aid—appeals which, unfortunately, were not soon answered.

The soldiers at Detroit had built temporary shelters, but work was soon begun on the new fort, to be called Fort Shelby. As the men settled down to more routine garrison duty, numerous instances of slovenly conduct crept into general orders and it was necessary to caution the soldiers repeatedly against selling their clothing, assaulting civilians, or increasing the provision problem by distilling grain. The greatest problem of the garrison was sickness; on November 28, Cass reported more than 1,300 ill. The official report of December 1 indicated only 643 enlisted men present for duty and 1,261 sick, 106 having died since the last monthly report and 23 having deserted.[22] Many of the sick could be available for emergency duty, but the situation greatly complicated Cass's effort to control Upper Canada.

The new definition of the British right front included all the territory they held west of Kingston. Some contact between Detroit and the new British right had been made by messengers. Only three days after the Battle of the Thames Procter had written Harrison requesting the return of private property belonging to British officers. However, Harrison furnished Procter's messenger, Lieutenant John Le Breton, transportation to Fort George and gave him a letter to carry to General Vincent, who was senior to Procter. In this, Harrison indicated that the property in question was under guard at Detroit solely because of American humanitarian considerations. He pointed out that the British had been remiss in caring for similar American property, and he emphasized that the British had allowed, perhaps approved, Indian atrocities.[23] Harrison cited three cases in point, but the crux of his letter was that, while he had restrained the Indians in the campaign on the Thames, he would in the future send his Indians against the people in Upper Canada unless the British restrained theirs.

230

General Vincent soon replied that he joined in any pledge to restrain the Indians' cruelty—indeed, he always had done so.[24] At long last the threat of effective retaliation might prevent the horror of unrestrained Indian warfare.

Cass was soon armed with full political power. He was appointed Governor of Michigan Territory on October 29 and, on December 2, he notified Secretary Monroe of his acceptance—the beginning of a long career in Michigan politics. As his soldiers increased in number, he ordered patrols sent into Upper Canada to buy provisions, administer oaths of loyalty, prevent communication between the inhabitants and the British army, and generally ascertain existing sentiment toward the Americans.

One such group, consisting of Lieutenant Larwill and 65 junior officers and men, left Detroit in December. On December 14 the force reached the Thames River, and camp that night was made around farmhouses on either side of the river. By daybreak the next morning a British patrol, under the command of Lieutenant Henry Medcalf of the Norfolk militia, opened fire on the camp on the south side of the river. The numbers of men engaged were fairly equal: The Americans had 39 officers and men, and the British, 33.[25] But the Americans were caught off guard by the opening volley through the doors and window of the farmhouse and never recovered from their initial confusion. After only token resistance, the Americans surrendered. They had five wounded; the British, none. Medcalf retreated with his prisoners, leaving the wounded at the house.

When Cass learned of the affair on December 17, he sent a detachment of 300 men to the area, only to find that the British had left. The commander of the American detachment, Major Angus Langham, had orders to destroy the property of any local resident who had aided the British, but no positive identification was made. This action at the farmhouse was but the first of a number of minor engagements in that area of Upper Canada.

In the middle of December Cass received orders to leave his command and report to Albany to serve as a witness at Hull's court-martial. Before leaving Detroit he prepared a summary of the situation there. He had already reported rumors of preparations for an Indian attack and had indicated that the appointment of Gabriel Godfroy as an official Indian Subagent in Michigan would help the situation. (The appointment was soon made.) He reported calling 200 Michigan militiamen into service, partly to be able to furnish them provisions legitimately and thus relieve the food shortage among civilians.[26] He further authorized Lieutenant-Colonel Anthony Butler of the Twenty-eighth Regiment, to whom he was to surrender his command, to call out the others if a strong enemy force were known to be approaching. Then Cass, Brigadier-General and Governor of Michigan Territory, left Detroit to become the principal witness against Hull.

Hull, released on parole by the British in October, 1812, had returned to Newton, Massachusetts, and immediately requested a review of his actions. The Secretary of War had promised such action when the state of the service permitted, and the court-martial was ordered for Philadelphia beginning on February 25, 1813, with General Wade Hampton presiding. But this court was dissolved by the President before meeting, and without explanation. A second court was ordered to meet in Albany on January 3, 1814, with Major-General Henry Dearborn presiding, and consisting of one general, four colonels, and eight lieutenant-colonels as members. This court met as ordered, with Martin Van Buren as Judge Advocate.

The first court might have been an unprejudiced body, but the second obviously was not. Dearborn never should have served, since he was presumably busy enough as the Senior Officer during the war and was indirectly involved in the controversy. Hull was hard put to maintain a defense because his own papers had been destroyed and he was refused all access to official government papers. Several of the regular army officers called as witnesses were impartial, but the former Ohio militia officers were uniform in their condemnation of Hull. The court-martial board accepted the worst possible interpretation of all testimony. It is not surprising, then, that he was found guilty on all counts of the charge of cowardice and on most of the charge of neglect of duty and unofficerlike conduct. The court had no choice but to find him innocent of the charge of treason, but still pronounced a death sentence, which President Madison commuted in view of Hull's services during the Revolutionary War.

The Administration had its scapegoat for the failure of the opening campaign. Hull returned home, broken in spirit. Not until Monroe's Presidency was he allowed access to official papers, and even then he found that many were missing. However, when he did obtain the documents, he was able to vindicate himself in the eyes of fair-minded persons by the publication of his memoirs before he died in 1825.

Notes to Chapter XI

1. Return of Right Division of Army of Upper Canada (undated), enclosed in Prevost to Bathurst, Montreal, Nov. 25, 1813, *MPHC, op. cit.*, Vol. XXV, p. 556.
2. Return of Troops arriving at Amherstburg enclosed in Chambers to Freer, Amherstburg, Aug. 12, 1813, *Ibid.*, Vol. XV, p. 353.
3. An eyewitness account of the council may be found in Casselman (ed.), *op. cit.*, pp. 204–07.
4. Esarey (ed.), *op. cit.*, Vol. II, p. 493.
5. Harrison to Armstrong, Seneca Towns, Sept. 8, 1813, *Ibid.*, pp. 537–38.
6. Portage River, Sept. 17, 1813, Burton Historical Collection, Duncan McArthur Papers, Vol. I.
7. McAfee, *op. cit.*, p. 394.
8. Harrison to Armstrong, Sandwich, Sept. 30, 1813, Esarey (ed.), *op. cit.*, Vol. II, p. 555.
9. *Ibid.*, p. 556.
10. Casselman (ed.), *op. cit.*, p. 242.
11. Procter certified that the *Ellen* was burned along the Thames and valued it at £500, *MPHC, op. cit.*, Vol. XV, p. 446. Possibly it had been sunk nearer the mouth of the Thames.
12. Casselman (ed.), *op. cit.*, pp. 224–25.
13. Harrison to Armstrong, Detroit, Oct. 9, 1813, *Ibid.*, p. 238. Casselman printed most of the pertinent letters of the retreat and battle and, on page 224, has a sketch of the distribution of men for both sides.
14. Enclosure, Prevost to Bathurst, Montreal, Nov. 25, 1813, *MPHC, op. cit.*, Vol. XXV, p. 556.
15. Harrison to Armstrong, Detroit, Oct. 9, 1813, Casselman (ed.), *op. cit.*, p. 240. Harrison also reported 601 prisoners.
16. The charges and finding are printed in *MPHC, op. cit.*, Vol. XVI, pp. 179–83.
17. Harrison to Armstrong, Detroit, Oct. 10, 1813, Esarey (ed.), *op. cit.*, Vol. II, pp. 573–74.
18. For terms, see Esarey (ed.), *op. cit.*, Vol. II, pp. 577–78.

19. *The Weekly Register* (Baltimore), Nov. 13, 1813.
20. *MPHC, op. cit.*, Vol. XL, pp. 536–37.
21. Cass to Armstrong, Detroit, Oct. 21, 1813, *Ibid.*, p. 539.
22. *Ibid.*, p. 555.
23. Nov. 3, 1813, Esarey (ed.), *op. cit.*, Vol. II, pp. 591–94.
24. Burlington Heights, Nov. 10, 1813, *Ibid.*, p. 599.
25. Medcalf to Lt.-Col. Bostwick, Dover, Dec. 25, 1813, *MPHC, op. cit.*, Vol. XV, pp. 458–59.
26. Cass to Armstrong, Detroit, Dec. 17, 1813, *Ibid.*, Vol. XL, p. 553.

CHAPTER XII

MACKINAC ISLAND; MINOR ACTIONS

THE BRITISH were not content to accept without a struggle the American occupation of Upper Canada. A complete shifting of the top generals in Upper Canada during December brought fresh viewpoints concerning possible action against the Americans. Major-General Phineas Riall succeeded Procter (who was allowed to return to England) in the command of the British right in Upper Canada; De Rottenburg was reassigned to Lower Canada to command the British left; and Vincent, to command the center. Lieutenant-General Gordon Drummond was now the military head and Lieutenant-Governor of Upper Canada.

Drummond soon wrote Prevost that the Detroit area was weakly garrisoned and could be reoccupied by the British. After Prevost requested details, Drummond, on January 21, 1814, submitted his plan. He reported the American force at Detroit to be 600 (actually there were more). He listed a detachment of his own, made up of 1,760 soldiers, militia, marines, and sailors, which he thought could capture and occupy the Detroit area, as well as destroy the naval vessels in winter anchorage in the Detroit River and at Put in Bay.[1] Most of these men would proceed overland and would need 300 sleighs to ride and to transport three weeks' provisions.

With sleighs, the force could advance an average of 30 miles a day, and would move down the Thames and seize Sandwich and Amherstburg before crossing the ice to capture Detroit and attack the naval vessels.

Prevost approved the plan, providing the entire operation could be completed by February 25. However, as Harrison had discovered the previous year, there was insufficient snow to warrant movement by sleigh, and the ice on Lake Erie was too thin to permit travel on it.[2] The expedition was called off, but patrols and small-scale detachments were maintained to the westward.

A number of British detachments were in American-held Upper Canada during the winter; some on routine patrol, some seeking information for Drummond's proposed expedition, and some attempting to deliver arms to the Indians. The latter action was taken after Matthew Elliott reported that Indian messengers had returned from Michigan with the news that the western Indians had only pretended to espouse the American cause and would, if supplied with arms, follow British orders.[3] Naturally, the British were interested in re-establishing control over these Indians, and attempted to arm those that had supposedly swung to the Americans.

Operations along the Niagara front had been confused and ineffective, and the men were finally moved into winter quarters. Harrison, convinced he could do little there, went to Washington to consult with Armstrong and, on December 22, left for Cincinnati. He had written that he feared the British would try to destroy American vessels on Lake Erie and capture Detroit that winter. Armstrong concurred on the danger to Detroit and, in a radical plan, suggested that the settlements in American-held Upper Canada be completely broken up, partly by turning the Indians against the British that spring.[4] But several days later he wrote that President Madison believed that plan too drastic. He suggested that Harrison refrain from using the Indians but move the male settlers of the region to Detroit. Even this plan would have created a kind of no man's land and, by leading the British to retaliate, would have increased American occupation

236

problems. Nevertheless, American officials again and again proposed some variation of the plan.

Harrison assumed active command of the Eighth Military District by January 19, but remained in Cincinnati. Cass was absent from Detroit, and Harrison ordered Brigadier-General Benjamin Howard to go there to assume command. However, before Howard had started, Armstrong countermanded the order in April. Actually, operations at Detroit that winter and in the spring of 1814 were actively commanded by Lieutenant-Colonel Butler and his several successors.

Toward the end of January Butler had a total of about 1,600 regulars and Ohio militia at Fort Shelby, Sandwich, and Fort Covington, a temporary and lightly fortified post outside the town of Amherstburg. But his sick list that winter constantly ran between 650 and 900.[5] It is doubtful that at any time he commanded an effective force much in excess of 400 at Detroit and another 400 divided between Sandwich and Malden. Besides the force mentioned, Butler had 200 men from the Michigan militia in service. Cass had authorized him to call out the remaining 402 Michigan militiamen, provided the British were known to be moving in force against the region. But these men were scattered over the area to afford some unofficial protection against marauding Indians, and it was doubtful that much more than another 200 would report if a general call were issued.

Forced by a shortage of provisions, Butler sent frequent expeditions deeper and deeper into Upper Canada to purchase foodstuffs. One of these parties approached the settlement of Delaware (west of London) late in January. The guide, Andrew Westbrook had been an active American adherent since Hull's days. The American party captured Lieutenant-Colonel Francis Baby, lately functioning as a Deputy Quartermaster General for the British, and seven other men, some of whom were Canadian militiamen guarding Westbrook's property. Westbrook removed his family and burned his own buildings before returning with the detachment to Detroit. The principal prisoners were forwarded to Harrison's headquarters.

237

The British sent a message protesting the seizure of the men but all but one were clearly connected with the British service. Butler informed General Riall that this particular man was seized in retaliation for the similar British capture of an American merchant and would be released when he was.[6]

Because of several other minor clashes between British and American detachments south of the Thames River, Butler decided to undertake a more sizable raid to discourage further British activity. On February 21 he ordered Captain Andrew H. Holmes, of the Twenty-fourth, to take two fieldpieces and advance a detachment along the shore of Lake Erie to raid the enemy post at Port Talbot. Holmes found travel difficult with his artillery and wagons and abandoned them at Tilbury East.[7] He proceeded to Rondeau and was there joined by Captain William Gill with a detachment. Holmes decided it would be impossible to surprise Port Talbot and moved overland to the Thames River, intending to raid the British post at Delaware.

Striking the Thames miles below the town, Holmes's advance gave chase to a British party but was unable to overtake them and continued up the river to an area called Longwood. Holmes, on learning that a British force was advancing down the river, withdrew his detachment a few miles to a position on the west side of Twenty Mile Creek (20 miles from Delaware), near its junction with the Thames to the north. Holmes's detachment consisted of regulars, Michigan militia, and rangers, probably 170 in all. Some of his original force had become ill and returned to Detroit; a few others functioned as a rear guard.

The British force, commanded by Captain William Caldwell, that was advancing along the Thames consisted of a party of Indians carrying arms to Michigan Indians who had made an armistice with the Americans.[8] On sighting the American force, Caldwell sent a messenger with the information to the post commander at Delaware, Captain Stewart of the Royal Scots. Stewart immediately ordered Captain James Basden to march the light companies of the Royal Scots and Eighty-ninth Foot to Caldwell's position and engage the enemy.

Basden joined Caldwell near Fourteen Mile Creek on March 4

and ordered the combined force of more than 200 to the American position, leaving a guide to direct some more Indians expected to arrive soon. Basden found the Americans occupying the high sides of a deep ravine. He detached his militia to circle to the rear and stormed the heights with his superior force. Amidst heavy fire from the Americans, who were partly protected by log breastworks, the British were forced to retreat. Some fire continued on both sides until it was nearly dark. Then the British withdrew. The Americans had no more than 8 casualties. The British had 14 killed (including 2 officers), 51 wounded (including Basden), and 2 captured.[9] The Battle of Longwood was an American victory. Holmes withdrew to Detroit, and the alarmed British moved their advance post from Delaware to Oxford. Butler had temporarily accomplished his objective.

Several promotions were made in February that affected the command at Detroit. Three new regular rifle regiments were ordered activated, and Butler was promoted to the rank of colonel and assigned to the command of the Second; George Croghan was promoted to the rank of lieutenant-colonel of the same regiment; and William Puthuff, McArthur's Adjutant during the Hull campaign, to the rank of major. Butler requested and received permission to leave Detroit and, in March, turned over the command to Croghan, who had arrived in February. Cass sent in his military resignation on March 3, and it was accepted, effective May 1.

On April 30 Armstrong wrote President Madison that he believed the British had no regulars stationed west of Burlington and that they appeared to consider Fort Erie as the westernmost objective for their summer campaign. He believed Perry's fleet might be employed in transporting troops to the eastward rather than attacking Michilimackinac. This had the effect of slowing up plans for the capture of Michilimackinac; eventually Armstrong wrote Harrison that, although two vessels and some men could proceed on that mission, the majority of the men should be prepared to move to Buffalo.[10] However, Harrison was convinced that his military usefulness was at an end. He had been virtually ignored by Armstrong (who had issued direct orders to

Harrison's subordinates) and by other easterners, and on May 11 had forwarded his resignation.[11] Armstrong accepted it immediately (effective May 31) and appointed Andrew Jackson to fill the vacant major-generalship. McArthur succeeded to the command of the Eighth Military District.

Shortly after May 1 Croghan ordered Captain Charles Gratiot to lead a detachment of 250 men from Detroit to the head of the St. Clair River and construct a permanent fort to hold 300 men. This post, soon named Fort Gratiot, was designed to cut off any water transport between the Thames River and British posts to the north. At the same time, a gunboat was sent on a scouting mission into Lake Huron but returned without any new information concerning British activity. Croghan also hoped to build forts at River Raisin, on Bois Blanc, and along the Thames River. Armstrong, on learning of Croghan's orders to construct Fort Gratiot, first ordered the project abandoned and then reluctantly approved it; there was little else he could do, for it had already been completed, armed with nine artillery pieces, and garrisoned with nearly 250 Ohio militia.

Negotiations now began for a formal treaty of peace with the Indians. A number of Indians had assembled at Fort Wayne in January to receive badly needed food rations, and had been informed at that time that a treaty council would be held later in the year. The next month at Dayton John Johnson had informed the assembled Indians of the general nature of the American proposals, chiefly that the Indians should be prepared to fight for the United States. Madison appointed Harrison, Shelby, and Colonel R. M. Johnson the official treaty commissioners, but the latter two declined to serve and Cass acted in their stead. The council was called to meet at Greenville on June 20. As usual, some Indians were late in arriving, and the council was delayed until July 8, when it convened on the spot where the Treaty of Greenville had been signed in 1795.

Armstrong and other officials had wanted land purchases or trades to be a subject of discussion, but the President had supported Harrison's view that this would only hurt chances of a real peace. The treaty, signed on July 22, bound the 1,450 Indians at the council to fight for the United States (receiving pay and rations)—the Indians were promised that no boundary changes would be made as a result of past actions. The Wyandot, Delaware, Shawnee, and Seneca were officially at peace with the United States, and the few men of those tribes still with the British were considered renegades. The treaty also involved most of the Miami, Potawatomi, Ottawa, and Kickapoo, but many members of these tribes were still British adherents. The Winnebago had not come to the council. Prime factors in the Indians' acceptance of the treaty were the American successes in Upper Canada and the knowledge that an American expedition had sailed in early July to attack Michilimackinac.

After the capture of Michilimackinac in 1812, Captain Charles Roberts had retained his headquarters on the island. He had been constantly faced with provision shortages because his was the last post in a long chain of forts and he frequently had had Indian detachments to provision. In June, 1813, he had applied for a transfer on the grounds of ill-health and, on September 14, had been relieved by Captain Richard Bullock of the Forty-first.

The victories of Perry and Harrison obviously had presented a serious threat to the security of Bullock's command. His first news of Harrison's presence on the Thames had come when the *Nancy*, a hired vessel en route to Malden, had reported it had been attacked at the rapids of the St. Clair River; on October 6 the vessel had been forced to return to Mackinac Island. Bullock had immediately laid plans to build a blockhouse on the hill commanding the fort and arrange an interior water supply for his main garrison. The need for small detachments of regulars and local British militia, the Michigan Fencibles, for expeditions to the west had further reduced the garrison. With the closing of navigation that fall, Bullock's most serious problem had been one of provision supply. New routes would have to be used.

To guarantee a means of supply independent of Lake Erie or the Detroit River, the British before the start of the war had negotiated with the Indians for the purchase of land between

Lake Simcoe and the eastern end of Lake Huron. This route permitted easy passage from Kingston or York via Lake Simcoe and Penetanguishene Bay or Matchadash (at the mouth of the Severn River) to Bullock's command. Bullock had sent a party to Matchadash in November to pick up provisions expected to be on deposit there, but nothing was found. Rations for the garrison had been reduced and, supplemented with Indian meal and fish, had lasted until navigation opened in the spring of 1814.

Orders had been issued by Drummond in the winter of 1813 to construct a number of bateaux to transport supplies that had been accumulating at Matchadash since December. A route via the Nottawasaga Bay had been chosen, since that way required less land passage. Bateaux had been built, but the hoped-for construction of larger craft had to be abandoned. Lieutenant-Colonel Robert McDouall had supervised the construction of the bateaux and had set off with them in late April for Fort Michilimackinac. On May 18 McDouall had assumed command of all British forces in the area, with but one dissenter, Lieutenant Newdigate Poyntz of the Royal Navy, who, although there were no regular naval vessels on Lake Huron, insisted he had sole command of everything afloat, including bateaux. McDouall had disputed the view and lost no time in appealing for a junior naval officer who would accept his orders and command the small detachment of sailors.

The construction of Fort George on Mackinac Island was completed in July. It was a stockaded blockhouse built on the highest point on the island, located several hundred yards to the rear and towering some 150 feet over Fort Michilimackinac.

The expedition against Mackinac was to have been commanded by Major Holmes. But Harrison and Croghan objected to the appointment (it was one of the final causes of Harrison's resignation). Eventually, Croghan was authorized to assemble a larger force and to command the expedition. On July 3 the troops sailed from Detroit, with Captain Arthur Sinclair commanding the naval vessels—the *Niagara, Lawrence, Caledonia, Scorpion,* and *Tigress.* Low water and contrary winds delayed their passage up the St. Clair flats so that it was July 12 before they entered Lake Huron.

Croghan had taken five companies of regulars from Detroit and most of the Ohio militia (commanded by Lieutenant-Colonel William Cotgreave) garrisoning Fort Gratiot, making a total land force of over 700. None of the Americans then knew the exact location of Matchadash Bay; after several days of searching through heavy fog, they abandoned the attempt to destroy the British installation known to be there, and sailed to St. Joseph Island, arriving there by July 20. Croghan found the fort deserted and destroyed it.

Off St. Joseph Island the Americans captured a North West Company vessel, the *Mink*, en route to St. Marys (Sault Ste Marie) to discharge a cargo of flour to another vessel for transhipment to Fort William. Major Holmes was detached to proceed to St. Marys, with Lieutenant Daniel Turner in command of the launches used for passage. Indians traveling in canoes were sighted but escaped with word of Holmes's approach, thus allowing the North West Company men and a force of Indians to get away. Turner discovered a vessel, the *Perseverance* (the one waiting for the *Mink*), on fire just above the falls. He extinguished the fire, stripped the vessel of everything removable, and succeeded in bringing her down to Lake Huron. But she had filled with water, and Turner ordered her beached and burned. Four small boats were captured and were filled with Indian Office goods; the rest of the British property at St. Marys was destroyed.[12]

By July 26 Croghan was anchored off Mackinac Island, and was joined two days later by Holmes and Turner, returned from the Sault. The attack on the island presented certain tactical problems. The guns of the fleet could not be sufficiently elevated to do much damage to Fort Michilimackinac and could not begin to reach Fort George. Too, the beach near the fort was dominated by steep hills. In 1812 the British had landed at the lowest part of the island two miles from the fort and much of the distance lay through dense woods, offering ample opportunity for ambush anywhere along the way. Croghan, with no idea of the number of Indians available to McDouall, waited several days hoping for better weather and more information. Considering the natural defenses of the island—a successive series of heights with the fort and blockhouse on the highest—he was reluctant to try any landing.

Finally, Croghan decided to land where the British had—on the west side of the island. He hoped to entice McDouall into leaving the fort and fighting in the open; if the Americans encountered superior forces, they could retreat to the cover of the guns of Sinclair's ships. Croghan landed on August 4, expecting to advance to a camp site suggested by a former resident and there await developments. He need have had no fear about McDouall's willingness to fight; before Croghan's lines had advanced more than a half mile, they were fired on by enemy fieldpieces.[13]

McDouall certainly did not have as large a force as he wished. At the first sign of American preparations to land, he had stripped the forts of all but a bare minimum of artillerists to man the guns and a garrison of 25 men in each post. He later reported that his disposable force for the field amounted to only 140 men, a probable reference to regulars only. But, inasmuch as some militia and some Indians were on the field, his total field force may have been less than 500. He had chosen to occupy a spot affording commanding ground, a clear-fire field in front, and dense woods on both flanks and the rear. His men protected by a natural breastwork fired their six- and three-pound fieldpieces on the Americans as they came into view.

Croghan ordered Holmes to advance the regulars to flank the British right. At first, the Indians on both flanks offered little resistance, but finally engaged the Americans fiercely—especially a band of Menominee. Croghan then ordered a frontal attack, using his own fieldpiece. Within a short time the Americans suffered a number of casualties, including Holmes who was killed and Captain Benjamin Desha, the second in command of the regulars, who was severely wounded. Further American advance was easily countered by the British occupying still higher ground, and Croghan ordered his men to retreat to the cover of Sinclair's guns. The probing attack had turned into a battle, and the battle into a British victory.

The next day a flag was sent to McDouall to recover Holmes's body and ensure that wounded prisoners were well treated. Sin-

244

clair then ordered sails set, and the Americans departed, hoping to return with a larger force. The American losses: Major Holmes and 12 privates killed; 3 officers and 48 men wounded (Captain Isaac Van Horne, Third Lieutenant Hezekiah Jackson, and a sergeant died shortly after the battle) ; and 2 prisoners—a total of 66 casualties.[14] Since they had fought from cover, the British had suffered only a few casualties. The Indian loss is only a matter of conjecture.

While the Americans were anchored off Mackinac Island, they had heard reports of the British capture of the most remote American outpost, Prairie du Chien.

Located above the Wisconsin River on the east bank of the Mississippi in Illinois Territory (modern Wisconsin), Prairie du Chien had long been important as a center for the Canadian fur traders and as a supply point for Indian lead mines located to the southward. In 1811 the town had a population of about a hundred families, mainly of mixed French and Indian blood, and boasted over thirty houses within the actual settlement.[15] American officials had never attempted to exert more than a shadowy control over either Prairie du Chien or Green Bay. Both areas were nominally under the authority of the Governor of Illinois, but the people felt closer to officials of Missouri, and closest of all to the British, since Canadian fur interests completely dominated the towns.

Despite the fact that thousands of Indians in the area isolated the position of Prairie du Chien and a fort there would need a chain of supporting posts along the Mississippi, Governor Edwards and General Howard (former Governor of the Missouri Territory) in 1813 had requested permission to establish a fort there. Armstrong had approved their request on July 29, but by the time Howard received the authority he considered it too late in the year, and the plans to build the fort were not carried out until almost a year later. Instead, Howard had determined to erect a fort at Peoria, a place of even greater importance to the main settlements to the southward.

In September, 1813, 1,300 men in three separate detachments

had advanced toward Peoria. Howard had ordered four companies of mounted militia from Missouri and Illinois and the available federal ranger companies to form in two groups and advance up both sides of the Illinois River. The third group, consisting of 200 regulars of the First Infantry under Lieutenant-Colonel Robert Nicholas, had been ordered to move up the Illinois River in armed boats. These separate detachments had forced the Indians to flee northward, and on September 29 the land forces had arrived at Peoria, where they learned that Nicholas' men had already beaten off a minor Indian attack. Large detachments had then destroyed the deserted Indian villages at the head of Lake Peoria. Fort Clark had then been built at the lower end of the lake, and a company of regulars left to garrison it.

To prevent large-scale Indian raids on the Mississippi and its tributaries, William Clark, Governor of the Missouri Territory, ordered the construction of large gunboats (such as the *Governor Clark*, with a six-pounder, a four-pounder, and several howitzers [16]), and these gunboats patrolled the Mississippi and its tributaries.

In the spring of 1814 the command of the Illinois and Missouri defenses was in confusion—General Howard had been ordered to Detroit, and Colonel Russell, second in command, was ill. Also, many of the regulars had been ordered away from the Territories, and the service of several ranger companies had expired. Into this vortex stepped Governor Clark, calling for 150 volunteers to serve for two months on the patrol gunboats.[17]

When Armstrong countermanded Howard's orders to Detroit, Howard resumed command at St. Louis on May 8. And fortunately so, for early in May, Clark had left St. Louis to accompany a detachment to Prairie du Chien, where a fort was now to be constructed.

The detachment to Prairie du Chien, consisting of 60 men of the Seventh Regiment (under Lieutenant Joseph Perkins) and 200 militia volunteers, traveled in three gunboats and arrived at its goal on June 2. The men landed without opposition. Twenty Winnebago were captured and some escaped, although several of these were killed in the process.[18]

Both fur company men and Indians at Prairie du Chien had long expected an American attempt to occupy the town. As far back as February, 1813, they had appealed to the British commander at Michilimackinac for aid,[19] their most influential argument being that the Americans, if successful, would gain the trade and support of 5,000 Indians of the area. Robert Dickson (in charge of recruiting Indians for the British) had appeared at the town in May, 1814, and had induced a number of Indians to go with him to Fort Michilimackinac. No British aid had been sent to Prairie du Chien, and only a few Indians and several militiamen (and those only semiofficially part of the Canadian militia) under Captain Dease were there—and they had fled at Clark's approach.

Clark's men occupied the old fur company building and began the construction of a post, named Fort Shelby. On June 5, Clark returned to St. Louis, leaving the regulars, 135 militia, and the two largest gunboats. On June 19 the exterior part of the fort was finished. For the first time an American flag flew on a public building in the modern state of Wisconsin.[20] The regulars moved inside, and the militiamen, except for the men under Captain Frederick Yeiser manning the *Governor Clark*, prepared to return to St. Louis for discharge. Fort Shelby was armed with a six-pounder in one blockhouse and a three-pounder in the other.

Meanwhile, British preparations were underway to retake Prairie du Chien. McDouall, at Mackinac, received his first information of Clark's victory on June 21, confirmed on the following day by some Winnebago who had escaped when Clark had landed at Prairie du Chien. They asserted that eleven Indians had been murdered, including the wife of La Feuille (the main Sioux war chief) and the brother of Tete de Chien (a Winnebago chief).[21]

At this news most of the western Indians that had arrived at Mackinac with Dickson demanded to return westward. McDouall was well aware of the military importance of Prairie du Chien to the Americans, and also that its continued possession by them would go far toward putting the fur trade of the whole Upper Mississippi region into American hands. He appointed William McKay, an old fur man, to the rank of major (he had been the captain of the Michigan Fencibles on the island), gave him the local rank of lieutenant-colonel, and assigned him to command an expedition to Prairie du Chien. McKay's force consisted of Sergeant James Keating of the Royal Artillery and twelve men of the Michigan Fencibles equipped with a three-pounder, as well as two companies of voyageurs and Canadian volunteers under specially commissioned captains, Thomas G. Anderson and Joseph Rolette. The force left in three gunboats, accompanied by 300 Indians traveling in canoes.

On his arrival at Green Bay, McKay was joined by a small company of Frenchmen hastily recruited by Captain Pierre Grignon under authority he had received at Mackinac Island. At the Fox River they were joined by more Indians. McKay moved up the Fox, portaged to the Wisconsin, and arrived in the vicinity of Prairie du Chien on the morning of July 17. Michael Brisbois, a former resident, had pushed ahead the previous night with three volunteers and brought back Brisbois' uncle, who lived a few miles outside the town. Having learned from him the strength of the American garrison, McKay ordered the advance into the town. His total force, he reported, consisted of 120 whites and 530 Indians, mainly Sioux, Winnebago, Fox, Sauk, and Kickapoo.

McKay sent the customary surrender request to the fort just past noon on Sunday, July 17. An equally customary refusal was returned from Lieutenant Perkins. McKay then ordered his artillery piece to commence firing, chiefly at the *Governor Clark* riding at anchor. The vessel, with a 40-foot keel, sails, and protected positions for 32 oarsmen, had as many men aboard as were in the fort, and the high sides protected them from small arms fire. But she had been designed for service against Indians and not to withstand even light artillery. After absorbing several direct hits in the next two hours, Yeiser was forced to slip his cable and float downstream to repair the worst leaks.

McKay turned his artillery against the fort, while vainly attempting to restrain the Indians from firing their muskets from an impossible range. By the morning of July 19 Perkins was in serious trouble. His garrison of 60 men was outnumbered more than ten to one; his ammunition for small arms, which had proved

248

to be defective, was nearly gone, and none was left for his artillery; his water supply was low; and the Indians had started to undermine the fort. When Perkins saw the British preparing to fire red-hot shot, he sent a surrender proposal to McKay. McKay accepted Perkins' terms: The garrison was to be accepted as prisoners of war, protected from Indian vengeance, and allowed to return southward on parole. The actual surrender was delayed until July 20 so that McKay could arrange for protection. The Americans in Fort Shelby had had five wounded, the British only three Indians wounded—an insignificant battle as far as casualties went, but of immense importance in the struggle for control of the Upper Mississippi. Perkins and his men were released on parole by the end of the month, but two of them were retained as British deserters and two others as British subjects.

Meanwhile, General Howard at his St. Louis headquarters was beset with Indian threats in several areas. Indians had killed a woman and five children in Illinois (only twenty-five miles from St. Louis) on July 10,[22] and a larger party of Indians was known to have set out from the Rock River area. Had Howard been in command at the time Clark had started northward, possibly he would never have established a post at Prairie du Chien without first establishing intermediate forts. He hoped to retain Fort Shelby and Fort Clark, but necessary supply expeditions to the forts would employ most of his ranger force, and so he appealed to Armstrong for more men. He had already ordered a detachment to reinforce Fort Shelby, not knowing it would be too late.

Major John Campbell[23] of the First Infantry had departed on July 4 to reinforce Prairie du Chien. His force consisted of 42 regulars (counting their families) under Lieutenant John Weaver in one gunboat and 66 rangers under Lieutenants Jonathan Riggs and Stephen Rector in the other two gunboats.[24] This force of about 100 fighting men proceeded until they met some Indians who told them that the Rock River (Sauk) Indians wanted to hold a council. Campbell beached his boats about four miles above the mouth of the Rock River and held the council, at which the Sauk promised to fight for the United States if furnished equipment.

Shortly after the Indians held the council with Campbell, they learned of the successful British attack on Prairie du Chien. The news came to them through Canadians aboard two gunboats on the Rock River, who had been pursuing the *Governor Clark,* which had escaped at Prairie du Chien on July 17. After learning of the British success, the Indians were determined to attack Campbell's men and aid the British.

By noon of July 21 Campbell's men entered the rapids several miles above the mouth of the Rock River, but the water was low and there was a strong wind. Campbell, in the boat carrying the regulars, was far in advance of the other boats. He was finally forced to land on the Illinois side, where he immediately posted guards on shore. An estimated force of 400 to 500 Indians soon killed the three guards and attacked the boat carrying Campbell and the regulars. Rector's boat moved to Campbell's support, but Riggs's was grounded when he attempted to move into better offensive position. After two hours of fighting the sails of Campbell's boat caught fire, and Rector quickly moved to transfer the regulars to his boat. Overloaded though it was, Rector's boat was of shallower draft, and he managed to get her into easily navigable water and out of musket range. Riggs's men engaged the enemy for some time before he was able to get away. The force proceeded down the river, abandoning Campbell's partly burned craft and giving up the attempt to reach Prairie du Chien. Campbell was himself wounded.

The American losses were as follows: 12 killed and 23 wounded (four of these, including a woman and a child, later died).[25]

The *Governor Clark* caught up with Campbell's command on the way down the Mississippi. When Yeiser arrived at St. Louis, he informed Howard of the attack on Fort Shelby, still unaware of its capture by the British. Howard immediately ordered Major Taylor to lead a force of over 350 regulars, rangers, and militia to relieve Prairie du Chien and evacuate the garrison. Reaching the Rock River on September 4, Taylor decided his eight boats were too large to proceed up the river to destroy the hostile Sauk villages and proceeded toward the rapids to anchor for the night, keeping his command on their vessels.

250

Meanwhile, Lieutenant-Colonel McKay had returned to Mackinac, leaving Captain Thomas Anderson in command of Fort Shelby at Prairie du Chien, now renamed Fort McKay. When Indians reported that a large American force had assembled to proceed up the Mississippi, Anderson ordered Lieutenant Duncan Graham to lead a detachment of 30 men, with a three-pounder and two swivel guns, to the Rock River to organize the Indians for another attack on the Americans. Graham left on August 27 and camped on Rock Island two days later. By the time the Americans were sighted, there were 1,200 Indian warriors present.[26] Many of these were Sauk Indians under a war chief destined to win lasting fame—Black Hawk.

Graham had hoped to delay his attack until the Americans were at the rapids but, on the night of September 4, Indians killed two Americans, and Taylor thus learned of the presence of hostile forces. At dawn one of the American boats was fired on from small arms, and Taylor ordered his men formed to land (the Indians were on the mainland). However, as a preparatory step to protect his potential flank, Lieutenant Rector took his boat upstream, where he met heavy fire from concealed artillery. The three British guns were brought to bear on all Taylor's boats and, because they fired from below a ridge, the American artillery was unable to silence them. Taylor ordered all his boats downstream, and the Indians pursued for a mile or two. Stopping only to bury the dead, Taylor abandoned his attempt to reach Prairie du Chien. The Americans had been fairly well protected from small-arms fire but had suffered the loss of 11 wounded, besides the men killed the previous night.[27]

Reaching the mouth of the Des Moines River, Taylor carried out his alternate orders and began construction of a fort, to be called Fort Johnson. On September 18 Howard died a natural death. A period of uncertainty set in until Colonel Russell arrived in October in St. Louis to take command of the area. Fort Johnson had been evacuated, and there were no American plans to recapture Fort McKay that winter.

Armstrong's orders authorizing Croghan's expedition against

Fort Michilimackinac had specified that he was to attack the British installations known to be in the Matchadash area.[28] On August 9, in his letter reporting the Battle on Mackinac Island, Croghan indicated that he was sending the militia and two companies of regulars back to Detroit on the *Lawrence, Caledonia,* and *Mink,* but was retaining the other vessels and the three companies of regulars to destroy British works on Nottawasaga Bay and to erect his own post. Sinclair anchored off the mouth of the Nottawasaga River on August 13, with the *Niagara, Scorpion,* and *Tigress*—British prisoners had been sufficiently informative for Sinclair to find the area this time.

When McDouall first learned of Croghan's presence off Mackinac Island, he had had a message slipped out ordering the *Nancy* to be taken as far as possible up the Nottawasaga River and a protecting blockhouse built. This had been done under the direction of Lieutenant Miller Worsley of the Royal Navy, recently arrived to replace Lieutenant Poyntz. Croghan landed a detachment on August 13 and discovered the *Nancy.* The next day Croghan and Sinclair set up howitzers on shore and shelled the British position. Worsley had too few men to defend his site and, either as the result of a direct hit by the American guns or because it was actually set by Worsley,[29] the *Nancy* caught fire and was destroyed. The British force fled in canoes farther up the river, and the Americans occupied the blockhouse. A small gunboat, three artillery pieces, and some official correspondence were captured. Croghan decided that the location was too risky for the establishment of an American post which might easily be taken by a force from York. Therefore, he loaded the guns on the American vessels, burned the blockhouse, and prepared to depart with Sinclair on the *Niagara.* The *Scorpion* and *Tigress* were detailed to blockade the river and patrol the whole area. A storm swept away the captured boats towed behind the *Niagara* on the way to Detroit. But that phase of the expedition was successful; there were no British vessels larger than small gunboats left on Lake Huron. Croghan, after arriving at Detroit, received orders to proceed to Kentucky on rest leave. His combat service in the war was over.

Lieutenant Daniel Turner, master of the *Scorpion* and the of-

ficer ordered by Sinclair to command the naval patrol in Lake
Huron, was under orders to prevent British passage between York
and Mackinac Island. Before the end of August he moved his vessels to the Detour (near Drummond Island). On August 31 Lieutenant Worsley, in a canoe, passed unobserved near the American
gunboats, reached Mackinac Island safely, and received McDouall's
permission to return to capture the American vessels. Four small
boats, two having fieldpieces fitted on them, left Mackinac Island
the next evening under Worsley's command. One boat carried
Worsley's sailors; the others, soldiers under Lieutenant Andrew
Bulger. A few Indians in canoes joined the expedition. Carefully
hiding during daylight, Worsley scouted the American position
and waited for darkness to fall on September 3 before closing to
attack the *Tigress.*

Turner, warned by Sinclair that the enemy would seek to capture his vessels, had been advised to keep shifting his position, but
had not done so. By 9:00 P.M. the British were sighted by the lookout on the *Tigress,* and the Americans quickly opened fire. Worsley
ordered his boats to approach both sides of the *Tigress* and the
British boarded. The *Tigress'* crew of 30, under Sailing Master
Champlin, was soon forced to surrender, her officers severely
wounded. The total loss of the *Tigress'* crew was three killed and
three wounded.[30] The next morning the prisoners were sent to
Mackinac Island, with Worsley and most of his men remaining on
the vessel.

The night of September 5, Turner brought the *Scorpion,* which
had been anchored over 15 miles below, to within two miles of the
Tigress and anchored. Worsley slipped his cable at dawn and got
within ten yards of the *Scorpion* before Turner's men noticed the
Tigress was now carrying a British crew. Worsley quickly boarded
and captured the vessel, two Americans being killed and two
wounded. The British loss for both captures was one officer
(Bulger) wounded, seven soldiers wounded, and three sailors
killed—a small price for the capture of vessels and stores valued
by the British at more than £16,000. With the *Tigress* mounting a
twenty-four-pounder and the *Scorpion* a twenty-four-pounder and
a twelve-pounder, the British navy was again in action on Lake

Huron. McDouall would not need to use another new supply route already organized.

During Croghan's absence on Lake Huron, Captain Alexander Gray of the Twenty-fourth, left to command at Detroit, had a force of 280 regulars and rangers at Detroit and Malden, besides the Michigan militia and a company of recently formed ranger scouts under James Audrain. With only some 500 men to guard the whole area, Gray was vulnerable to attack. In early July Andrew Westbrook led a patrol as far as Moravian Town, where he encountered a group of McGregor's and Caldwell's men and killed three of them.[31] But for the most part Gray kept his men close to their posts because he had heard rumors of British preparations to attack Detroit.

Hastily appealed to at Greenville, Cass, as soon as the treaty council had closed, rushed to Detroit with 600 Indians. These he sent on two raids in August, one to the area of Oxford, the other toward Port Talbot. The few militia on the raids could not deter the Indians from plundering the residents' property. Cass, convinced that the Indians were too difficult to handle, discharged them. About the same time a few hostile Indians from the area of Saginaw Bay entered Detroit. They pretended to be friendly until issued rations; then they killed four people, and only artillery fire from the fort prevented them from stealing a number of cattle. All indications pointed to increased British and Indian activity, and Cass appealed to McArthur to send a mounted force to Detroit.

McArthur had been earlier ordered by Armstrong, on August 2, to assemble a force of 1,000 mounted men, collect loyal Indians and proceed against the openly hostile Potawatomi villages of Michigan. In co-operation with the fleet, a post was to be built at the mouth of the St. Joseph River, where the ships taking part could then winter under cover of the fort's guns.[32] However, when British attacks had increased along the American center, the fleet had been sent to that area. McArthur had already issued a call to Kentucky and Ohio for 1,000 mounted volunteers to assemble at Urbana on September 20. He visited Detroit on August 19 and ordered the construction of a permanent fort at the southwest corner of old Fort Malden. When Colonel John Miller, of the Seventeenth, arrived on August 22, McArthur appointed him to command the entire region and departed for Ohio to organize his own expedition.

Miller, who had brought a reinforcement of 300 regulars, was thus able to resume activities in Upper Canada. On August 29 a party of rangers, guided by Westbrook, reached Delaware and captured a few militiamen at Oxford the next day. On their return march they were attacked, and four were wounded and the senior officer wounded and captured.[33] Miller immediately sent out a larger body of rangers, who marched to Port Talbot, burned mills there, and destroyed arms found at Kettle Creek (south of modern St. Thomas), but without any real fighting.[34]

As McArthur prepared for his expedition, a series of conflicting orders were issued from the War Department. The war had not gone well in the East or in the Niagara area. After the entrance of the British into the city of Washington in August, Madison accepted Armstrong's resignation. James Monroe was first Acting Secretary and, after September 27, official Secretary of War. The regulars at Detroit were ordered eastward in September; the order was countermanded in October, and those who had left Detroit were ordered to return; but later that order was countermanded, and the regulars were ordered to stay in the Niagara area. Thus, most of the regulars had left Detroit by the middle of October. Coupled with this was McArthur's failure to raise the 1,000 men for his expedition. The Kentucky men would have flocked to Harrison's standard but were less willing to fight under anyone else, especially since there was a general dissatisfaction in the West with the way the Administration was running the war.

McArthur learned that the Indians of northern Michigan were preparing to move southward to dispute his passage. He had difficulty in arranging for forage for his horses; he could not employ naval vessels; and he had only 650 mounted men. He therefore abandoned his expedition against the Potawatomi but prepared to move his mounted men and 70 Indians from Urbana to Detroit in answer to Cass's appeals for aid. First, he ordered several companies of Kentucky militia, just forming, to reinforce Fort Wayne and Detroit and left for the latter place. Near River Raisin his men captured a few hostile Indians that had gone back on their pledge of peace.

Arriving at Detroit on October 9, McArthur found that Colonel Miller had left with his men and that Captain Charles Gratiot commanded the area, with Captain Joel Collins commanding Fort Shelby. Cass had awarded Gratiot a brevet commission of colonel in the Michigan militia to permit him more effectively to command the Michigan men on active duty. McArthur was pleased with this arrangement and, since he knew Major-General George Izard was experiencing difficulties to the eastward, determined to create a diversion in his favor and at the same time secure the safety of Michigan for the winter. He would undertake a large-scale raid in Upper Canada, attack Burlington, and join forces with Izard. But American expeditions from Detroit had never been secret, because the residents gossiped and men of British sentiment quickly informed the British of American plans. To preserve secrecy McArthur announced that his operation was to be against the Indians of the Saginaw Bay region.

On October 23 McArthur led his mounted men out of Detroit up the west side of Lake St. Clair, crossed the St. Clair River, and reached Baldoon on October 27. Forced to wait for boats to cross Big Bear Creek, he then rode to Moravian Town, reached Oxford on November 4, advanced to Burford, and arrived at Brantford on the Grand River on November 6.[35] There he found the river too high to ford and learned that a British force lay between that point and Burlington. Until now his advance had been so rapid and security measures so strict that the British had not been able to form any force to oppose him. McArthur left some of his men at the Grand River, where they successfully engaged a force of British regulars, and took the rest of the men to Malcom's Mills (near Burford), engaging and defeating a body of militia at that point. Learning that Izard had left Canada, McArthur abandoned his plans to advance farther and moved southward to destroy some mills at Dover. Then he swung westward and returned to Detroit, reaching Sandwich on November 17.

McArthur's twenty-four-day trip had destroyed most of the flour mills in Upper Canada west of the Grand River and thus forced the British to revise their plans for feeding their regulars that winter; he had also destroyed some arms and secured the safety of Michigan from British (but not Indian) attacks that winter. He reported his total loss as one killed and 6 wounded, asserting the British had had 18 killed and 120 prisoners in the engagements near the Grand River.[36]

Rations at Detroit were still not abundant. A proclamation was issued on November 5 requiring residents of American-held Upper Canada to deliver all surplus flour, wheat, and oats to Detroit, Dover, or Amherstburg for sale to the American government.[37] Carrying out these orders required a number of American detachments in Upper Canada but, all in all, 1814 closed with the situation well in hand for the Americans in the West. McArthur returned to Ohio to contemplate attempts to recover Mackinac and further harass Upper Canada in the next campaign.

Notes to Chapter XII

1. Drummond to Prevost, Kingston, Jan. 21, 1814, *MPHC, op. cit.*, Vol. XV, pp. 473–76.
2. Drummond to Prevost, York, Feb. 19, 1814, *Ibid.*, p. 493.
3. Elliott to Maj. Glegg, Beach, Jan. 31, 1814, *Ibid.*, pp. 484–85.
4. Dec. 29, 1813, Esarey (ed.), *op. cit.*, Vol. II, pp. 613–14.
5. These and other returns may be found in the Burton Historical Collection, Duncan McArthur Papers, Vol. I.
6. Mar. 5, 1814, *MPHC, op. cit.*, Vol. XV, pp. 501–02.
7. Fred C. Hamil, *op. cit.*, p. 96. The British later burned the wagons and gun carriages and carried the guns deeper into the swamp to prevent American recovery.
8. Drummond to Prevost, York, Mar. 5, 1814, *MPHC, op. cit.*, Vol. XV, p. 503.
9. Gen. orders, Quebec, Mar. 18, 1814, Wood (ed.), *Documents of the Canadian War, op. cit.*, Vol. II, p. 350. Wood reprints most of the pertinent documents but a sketch of the battleground may be found in *MPHC, op. cit.*, Vol. XV, p. 510.
10. May 14, 1814, Burton Historical Collection, Duncan McArthur Papers.
11. See Cleaves, *op. cit.*, Ch. XVII, for a discussion of Harrison's reasons for resigning.
12. Most of the letters reporting the action may be found in *The Weekly Register*, supplement to Vol. VII.
13. The best report of the action on the American side is a ten-page letter, Croghan to Armstrong, on board the *Niagara*, Aug. 9, 1814, National Archives (printed in *The Weekly Register*, Vol. VII). For the British see McDouall to Prevost, Michilimackinac, Aug. 14, 1814, Wood (ed.), *Documents of the Canadian War, op. cit.*, Vol. III, pp. 273–77.

14. Enclosure in Croghan to Armstrong, Aug. 9, 1814, *Ibid.*
15. The description of Prairie du Chien is taken from N. Boilvin to Eustis, Washington, Feb. 2, 1811, Washburne (ed.), *Edwards Papers*, pp. 60–63.
16. Clark to Armstrong, St. Louis, Feb. 2, 1814, Carter (ed.), *op. cit.*, Vol. XIV, p. 739.
17. Clark to Armstrong, St. Louis, Mar. 28, 1814, *Ibid.*, p. 747.
18. Clark to Armstrong, St. Louis, June 28, 1814, Carter (ed.), *op. cit.*, Vol. XIV, p. 776.
19. See La Feuille to Roberts, Prairie du Chien, Feb. 5, 1813, and also, principal inhabitants of Prairie du Chien to Roberts, Feb. 10, 1813, Wood (ed.), *Documents of the Canadian War, op. cit.*, Vol. III, pp. 245 and 251–52.
20. Louise P. Kellogg, *The British Regime in Wisconsin and the Northwest* (Madison: State Historical Society of Wisconsin, 1935), p. 315.
21. McDouall to Drummond, Michilimackinac, July 16, 1814, Wood (ed.), *Documents of the Canadian War, op. cit.*, Vol. III, pp. 255–56.
22. Howard to Armstrong, St. Louis, July 15, 1814, Carter (ed.), *op. cit.*, Vol. XVI, p. 445.
23. Heitman, *Register of the Army*, Vol. I, p. 278, states Campbell was promoted to captain on May 2, 1814. However, he may not have known about it by early July as he signed his report of the expedition as a lieutenant. He was a brigade-major and, since all the letters of the other officers refer to him as major, the present writer has followed suit.
24. Morning Report, Camp Hard Water Number 15, July 19, 1814, *MPHC, op. cit.*, Vol. XV, p. 622.
25. See Howard to Armstrong, St. Louis, Aug. 1, 1814, and enclosures (reports of Campbell and Riggs), Carter (ed.), *op. cit.*, Vol. XVII, pp. 3–8.
26. Anderson to McDouall, "Anderson's Journal," *Wisconsin Historical Collections*, Vol. IX, p. 232.
27. Taylor to Howard, Fort Madison, Sept. 6, 1814, *The Weekly Register*, Vol. VII, Supplement, p. 137.
28. Armstrong to Croghan, War Dept., June 2, 1814, National Archives, Military Book 7.
29. Both Sinclair and Croghan insisted their shells caused the fire, but British reports refer to Worsley's burning her to avoid capture. See *The Weekly Register*, Vol. VII, p. 18, and Supplement, p. 131; also *MPHC, op. cit.*, Vol. XV, p. 636. Worsley had one seaman killed and one wounded.
30. Bulger to McDouall, Michilimackinac, Sept. 7, 1814, Wood (ed.), *Documents of the Canadian War, op. cit.*, Vol. III, p. 280.
31. Gray to McArthur, Ft. Shelby, July 14, 1814, Burton Historical Collection, Duncan McArthur Papers, Vol. I.
32. Armstrong to McArthur, War Dept., Aug. 2, 1814, National Archives, Military Book 7.
33. Lt. William Rayburn to Miller, Amherstburg, Sept. 4, 1814, Burton Historical Collection, Duncan McArthur Papers, Vol. II.
34. Capt. McCormick to Miller, Ft. Malden, Sept. 16, 1814, *Ibid.*
35. See Lossing, *op. cit.*, p. 852, for a map of the expedition.
36. See McArthur to Izard, Detroit, Nov. 18, 1814, and McArthur's General Orders of that date, Burton Historical Collection, Duncan McArthur Papers, Vol. III.
37. Signed by Col. John Miller, Ft. Malden, Nov. 5, 1814, Wood (ed.), *Documents of the Canadian War, op. cit.*, Vol. III, pp. 296–97.

CHAPTER XIII

PEACE

IN EARLY 1815 THE BRITISH were laying plans to renew their efforts in Upper Canada, re-establish a strong navy (especially at yards to be built at Turkey Point), and induce large-scale attacks on American posts by the northern Indians. For his part, McArthur was appealing for final authority to lay waste to American-held Upper Canada.

But, while the British and Americans made war plans, a calmer group of men had concluded peace terms at Ghent on December 24, 1814—a peace desired by both governments. President Madison learned of the terms on February 14 and arranged for the exchange of official ratifications on February 17. The war had officially ended.

As it affected the Northwest, the treaty provided for the mutual restoration of all forts (including artillery and official records), Indian lands, and all territory to the possessor in 1811. Later, special commissioners were to describe the boundaries along the Great Lakes water system, in agreement with the Treaty of 1783. The keynote of the Treaty of Ghent was the status quo as of 1811. Most of the issues leading to war were not even mentioned.

It was decided to arrange a simultaneous exchange of Mackinac

Island and American-held Upper Canada. This was unfortunate since the weather prevented immediate departure of American forces to occupy Mackinac Island and encouraged British officials to delay the exchange as long as possible, creating further bad feelings.

British fur men were alarmed by the proposed surrender of Fort Michilimackinac and addressed communications to Drummond and Prevost urging that a strong post be built as near there as possible—the alternative: loss of the Indian trade. For his part, Prevost wrote Drummond concerning the exchange of Mackinac, saying, "I am disposed to think as much procrastination should be resorted to as may admit of your receiving the specific commands of His Majesty's Government on that Subject." [1] Drummond needed no prompting; he had already ordered stalling tactics.

Colonel Anthony Butler was designated to represent the United States in the dual exchange of posts. McDouall was prompt to notify him it would be some time before the British could evacuate Mackinac Island: artificers would have to be sent and a post built for the British garrison on another island before evacuation could be considered. Meanwhile, American customs officials were barred from the area, and Butler was sure the British were working night and day to further prejudice the Indians against the United States. When Prevost was ordered to England to stand trial on charges brought by Commodore Yeo, Drummond succeeded to his position and Lieutenant-General George Murray to Drummond's. But Murray did nothing to speed the exchange of posts.

The island of Bois Blanc, off Malden in the Detroit River, became a further pretext for delay. The Treaty of 1783 was interpreted to provide boundaries based on the normal ship channel, which would make the island American. However, the British had once had a few men stationed on this island and, since the Americans had not objected at the time, they used this as the basis of a claim to possession. This controversy gained the British further time, but the move could not long be postponed without reopening the war.

On June 25 Butler and Lieutenant-Colonel William James agreed that Butler would evacuate the Malden area by July 1, that the question of ownership of Bois Blanc would be submitted to the commissioners, and that Fort Michilimackinac would be turned over by July 15.[2] It was just in time; tempers were wearing thin.

McDouall had long had temporary quarters prepared on St. Joseph Island for his garrison and had begun construction of a post on the west end of Manitoulin Island (Drummond Island, later awarded to the United States). Most of his energy had been spent in explaining to the Indians that evacuation of Mackinac did not mean the British were weak or that they were abandoning the Indians. He had dispensed hundreds of pounds' worth of goods, hastily requisitioned from private merchants, to help prove his point to the Indians. Finally, on July 18, Mackinac Island was turned over to Colonel Butler. The smaller fort immediately was named Fort Holmes.

The situation in Illinois was even more critical. Indians in that area, unaware that the war was over, sent out a number of small parties in April and May. Lieutenant Andrew Bulger, who had taken command at Fort McKay about December 1, received orders on May 22 to evacuate his fort. Since the Americans had not occupied the area in 1811, the British felt no compulsion to surrender the post intact to the Americans but they did have to evacuate the territory. Bulger held an Indian council to try to reconcile the Indians to the British withdrawal from Prairie du Chien. He then burned the fort and departed. On his arrival at Mackinac Island he turned over the American artillery captured at Prairie du Chien and it was included in the ordnance surrendered to Colonel Butler.

Thus, by July 18, the exchange of posts in the West had been completed. Harrison, McArthur, and John Graham were appointed commissioners to arrange Indian treaties and, in sessions at Spring Wells in August and September, arranged peace terms with the tribes of Ohio, Indiana, and Michigan. Only the Prophet and his immediate followers remained aloof and eventually even he sought to return to the United States. Governors Clark and Edwards and Auguste Chouteau concluded treaties with the western Indians between July and October. The United States was now at peace with everybody.

Yes, peace had come, but it would be many years before the Canadian-American frontier would aptly demonstrate peaceful co-existence to the peoples of the world.

It is often asserted that the War of 1812 accomplished nothing. This is far from the truth, particularly in the West, the scene of most American victories. The war did much to end the Indian menace in the Old Northwest and made it possible to extend American settlements with remarkably little more bloodshed. Many new settlers on the frontier were men who had first visited these areas during their military service. Too, the war increased the power and prestige of the United States, resulted in a clearer delineation of actual boundaries, and, more important than anything else, ensured the rapid and permanent economic independence of the unsettled American areas from the hands of British fur traders.

Certainly not the least important result of the war in the West was the multitude of political leaders it first brought to the fore— William Henry Harrison and Zachary Taylor, both of whom were later to serve as United States presidents; Richard M. Johnson, who was to become vice president; Lewis Cass, who was to become a United States Senator, Minister to Paris and a Secretary of State, in addition to his post as Territorial Governor of Michigan; and Duncan McArthur and Robert Lucas, who were later governors of Ohio.

Notes to Chapter XIII

1. Quebec, Mar. 31, 1815, *MPHC, op. cit.*, Vol. XXV, pp. 622–23.
2. Butler to James, Detroit, June 25, 1815, *MPHC, op. cit.*, Vol. XVI, pp. 141–42. All the important documents are printed in this source for the exchange of posts.

BIBLIOGRAPHY

PRIMARY SOURCES

Manuscripts

Chicago Historical Society:
  Letter, James Wilkinson to David Holmes, New Orleans, September 14, 1812.
William L. Clements Library, University of Michigan:
  Cass, Lewis, Papers, 1772–1819 (one box).
  Papers Relating to Michigan (one box).
Department of Public Records and Archives of Ontario (Toronto):
  Letter, J. Grant to I. Brock, Amherstburg, February 1, 1808.
Detroit Public Library, Burton Historical Collection:
  Bishop, Levi, Papers (one folder).
  Burton, C. M., Papers, Detroit-History, War of 1812 (one folder).
  Cass, Lewis, Papers, 1780–1818 (one box).
  Clay, Green, Papers (one box).
  Farmer, Silas, Papers, ZH877 (one folder).
  Godfroy, Gabriel, Papers, 1808–27 (one box).
  Hull, William, Papers (one folder, copies of letters to Hull).
  Kingsbury, Jacob, Papers (copies, two boxes).
  Lossing, Benson J., Papers, 1810–20 (one folder).
  McArthur, Duncan, Papers (photostats, 4 volumes).
  Porter, Augustus S., Papers (one folder).
  Pringle, Alexander, Papers (photostats, one folder).
  Reynolds, Lawrence, Papers (one folder).
  Robison, John, Diary (photostats).
  Smyth, Richard, Papers (muster roll).
  Taylor, James, Papers (three boxes).
  United States War Department Photostats (two boxes).
  Winchester, James, Papers (Orderly Book).
  Witherell, B. F. H., Papers, 1796–1924 (one box).
  Woodbridge, William, Papers (two boxes).
  Woodward, Augustus B., Papers, 1809–19 (one box).
  Zug, Samuel, Papers, 1788–1872 (one folder).
Library of Congress:
  Madison, James, Papers, letter, William Eustis to James Madison, September 25, 1812.
Michigan Historical Collection, University of Michigan:
  Anderson, John, Papers (one box).
The National Archives:
  Military Books 5, 6, 7, 8 (letters sent by the Secretary of War).
  Letter, George Croghan to J. Armstrong, U. S. sloop *Niagara* off Thunder Bay, August 9, 1814.

263

Ohio Archaeological and Historical Society (Columbus, Ohio):
  Hatch, William S., Papers (one box).
  McArthur, Duncan, Letters (one folder).
  Meigs, Return J., Letters (Governor's Papers).
  Williams, Samuel, Memoirs (two volumes).
Ohio Historical and Philosophical Society (Cincinnati):
  Hatch, William S., Journal Book.
Public Archives of Canada (Ottawa):
  Chaplaincies, 1792–1813 (one volume).
  Embodied Militia, 1812–14, Pension List for Upper Canada.
  Essex Militia Muster Rolls and Pay lists, 1812–15.
  Forty-first Regiment, 1811–13 (one volume).
  General Orders, 1811–13 (one volume).
  Indians, 1809–12.
  McCoy, William, Journal (photostat).
  Medical, 1809–12.
  North West Fur Company, Letters and Reports (C363).
  Royal Veteran Battalions, 1807–14.
  War of 1812, 1806–12 (two volumes, C676, C677).
  War of 1812, Prisoners, 1812–13 (C689).
Ross County Historical Society (Chillicothe, Ohio):
  McArthur, Duncan, Letters (photostats, one folder).
  Receipt roll of artificers surrendering at Detroit.
  Williams, Samuel, Letters from the Front (one folder).
  Worthington, Thomas, Letters (one box).
University of Michigan Library (Rare Book Room):
  Letters of the Secretary of War, 1800–16 (Copied from originals by Colonel Oliver Spaulding.)
Western Reserve Historical Society (Cleveland):
  Letter, William Hull to Captain Campbell, Sandwich, July 15, 1812.
  Letter, William Hutt to John Hutt, River Raisin, August 11, 1812.

Printed Sources, Journals

Casselman, Alexander C. (ed.), *Richardson's War of 1812*. Toronto: Historical Publishing Co., 1902.

Crawford, Mary M. (ed.), "Mrs. Lydia B. Bacon's Journal 1811–12," *Indiana Magazine of History*. Part One, Vol. XL (December, 1944); Part Two, Vol. XLI (March, 1945).

Esarey, Logan (ed.), *Messages and Letters of William Henry Harrison*. Indianapolis: Indiana Historical Commission, 1922. Two volumes.

Fairchild, G. M. (ed.), *Journal of an American Prisoner at Fort Malden and Quebec in the War of 1812*. Quebec: Frank Carrel, 1909.

Gordon, Nelly K. (ed.), *Lieutenant Linai T. Helm The Fort Dearborn Massacre*. Chicago: Rand McNally & Company, 1912.

Lindley, Harlow (ed.), *Captain Cushing in the War of 1812*. Columbus: The Ohio Archaeological and Historical Society, 1944.

264

Parish, John C. (ed.), *The Robert Lucas Journal of the War of 1812. During the Campaign under General William Hull.* Iowa City: State Historical Society of Iowa, 1906.

Quaife, Milo M. (ed.), *War on the Detroit—The Chronicles of Thomas Verchères de Boucherville and The Capitulation by an Ohio Volunteer.* (The Lakeside Classics, number 38) Chicago: The Lakeside Press, 1940.

Walker, Adam, *A Journal of Two Campaigns of the Fourth Regiment of U. S. Infantry in the Michigan and Indiana Territories Under the Command of Col. John P. Boyd, and Lt. Col. James Miller During the Years of 1811 & 12.* Keene, New Hampshire: Adam Walker, 1816.

Williams, Samuel, "Two Western Campaigns in the War of 1812" (in Ohio Valley Historical Series entitled *Miscellanies*). Cincinnati: Robert Clarke & Co., 1871.

Wood, William (ed.), "Extract of the Journal of Charles Askin," *Select Britsh Documents of the Canadian War of 1812*, Vol. I. Toronto: The Champlain Society, 1920.

Printed Sources, Documents, and Contemporary Writings

Aggregate Amount of Persons Within the United States in the Year 1810. Washington: 1811.

American State Papers, Documents Legislative and Executive of the Congress of the United States. *Indian Affairs*, Vol. I. Washington: Gales and Seaton, 1832.

American State Papers, Documents Legislative and Executive of the Congress of the United States. *Military Affairs*, Vol. I. Washington: Gales and Seaton, 1832.

An Appeal to the People Or, an Exposition of the Official Conduct of Return Jonathan Meigs, Governor of the State of Ohio. Printed for the People, 1812.

Armstrong, John, *Notices of the War of 1812.* New York: Wiley & Putnam, 1840. Two volumes.

Blume, William Wirt (ed.), *Transactions of the Supreme Court of the Territory of Michigan 1805–14,* Vols. I and II. Ann Arbor: University of Michigan Press, 1935.

B[oyle], D[avid] (ed.), "The Cameron Rolls, 1812," *Ontario Historical Society Papers and Records*, Vol. I (1899).

Brannan, John (ed.), *Official Letters of the Military and Naval Officers of the United States during the War with Great Britain in the Years of 1812, 13, 14 & 15.* Washington: John Brannan, 1823.

Brown, Samuel R., *Views of the Campaigns of the North-Western Army.* Troy, New York: Printed by Francis Adancourt, 1814.

Carter, Clarence E. (ed.), *The Territorial Papers of the United States,* Vols. VIII, X, XIV, XV, XVI, XVII. Washington: United States Government Printing Office, 1939–51.

Collections of the State Historical Society of Wisconsin, Vols. II–XVII. Madison: State Historical Society, 1856–1906.

Coxe, Tench (ed.), *A Statement of the Arts and Manufactures of the United States of America for the Year 1810.* Philadelphia: A Cornman, Junr., 1814.

Coyne, James H. (ed.), "The Talbot Papers," *Proceedings and Transactions of The Royal Society of Canada,* Third Series, Vol. I (May, 1907).

Cruikshank, E. A. (ed.), *Documents Relating to the Invasion of Canada and the Surrender of Detroit 1812.* Ottawa: Government Printing Bureau, 1913.

————, *Inventory of the Military Documents in the Canadian Archives.* Ottawa: Government Printing Bureau, 1910.

D., L. C. (ed.), "Lawe and Grignon Papers, 1794–1821," *Report and Collections of the State Historical Society of Wisconsin,* Vol. X (1883–85).

The Debates and Proceedings in the Congress of the United States. Twelfth Congress, First Session. Washington: Gales and Seaton, 1853. Two volumes.

Duane, William, *The American Military Library: Or Compendium of the Modern Tactics.* Philadelphia: William Duane, 1809. Two volumes.

————, *A Military Dictionary or Explanation of the Several Systems of Discipline of Different Kinds of Troops.* Philadelphia: William Duane, 1810.

Forbes, James G., *The Trial of Brig. General William Hull.* New York: Eastburn, Kirk, and Co., 1814.

Ford, Paul L. (ed.), *The Writings of Thomas Jefferson,* Vol. IX. New York: G. P. Putnam's Sons, 1898.

Hamilton, Stanislaus M. (ed.), *The Writings of James Monroe,* Vol. V. New York: G. P. Putnam's Sons, 1901.

Hull, William, *Memoirs of the Campaign of the North Western Army.* Boston: True & Greene, 1824.

————, *Defence of Brigadier General W. Hull.* Boston: Wells and Lilly, 1814.

Hunt, Gaillard (ed.), *The Writings of James Madison,* Vol. VIII. New York: G. P. Putnam's Sons, 1908.

Michigan Pioneer and Historical Collection. Lansing: 1877–1929. Forty volumes.

Palmer, T. H. (ed.), *The Historical Register of the United States,* Vol. I. Washington: T. H. Palmer, 1814.

Quaife, Milo M. (ed.), *The John Askin Papers,* Vol. II (1796–1820). Detroit: Detroit Library Commission, 1931.

Robertson, Nellie A. and Riker, Dorothy (eds.), *The John Tipton Papers,* Vol. I. Indianapolis: Indiana Historical Bureau, 1942.

Roster of Ohio Soldiers in the War of 1812. The Adjutant General of Ohio, 1916.

"Selections from the Gano Papers," *The Quarterly Publication of the Historical and Philosophical Society of Ohio.* Part I, Vol. XV (January–June, 1920); Part 2, Vol. XVI (July–September, 1920).

Wallace, W. Stewart (ed.), *Documents Relating to the North West Company.* Toronto: The Champlain Society, 1934.

Wood, William (ed.), *Select British Documents of the Canadian War of 1812.* Toronto: The Champlain Society, 1920. Three volumes.

Newspapers

The Albany Register.
Columbian Sentinel (Boston).
Liberty Hall (Cincinnati).

National Intelligencer (Washington, D. C.).
Niles Weekly Register (Baltimore). (Originally a newspaper.)
Poulson's American Daily Advertiser (Philadelphia).
The Scioto Gazette.
The Supporter (Chillicothe).
The United States Gazette for the Country (Philadelphia).
Weekly Aurora.
The Western Spy (Cincinnati).
The Western Star and Harp of Erin (New York).
Upper Canada Gazette (York, Upper Canada).

Periodicals

American Historical Review, Vol. XVII.
Bulletin of the Johns Hopkins Hospital, Vol. XLVI.
Burton Historical Collection Leaflets (Detroit, Numbers I, IV, VIII).
Canadian Historical Review, Vol. XXXIV.
The Indiana Magazine of History, Vols. IX, XXX.
Magazine of American History, Vol. XXVII.
Michigan History Magazine, Vols. XII, XIII.
Mississippi Valley Historical Review, Vols. VII, X, XIII, XV, XVIII, XIX.
Ohio Archaeological and Historical Publications, Vols. III, IX, XXVIII, XXXIII, XLVII.
Ontario Historical Society Papers and Records, Vols. X, XII, XIX, XXIV, XXVII, XXXVI, XXXVII.
Proceedings and Transactions of the Royal Society of Canada, Third Series, Vols. I and VI.
Western Reserve Historical Society Publications, Number 1, 22.

SECONDARY SOURCES

Adams, Henry, *History of the United States of America During the First Administration of James Madison.* New York: Charles Scribner's Sons, 1890. Two volumes.

Bald, F. Clever, *Detroit's First American Decade 1796 to 1805.* Ann Arbor: University of Michigan Press, 1948.

Bayliss, Joseph and Estelle, *Historic St. Joseph Island.* Cedar Rapids: The Torch Press, 1938.

Beirne, Francis F., *The War of 1812.* New York: E. P. Dutton & Co., Inc., 1949.

Bull, William P., *From Brock to Currie.* Toronto: The Perkins Bull Foundation, 1935.

Burt, A[lfred] L., *The United States Great Britain and British North America From the Revolution to the Establishment of Peace After The War of 1812.* (Unnumbered volume in the series, The Relations of Canada and the United States.) New Haven: Yale University Press, 1940.

Burton, Clarence M. (ed.), *The City of Detroit Michigan 1701-1922,* Vol. I. Detroit: S. J. Clarke Publishing Company, 1922.

Burton, Clarence M. and Burton, M. Agnes (eds.), *History of Wayne County,* Vol. I. Detroit: S. J. Clarke Publishing Company, 1930.

Campbell, (Mrs.) Maria, *Revolutionary Services and Civil Life of General William Hull* and *History of the Campaign of 1812* (by James F. Clarke). New York: D. Appleton & Co., 1848.

Clarke, James F., *William Hull and the Surrender of Detroit*. Boston: George H. Ellis Co. (undated).

Clarke, Samuel C., *Memoir of Gen. William Hull*. Boston: David Clapp & Son, 1893.

Cleaves, Freeman, *Old Tippecanoe*. New York: Charles Scribner's Sons, 1939.

Coffin, William F., *1812: The War and Its Moral*. Montreal: 1864.

Cullum, George W., *Campaigns of the War of 1812–15 Against Great Britain Sketched and Criticised with Brief Biographies of the American Engineers*. New York: James Miller, Publisher, 1879.

Dawson, Henry B., *Battles of the United States by Sea and Land*. New York: Johnson, Fry, and Company, 1858. Two volumes.

Dearborn, Henry A. S., *Defence of Gen. Henry Dearborn Against the Attack of Gen. William Hull*. Boston: Edgar W. Davies, 1824.

Dillon, John B., *A History of Indiana*. Indianapolis: Bingham & Doughty, 1858.

Dobbins, W. W., *History of the Battle of Lake Erie* (2nd ed.). Erie: Ashby Printing Co., 1913.

Drake, Benjamin, *Life of Tecumseh and of His Brother the Prophet, With a Historical Sketch of the Shawanoe Indians*. Cincinnati: H. M. Rulison, Queen City Publishing House, 1841.

Farmer, Silas, *The History of Detroit and Michigan*. Detroit: Silas Farmer & Co., 1884.

Fortescue, John W., *A History of the British Army*, Vol. VIII. London: The Macmillan Company, 1917.

Fuller, George N. (ed.), *Michigan—A Centennial History of the State and Its People*, Vol. I. Chicago: The Lewis Publishing Company, 1939.

Gilleland, J. C., *History of the Late War Between the United States and Great Britain* (3rd ed.). Baltimore: Schaeffer & Mound, 1818.

Hamil, Fred C., *The Valley of the Lower Thames 1640 to 1850*. Toronto: University of Toronto Press, 1951.

Hatch, William S., *A Chapter of the War of 1812*. Cincinnati: Miami Printing and Publishing Company, 1872.

Heitman, Francis B., *Historical Register of the United States Army*. Washington: The National Tribune, 1890.

Howe, Henry, *Historical Collections of Ohio in Three Volumes*. Columbus: Henry Howe & Son, 1891.

Ingersoll, Charles J., *Historical Sketch of the Second War Between the United States of America and Great Britain*, Vol. I. Philadelphia: Lea and Blanchard, 1845.

Irving, L. Homfray, *Officers of the British Forces in Canada During the War of 1812–15*. Welland: Welland Tribune Print., 1908.

Jacobs, James R., *The Beginning of the U. S. Army 1783–1812*. Princeton: Princeton University Press, 1947.

James, William, *A Full and Correct Account of the Military Occurrences of the Late War Between Great Britain and the United States of America*, Vol. I. London: William James, 1818.

Kellogg, Louise P., *The British Regime in Wisconsin and the Northwest.* Madison: State Historical Society of Wisconsin, 1935.

Knapp, Horace S., *History of the Maumee Valley Commencing with its Occupation by the French in 1680.* Toledo: Blade Mammoth Printing and Publishing House, 1872.

Lomax, David A. N., *A History of the Services of the 41st (the Welch Regiment, [Now 1st Battalion the Welch Regiment]) From its Formation in 1719, to 1895.* Devonport: Hiorns & Miller, 1899.

Lossing, Benson J., *The Pictorial Field Book of the War of 1812.* New York: Harper & Brothers, 1868.

Lucas, Charles P., *The Canadian War of 1812.* Oxford: Henry Frowde, 1906.

McAfee, Robert B., *History of the Late War in the Western Country.* Lexington: Worsley & Smith, 1816.

Mann, James, *Medical Sketches of the Campaigns of 1812, 13, 14.* Dedham: H. Mann & Co. 1816.

Pirtle, Alfred, *The Battle of Tippecanoe.* Louisville: Filson Club, 1900.

Powell, William H., *List of Officers of the Army of the United States from 1799 to 1900.* New York: L. R. Hamersly & Co., 1900.

Pratt, Julius W., *Expansionists of 1812.* New York: The Macmillan Company, 1925.

Quaife, Milo M. and Glazer, Sidney, *Michigan: From Primitive Wilderness to Industrial Commonwealth.* New York: Prentice-Hall, Inc., 1948.

Steele, Matthew F., *American Campaigns,* Vol. I. Washington: War Department, 1909.

Thompson, David, *History of the Late War Between Great Britain and the United States of America: With a Retrospective View of the Causes from whence it Originated.* Niagara: T. Sewell, 1832.

Thompson, John L., *Historical Sketches of the Late War Between the United States and Great Britain; Blended with Anecdotes* (4th ed.). Philadelphia: Thomas Desilver, 1817.

Tupper, Ferdinand B., *Life and Correspondence of Major General Sir Isaac Brock, K. B.* London: Simpkin, Marshall and Co., 1845.

Updyke, Frank A., *The Diplomacy of the War of 1812.* Baltimore: The Johns Hopkins Press, 1915.

Utley, Henry M. and Cutcheon, Byron M., *Michigan as a Province, Territory and State,* Vol. II *(Michigan as a Territory).* New York: Publishing Society of Michigan, 1906.

Wing, Talcott E. (ed.), *History of Monroe County Michigan.* New York: Munsell & Company, 1890.

Winter, Nevin O., *A History of Northwest Ohio,* Vol. I. Chicago: The Lewis Publishing Company, 1917.

Wood, Edwin O., *Historic Mackinac.* New York: The Macmillan Company, 1918. Two volumes.

Wood, William, *The War with the United States.* (Chronicles of Canada Number 14). Toronto: Glasgow, Brook and Company, 1920.

Woodford, Frank B., *Mr. Jefferson's Disciple: A Life of Justice Woodward.* East Lansing: Michigan State College Press, 1953.

Boswell, Lieutenant-Colonel William, 185
Boyd, Colonel John P., 8, 9, 11, 14, 20
Brevoort, Captain Henry B.: plans for capture of *Queen Charlotte*, 86; at Monguagon, 100
Brisbois, Michael, 248
British: in Old Northwest, 3; and threat of war, 21; in Michigan, 24; enlist aid of Indians, 24; Indian alliance with, 25, 68, 91, 195–96; fur traders, 25, 26; gifts to Indians, 26; forces in Canada, 46–47; and Declaration of War, 54, 67; custom of awarding shares in captured property, 58; fort at Detroit, 63; army chain of command, 69–70; attempt to win allegiance of Canadians from, 73, 74; and disaffection of Canadians, 93–94; did not desire war with Americans, 132; trade restrictions, 132; and Dearborn Armistice, 132–34; and provision problems, 160–61; shift in top generals, 235; and peace, 259. *See also* England, Great Britain
Brock, Major-General Sir Isaac, 70; and Declaration of War, 54; orders preparations for offensive, 57; issues proclamation, 88; on disaffection of Canadians, 93; goes to Malden, 105; plans offensive against Detroit, 109, 124 (n. 1); demands Hull's surrender, 112; and attack on Detroit, 115, 116; surrender of Detroit, 117, 121; and Fort Dearborn, 128; and Dearborn Armistice, 133; proclamation to Michigan citizens, 158; departs for Fort George, 159; killed at Queenston, 160
Brown, Noah, 208
Brown, Captain Return, 81
Brownstown, Michigan Territory, 25; council at, 38, 79; Battle of, 96–97; British prepare ambush at, 100
Brush, Colonel Elijah: commands Michigan militia at Detroit, 115, 117; signs surrender terms, 118; protests Procter's orders to leave Detroit, 181

Brush, Captain Henry: leads provision train, 95; at River Raisin, 103, 110, 111, 114; ignores Hull's orders to surrender, 119–20
Bruyeres, Lieutenant-Colonel R. H., 84 (n. 6)
Buck, Reverend W., 34
Buford, Thomas, 140
Bulger, Lieutenant Andrew, 253, 261
Bullock, Captain Richard, 241, 242
Bureau River, Illinois Territory, 198
Burnet's Creek, Indiana, 16
Busseron, Indiana Territory, 6; cavalry at, 12; Hopkins' men camp at, 147
Butler, Lieutenant-Colonel Anthony: in command at Detroit, 232, 237–38; in command of Second Regiment, 239; represents United States in exchange of posts, 260
Butler, Captain James, 154

Caldwell, William: and command of Canadian rangers, 182; in Battle of Longwood, 238–39
Caledonia: described, 67; at Mackinac, 89; captured by Americans, 159; at Battle of Lake Erie, 210
Campbell, Alexander, 61 (n. 6)
Campbell, Major John: leads expedition to Prairie du Chien, 249, 258 (n. 23); in Indian fight near Rock River, 250
Campbell, Lieutenant-Colonel John B., 153–54
Camp Edwards, Illinois Territory, 130
Camp Meigs, Ohio, 36
Canada: white population of Upper, 27; American confidence in conquest of, 45–46; preliminary war campaigns against, 45, 46; and Great Britain in war, 70; American migrants to, 73; Brock's proclamation to people of, 88. *See also* Upper Canada
Canadian militia, 68–69: encouraged to desert, 59–60; desertion of, 79, 88; Harrison offers parole to, 229
Canard River, Upper Canada: American forces at, 79–82, 83, 85 (n. 31), 92; Indian action near, 87

Dearborn Armistice, 133–34; at Hull's court-martial, 232
Dearborn. *See* Fort Dearborn
Dearborn Armistice, 132–34
Declaration of War, 47, 52, 54
Delaware, Upper Canada, 94, 223
Delaware Indians: sign treaty, 5; chiefs aid Harrison, 13; at Piqua council, 128; hostiles appeal for peace, 220; at Greenville Council, 241
Denny, Major James: First Regiment, 32; accompanies boats from Thames, 78; in Indian action near Canard River, 87; commands Fort Hope, 99
Dequindre, Captain Antoine (Michigan Detached Militia), 100
De Rottenburg, Major-General Francis: commands in Upper Canada, 201; releases regulars to Procter, 214; exchanges letters regarding Procter's position, 215–16; to Lower Canada, 235
Desha, Captain Benjamin, 244
Desha, General Joseph (Kentucky militia), 225
Detroit, Michigan Territory: fire of 1805, 24; as strategic post, 25, 28, 29; citizens petition after Tippecanoe, 27; citizens guard, 57; described, 63–64; garrison at, 65; Hull recrosses to, 86; Michilimackinac garrison at, 91; Hull's army returns to, 99; attack on, 113, 115–18; surrender of, 118–19; citizens ransom prisoners of River Raisin, 170; Procter forces residents to leave, 181; British retreat from, 217
Detroit: new vessel constructed at Malden, 209; British flagship at Battle of Lake Erie, 211–12
Detroit. See Adams
Detroit Historical Society, 108 (n. 38)
Dickson, Robert: aids in capture of Mackinac, 89; appointed British Indian agent, 195–96; at Prairie du Chien, 247
Dill, Captain Andrew, 49
Dixon, Captain Matthew (Royal Engineers), 84 (n. 6): at Fort

Meigs, 183; wounded at Fort Stephenson, 207
Dobbins, Captain Daniel: at Mackinac, 90; builds fleet at Presqu' Isle, 208
Dolsen's, Upper Canada, 78, 221
Dousman, Michael, 90
Drummond, Lieutenant-General Gordon, 235, 236, 260
Drummond Island, 261
Dubois, Touissant: sends message to Harrison, 10; at Tippecanoe, 15; guide for Hopkins, 148
Dudley, Lieutenant-Colonel William (Kentucky militia): at Fort Meigs, 185 ff.; killed, 187; his standards regained, 226
Dunlap, Colonel James (Ohio militia), 139
Dyson, Captain Samuel (United States Artillery): in Canada, 76, 92–93; in attack on Detroit, 114, 116

Eastman, Lieutenant John, 100, 122
Ecorse River, Michigan Territory, 95, 97
Edwards, Doctor Abraham, 39
Edwards, Ninian (Governor, Illinois Territory): and Indian threats, 7, 8–9; believes Peoria center of hostiles, 129; in raid on Peoria, 149; orders arrest of Peoria Indians, 194; measures dealing with Indian raids, 198; field service ends, 199; concludes peace treaties, 261
Eighth Military District, 192
Eliza: shells Fort Meigs, 183; abandoned by Procter, 222
Elkswatawa: *See* Prophet, The
Ellen, 222, 233 (n. 11)
Elliott, Lieutenant Jesse D. (United States Navy), 159
Elliott, Colonel Matthew, 68: reports Indian force at the Rapids, 152; age hinders service, 195; reports Indians willing to return to British, 236
Elliott, Captain William, 119–20
Ellison, Ensign Andrew, 97
England: trade difficulties of U. S. with, 31; and Indian allies, 44. *See also* British, Great Britain

at, 68; militia at, 69; Hull authorized to attack, 72; Procter commands, 93; Hull's plan for attack on, 86, 92, 98; British retreat to, 101; Brock leaves token guard, 110. *See also* Amherstburg

Fort Meigs, Ohio: constructed, 175; changes of command at, 175; Harrison at, 180; siege of, 183 ff.; second British siege of, 201–05, 213 (n. 18)

Fort Miami, 21 (n. 1)

Fort Michilimackinac, Michigan Territory: described, 88–89, 106–07 (n. 7); British capture, 90–91; Harrison delays attack on, 228–29; British activities at, 241; American attack on, 242–45; surrendered to Americans, 260

Fort Necessity, Ohio, 50

Fort Portage, Ohio, 51

Fort St. Joseph, Upper Canada, 89, 243

Fort Seneca, Ohio, 157

Fort Shelby (Prairie du Chien), Illinois Territory: built, 247; captured by British, 249; renamed Fort McKay, 251

Fort Shelby, Michigan Territory: new fort at Detroit, 230; Butler commands, 232; Croghan commands, 239; Gray commands, 254; Collins commands, 256

Fort Stephenson, Ohio: constructed, 157; British attack, 205–07

Fort Vallonia, Indiana Territory, 196, 197

Fort Washington (Cincinnati), 4

Fort Wayne, Indiana Territory, 126, 127, 128: history of, 132; Indian attack on, 134–37

Fort Wayne, Treaty of, 5, 13

Fort William, Upper Canada, 91

Fort Winchester, Ohio, 155, 157

Forty-first Regiment of Foot: location in 1812, 66–67; detachment to Moravian Town, 93; reinforcements, 105; at Fort Meigs, 186; at Malden, 214–15

Foster, Augustus J., 133

Fourth Regiment, United States Infantry: ordered to Indiana Territory, 7; at Vincennes, 9; at Tippe-

canoe, 10–19; to join Hull, 29; ordered to Ohio, 36; put down mutiny at Urbana, 48; in advance of Hull's army, 52; strength of, 65; at Canard River, 80; some men with Brush, 95; at Monguagon, 99–104; surrenders at Detroit, 118–19

Fox Indians, 129

France: and Michigan area, 23; and War of 1812, 61 (n. 6)

Freegoodwill, 90

French: in Old Northwest, 3; in Michigan, 24; fort at Detroit, 63

Frenchtown (Monroe, Michigan), 52. *See also* River Raisin

Fuller, Captain Charles, 112

Funk, Captain Peter, 10

Fur trade, 26, 91–92, 247

Gano, Major-General (Ohio militia), 84–85 (n. 24)

Garrard, Captain William, 135, 142

Geiger, Captain Frederick, 10, 17

General Hunter: captures the *Cayauga*, 54; described, 67; cuts off American retreat, 101–02; fires at Detroit, 113

General Myers, 222

George III, 69

George IV, 69

Ghent, Treaty of, 259

Gilchrist, Captain Robert, 97

Gill, Captain William, 238–39

Glegg, Captain John B., 112, 118

Godfroy, Colonel Gabriel (Michigan militia): meets wounded, 102, 107 (n. 31); signer of Cass round robin, 106; to guide Cass and McArthur, 112; appointed Indian subagent, 232

Godfroy's Trading Post, Michigan Territory, 111

Gooding, Lieutenant George, 54

Governor Clark, 246, 248

Graham, Lieutenant Duncan, 251

Graham, John, 261

Grand River, Upper Canada, 105

Gratiot, Captain Charles: engineer officer for Harrison, 143; builds Fort Gratiot, 240; commands Detroit area, 256

Gray, Captain Alexander, 254

281

Port Dover, Upper Canada, 105
Porter, Augustus, 36, 42 (n. 18), 72, 94
Porter, General Peter B., 29, 42 (n. 18)
Port Miami, 51
Posey, Thomas, 196
Potawatomi Indians: sign Treaty of Fort Wayne, 5; murders in Missouri, 7; receive annuities, 25: at Brownstown council, 79; attack Fort Dearborn garrison, 127–28; build settlement along Huron River, 201; Harrison's plans against, 220; provisional armistice with, 228; at Greenville Council, 241
Pothier, Toussaint, 89
Powers, Avery, 87
Poyntz, Lieutenant Newdigate (Royal Navy), 242, 252
Prairie du Chien, Illinois Territory: American fort at, 245, 247: British capture of, 248 ff.; British withdrawal from, 261
Presqu' Isle (Erie), Pennsylvania, 201, 208–09
Prevost, Sir George: Governor-General of Canada and Commander of all forces, 70; sends reinforcements to Brock, 105; and the Dearborn Armistice, 132–33; reports on British defeat at Fort Stephenson, 207; orders Barclay's fleet to be sacrificed, if necessary, 212; exchanges letters concerning Procter's position, 215–16; reports on Battle of the Thames, 226; approves plan to attack Detroit, 236; advocates delay in surrendering Mackinac, 260; court-martial of, 260
Prize Pay Lists (Brock's force at Detroit), 121
Proclamations: Hull's to Canadians, 59, 73–74; Hull's to Indian council, 79; Brock's to Canadians, 88; Brock's to Michigan citizens, 158; Harrison's to people of Michigan, 227; Harrison's to Canadians, 229; at Detroit, 257
Procter, Colonel Henry, 107 (n. 14): commands at Malden, 93; on Battle

of Monguagon, 103–04; Tecumseh's opinion of, 105; in command of Detroit attack, 109–10; and Fort Wayne attack, 134, 141; civil governor of Michigan, 159; reports forces in area, 160–61; at Battle of River Raisin, 166 ff., 170; forces Detroit residents to leave, 181; promoted to brigadier-general, 182; at siege of Fort Meigs, 183 ff., 187, 202; loses chance to take offensive, 190–91; fails to get reinforcements, 201; at Fort Stephenson, 206–07; error in not attacking Presqu' Isle, 208; influence of naval policies, 209; retreats, 214–17; at Battle of the Thames, 225; court-martial of, 227; requests return of officers' property, 230; returns to England, 235
Prophet, the: at Prophet's Town, 4; sends messengers to Harrison, 13; at Tippecanoe, 14, 16 ff.; on Wild Cat Creek, 20; accepts peace, 261
Prophet's Town, Indiana Territory, 4, 8, 9: Harrison's force approaches, 15; destroyed by Harrison, 19; burned by Hopkins, 149; Russell leads raids on, 197
Puthuff, Major William, 239
Put in Bay, 211

Queen Charlotte: described, 67; and Hull's invasion of Canada, 82, 83, 86; and attack on Detroit, 110, 113; Harrison orders destroyed, 176; at Battle of Lake Erie, 211–12
Queenston, Battle of, 160

Race, Andrew, 52
Raisin River, 52. See also River Raisin, River Road
Rangers, United States, 30–31, 34
Rector, Lieutenant Stephen, 249
Reiffenstein, Staff-Adjutant John, 226
Reynolds, Major Ebenezer, 164, 166
Reynolds, Doctor James, 52, 116
Rhea, Captain James, 132, 135
Riall, Major-General Phineas, 235
Richardson, John, 97
Rife, Colonel Christopher, 219

commands right on invasion of Canada, 219

Shipp, Lieutenant Edmund, 206

Short, Lieutenant-Colonel William, 207

Silver Heels' Town, Indiana Territory, 154

Simrall, Lieutenant-Colonel James (Kentucky dragoons), 139–40

Sinclair, Captain Arthur, 242, 252, 258 (n. 29)

Sioux Indians: reported at Brownstown, 53; at capture of Mackinac, 89

Sloan, Captain James: ordered to Thames River, 77; at Battle of Monguagon, 100

Smyth, Brigadier Alexander, 160

Smyth, Captain Richard, 78

Snelling, Captain Josiah: at Tippecanoe, 18; at Canard River, 79–82; reinforces Van Horne, 97; at Battle of Monguagon, 100; brevetted, 104; at Hanks's court-martial, 112; at attack on Detroit, 114, 118

South West Fur Company, 26

Spencer, Captain Spier, 18

Spafford, Amos, 51

Springer, Captain Daniel, 93, 107 (n. 15)

Spring Wells, Michigan Territory, 56, 57, 71, 113

Stansbury, Lieutenant Dixon, 99–104

Staunton, Ohio, 37

Stephens, Blackhall, 75

Stickney, Benjamin, 132

Stoddard, Major Amos (United States Artillery): at Fort Meigs, 180; mortally wounded, 193 (n. 21)

Stony Creek, 166

Tallon, Captain Joseph, 109

Taylor, James: appointed quartermaster-general, 39; authorized to advance pay, 47; delays in issuing provisions, 111

Taylor, Major Waller, 10, 15, 17

Taylor, Captain Zachary: at Fort Harrison, 39; in Indian attack on Fort Harrison, 137–38; brevet major, 139; on Rock River expedi-

tion, 250–51; prominence gained in war, 262

Tecumseh: youth, 3; at Prophet's Town, 4; and Treaty of Fort Wayne, 5; councils of 1810 and 1811, 5–7; on southern trip, 7; Harrison appraises, 8; believed in Malden area, 53, 62 (n. 18); at Battle of Brownstown, 97; at Battle of Monguagon, 100–03; and Brock, 105, 108 (n. 36); and frontier Indian raids, 139; and Battle of River Raisin, 167; at siege of Fort Meigs, 183 ff., 187, 204–05; requests Indian villages be moved, 197; followers settle along Huron River, 201; and retreat from Malden, 216; agrees to move up the Thames River, 217; killed at Battle of the Thames, 224–25

Tenth Royal Veteran Battalion, 89

Terre Haute, 13

Thames River, Upper Canada: McArthur Expedition to, 77–78; detachment of the Forty-first at, 93; the Battle of, 224 ff., 233 (n. 13), 233 (n. 15)

The Forks, Indiana Territory, 196–97

The Prophet. *See* Prophet, The

The White Horse, 15

Third Regiment of Ohio Volunteers, 33, 49, 51

Thompson, James, 39

Tigress: at Battle of Lake Erie, 210 ff.; at Mackinac, 242; at Nottawasaga Bay, 252; captured by British, 253

Tippecanoe, Battle of, 17–19, 22 (n. 19), 22 (n. 20); American forces en route to, 10–16; reaction at Detroit to, 27

Tippecanoe River, 4

Tipton, Major John, 197

Trade: between British and American fur traders, 26; British restrictions on, 132

Trimble, Colonel Allen (Ohio militia), 153

Trimble, Major William, 32, 83

Trippe, 210 ff.

Tupper, Brigadier-General Edward (Ohio militia): at Urbana, 143;

expedition to the Rapids, 150–53; protects provisions at Fort Mc-Arthur, 156
Turkey Creek, Upper Canada, 77, 79
Turkey Point, Upper Canada, 259
Turner, Lieutenant Daniel, 243, 253
Twenty-fourth Regiment, United States Infantry, 177
Twenty-sixth Regiment, United States Infantry, 203

Ulry, Captain Henry, 77, 97
United States Artillery, 65
United States Rangers, 30–31, 34
Upper Canada: militia of, 68–69; revises militia laws, 69; Procter proclaims limited martial law in, 215; Harrison's proclamation to, 229; shift of top British generals in, 235. *See also* Canada, Malden, Sandwich, Thames River
Urbana, Ohio: Hull to advance to, 37; Hull's army at, 38–48; Brush leaves, 95

Van Buren, Martin, 232
Van Horne, Captain Isaac, 245
Van Horne, Major Thomas: Second Ohio Volunteers, 33; ordered to River Raisin, 95; at Battle of Brownstown, 96–97, 107 (n. 21); at Battle of Monguagon, 100
Van Rensselaer, General Stephen, 46, 160
Varnum, Joseph B., 25
Verchères de Boucherville, Thomas, 62 (n. 20), 107 (n. 29)
Vermilion River, Indiana Territory, 14
Vincennes, Indiana Territory: regulars moved to, 6; Indian councils at, 6–7; Harrison at, 9; petition by citizens of, 7; Harrison's force returns to, 19; Fourth Regiment leaves, 39; force to relieve Fort Harrison gathered at, 138
Vincent, Brigadier-General John: delays sending reinforcements to Procter, 201; becomes major-general, 201; against unrestrained Indian warfare, 231; in command of British center, 235

Wabash River, Indiana Territory, 6, 9, 12–15
Wadsworth, Major-General Elijah (Ohio militia), 156
Walk-in-the-Water (Wyandot), 228
Wallace, Robert, 39
Warburton, Lieutenant-Colonel Augustus: to replace St. George, 182; awaits orders to destroy Fort Malden, 217; commands during Procter's retreat, 223
War Hawks, 47
Warwick, Captain Jacob, 18
Washington, D.C., 255
Watson, Joseph, 73, 88
Watson, Simon Z., 78, 93
Waubunsee, 22 (n. 22)
Wayne, General Anthony, 4, 12, 21 (n. 1), 25, 36
Weaver, Lieutenant John, 249–50
Wells, Major Samuel: at Tippecanoe, 18; colonel of Seventeenth Infantry, 130–31; destroys Five Medal's Towns, 139; opposes Winchester's advance to River Raisin, 164; at River Raisin, 165, 169; at Lower Sandusky, 203
Wells, Captain William, 127, 128
Westbrook, Andrew: aids American cause, 78, 93; burns his own property, 237; leads patrol to Moravian Town, 254
Whistler, Captain John, 57, 71
Whistler, Lieutenant William, 100
White Horse, The, 15
White Pigeon's Town, Michigan Territory, 153
Wild Cat Creek, Indiana: the Prophet at, 20; Indians attack of, 149
Wilkinson, Brigadier-General James, 4, 123
Williams, Samuel, 107 (n. 18)
Wilson, Reverend Joshua, 34
Wilson, Captain Waller, 6
Winchester, Brigadier-General James: and recruits to Detroit, 104; assembles force, 130–31; allows Harrison to take temporary command, 131; Harrison comments on, 136; at Fort Wayne, 140; moves down Miami River, 141 ff.; in command of Harrison's left

wing, 144-45; friction with Ohio men, 150-51; advances to the Rapids, 155-58; at Battle of River Raisin, 164 ff.; captured by British, 168; his standards regained, 226

Winnebago Indians: at Mackinac, 89; and Greenville Council, 241; captured at Prairie du Chien, 246

Winnemac (Winnimeg), 15, 158

Witherell, B. F. H., 108 (n. 38)

Witherell, Major James, 65

Wood, Captain Eleazer, 175

Woodward, Judge Augustus B.: and invasion of Canada, 75; and attack on Detroit, 113; after surrender of Detroit, 159; leaves Detroit, 181

Worsley, Lieutenant Miller (Royal Navy), 252, 253, 258 (n. 29)

Worthington, Senator Thomas: opposes Hull's appointment, 29; opposes war declaration, 47

Wyandot Indians: ignore the Prophet, 13; receive annuities, 25; relations with Hull, 25; report capture of the *Cayauga*, 53; report to Hull, 56; at Brownstown council, 79; join British, 93; appeal for peace, 220; armistice with, 228; at Greenville Council, 241

Yeiser, Captain Frederick, 247, 248 ff.

Yeo, Commodore James, 209, 260